VOICES
in Texts and Contexts

Published by Sunway University Press
An imprint of Sunway University Sdn Bhd

No. 5, Jalan Universiti
Bandar Sunway
47500 Selangor Darul Ehsan
Malaysia

press.sunway.edu.my

ISBN 978-967-5492-55-6

Perpustakaan Negara Malaysia Cataloguing-in-Publication Data

VOICES : IN TEXTS AND CONTEXTS / Editors Toshiko Yamaguchi, Jariah Mohd Jan, Sheena Kaur.
ISBN 978-967-5492-55-6 (hardback)
1. Voice.
2. Communication.
3. Language and languages.
I. Yamaguchi, Toshiko. II. Jariah Mohd. Jan.
III. Sheena Kaur.
612.78

Edited by Hani Hazman
Designed and typeset by Rachel Goh
Printed and bound by CPI Group (UK) Ltd,
Croydon, CR0 4YY

CONTENTS

This page is intentionally left blank.

ABOUT THE CONTRIBUTORS

ANG, Pei Soo
angps@um.edu.my

Pei Soo Ang, PhD is a Senior Lecturer at the Faculty of Languages and Linguistics, Universiti Malaya. Her areas of research interest include discourses of disability, critical disability studies, critical discourse analysis, social semiotics, and multimodality. Her research centres on characterising the discourses of disability as represented in the Malaysian news media, employing a critical semiotic theoretical approach and a multi-perspectival methodology.

BALWANT SINGH, Manjit Kaur
manjitbal49@gmail.com

Manjit Kaur Balwant Singh retired from Berjaya in 2006 after working there for 32 years. To fulfil her lifelong learning desire, she pursued her TESL degree at Open University Malaysia from 2010 to 2014, followed by her Masters (MESL) at Universiti Malaya from 2016 to 2019. Her keen interest in Malaysian English led her to research the loanwords of Sanskrit origin borrowed by the skillful multilinguals in Malaysia. She presented her paper on the subject at the 7th UM International Conference on Discourse and Society and has a passion for researching further.

CHOWDHURY, Tanzeel

tanzeel.chowdhury@yahoo.com

Tanzeel Chowdhury obtained her MA degree from the Faculty of Languages and Linguistics, Universiti Malaya in 2019. She was with Oncosys International, Bangladesh before becoming a lecturer at Independent University, Bangladesh. Her Masters' research focus is on language learning experience and identity formation of Bangladeshi migrant workers in Malaysia. She presented papers at the 17th Asia TEFL International Conference and 6th FLLT International Conference 2019 in Bangkok, Thailand, and Universiti Malaya's Discourse and Society's 2019 international conference in Kuala Lumpur, Malaysia.

CHRZANOWSKA-KLUCZEWSKA, Elżbieta

elzbieta.chrzanowska-kluczewska@uj.edu.pl

Elżbieta Chrzanowska-Kluczewska, PhD is a Professor of Linguistics at the Institute of English Studies, Jagiellonian University in Krakow, Poland. Her main areas of interest cover literary semantics, stylistics, poetics, philosophy of language, and artistic semiotics. Her monographs include *Language-Games: Pro and Against* (Universitas, 2004) and *Much More than Metaphor: Master Tropes of Artistic Language and Imagination* (Peter Lang, 2013), and she co-edited a collected monograph *Language–Literature–the Arts: A Cognitive-Semiotic Interface* (Peter Lang, 2017). She is a board member of the International Association of Literary Semantics and served on the editorial board of *Journal of Literary Semantics* from 2005 to 2020.

HALL, Stephen J

stephenh@sunway.edu.my

Stephen J Hall is Professor and Head of the Centre for English Language Studies, Sunway University, where he has worked for over 13 years. He has managed Malaysian national education projects, been in business as a corporate trainer in Singapore, and trained teachers ASEAN-wide. Dr Hall has over 45 publications, including seven books, and recently co-authored *Manglish: Malaysian English at Its Wackiest* (2nd edition) with Lee Su Kim. He has been involved in TESOL for over 40 years and is passionate about teaching and learning in the digital age of great change.

HOW, Cherish

cherishhow@gmail.com

Cherish How studied pragmatics and sociolinguistics at the Faculty of Languages and Linguistics, Universiti Malaya and teaches English to undergraduate students. Her research areas include speech act of concern on children from foster homes and impoliteness in reality TV shows. She has published in *GEMA Online Journal of Language Studies, Malaysian Journal of Social Sciences and Humanities*, and *Pertanika Journal of Social Sciences and Humanities*. She has also presented papers in international conferences held in Australia, Indonesia, and Italy.

KADHIM, Kais Amir

kalwan@su.edu.om

Kais Amir Kadhim is an Assistant Professor of Linguistics and Translation at the Faculty of Language Studies, Sohar University, Oman. He obtained his PhD in translation from Universiti Sains Malaysia, and teaches linguistics and translation. In 2015, he was awarded a DAAD scholarship to advance his research work at Munich University, Germany. His research interests include stylistics, discourse of media, and the structure of the English language. His latest publication is *The Functional Use of Imperative in the Translated Chapter of Joseph* in *SKASE Journal of Translation and Interpretation.*

KAUR, Sheena

sheena@um.edu.my

Sheena Kaur is a Senior Lecturer at the Faculty of Languages and Linguistics, Universiti Malaya, and currently Deputy Dean of Postgraduate Studies. She obtained her doctoral degree in Applied Linguistics from Lancaster University. Her research interests include applied linguistics, internationalisation of higher education, sociolinguistics, and the use of corpus methodology. She has presented at several national and international conferences and is a reviewer for several journals. Her most recent publications include a commentary on the coronavirus pandemic in Malaysia in the journal *Psychological Trauma: Theory, Research, Practice, and Policy.*

KAZZAZ, Mourhaf
mmkazzaz@jgu.edu.in

Mourhaf Kazzaz is a PhD candidate at the Jindal School of International Affairs, OP Jindal Global University, India. He studied English Language and Literature at Aleppo University, Syria before pursuing his Masters at Mangalore University, India on an Indian Council for Cultural Relations scholarship. His research is centred on the link between political paradigms and their linguistic representation in the context of contemporary Middle East politics. He also worked as a full-time lecturer of English for Special Purposes at Al Furat University, Syria.

MOHD JAN, Jariah
jariah@um.edu.my

Jariah Mohd Jan is an Associate Professor at the Department of English Language and former Dean at the Faculty of Languages and Linguistics, Universiti Malaya. Her main area of research specialisation is sociolinguistics, and she has published widely on gender and power in relation to language, pragmatics, and discourse. Her recent research interest and publications focus on (im)politeness, speech acts, women and leadership, discourse at the workplace, academic concerns of children in foster care, and language and culture of the Kerinchi community.

NG, Lee Luan
ngleeluan@um.edu.my

Lee Luan Ng obtained her MA in applied linguistics from Ohio University, the United States and a PhD from the University of Otago, New Zealand. She teaches postgraduate courses related to research methodology, social dimensions of language, and language acquisition. Her research interests include computer-assisted language learning, blended learning, and interdisciplinary research that relates to health sciences. She is also a certified trainer for the software Nvivo. Her publications include *Translanguaging Practices and Identity Construction of Multilingual Malaysian University Graduates in Digital Media* in the journal *English Teaching & Learning*.

WAHYUDI, Ribut

ribut@bsi.uin-malang.ac.id

Ribut Wahyudi is a lecturer at the Faculty of Humanities, Universitas Islam Negeri Maulana Malik Ibrahim Malang, Indonesia. He gained his MEd in TESOL from University of Sydney, Australia in 2010 and PhD in critical and interdisciplinary ELT from Victoria University of Wellington, New Zealand in 2018. He has published book chapters, among other things, with Palgrave Macmillan and Routledge, and an article in *Journal of IATEFL ESP SIG 2016*. He has reviewed articles for major international journals.

YAMAGUCHI, Toshiko

yamag@um.edu.my; toshikoyamag@gmail.com

Toshiko Yamaguchi is an Associate Professor at the Faculty of Languages and Linguistics, Universiti Malaya, and teaches linguistics to postgraduate students. In her earlier academic career, her research centred on synchronic and diachronic aspects of the Japanese language. She is currently engaged in two book projects, both concerning second language or L2 users/learners: one on Japanese English grammar and the other on Japanese linguistics for L2 learners.

YEO, Siang Lee

yeosl@um.edu.my

Siang Lee Yeo, PhD is a Senior Lecturer at the Faculty of Languages and Linguistics, Universiti Malaya, Kuala Lumpur. His main research interest is on interactions of individuals with communication disorders, particularly those diagnosed with autism. His current research focuses on the interactions between a small group of children with autism and their teachers in an educational setting.

LIST OF ABBREVIATIONS

CEO	Chief Executive Officer
CofP	Community of Practice
DS	Discourse Space
ELF	English as Lingua Franca
ELT	English Language Teaching
ICE	Inner Circle Englishes
IDC	Inside-Deictic-Circle
IR	International Relations
MD	Metadiscourse
ME	Malaysian English
MPA	Multiple-Perspectival Approach
NST	New Straits Times
ODC	Outside-Deictic-Circle
P	Participant
ST	Source Text
STAR	Suara Tunku Abdul Rahman ("Voice of Tunku Abdul Rahman")
TA	Thematic Analysis
TESOL	Teaching English to Speakers of Other Languages
TT	Target Text
WE	World Englishes
WMD	Weapons of Mass Destruction
WHO	World Health Organisation

Chapter 1

Introduction

Toshiko Yamaguchi*

This edited volume, *Voices in Texts and Contexts*, grew out of two conferences, the 6th and 7th International Conferences on Discourse and Society, organised by the Faculty of Languages and Linguistics, Universiti Malaya held in Kuala Lumpur (2017), the capital of Malaysia, and in Subang Jaya (2019), near Kuala Lumpur. Five of the nine chapters were written by scholars who presented their original research at one of these conferences and the other four are contributions by invited scholars whose academic interests intersect with the theme of the volume. The three terms "voices", "texts", and "contexts", comprising the title of the book, immediately inform the reader what the book is concerned with. Each chapter has its own research design or theoretical framework and seeks to present or interpret "voice" or "voices" in light of selected texts and specific contexts. This volume is thus a rich repository of the same concept emerging from a wide range of language choices, social and cultural phenomena, and human interactions and psychology. It also provides the reader with a tapestry of experiences: from attitudes towards Standard English and localised English in Indonesia to the translator's delicate tasks in converting English into Arabic, as well as interpretations of presidential speeches in the United States (US) and Western fantasy literature and painting. Six chapters give special focus to Malaysia at the macro level: the naming of disabled people, mastery of the Malay language by migrants, learning obstacles inherent in the experience of foster children, loanwords of Sanskrit origin in Malaysian English, and academic report writing by adult L2 English users. The unity in the diversity that frames the book will interest readers in Malaysia and beyond.

* Universiti Malaya, Malaysia

This introductory chapter has two parts. It begins with a brief explanation of the three notions underlying the volume, and then outlines how each chapter contributes to the concept of voice on the basis of the chosen texts and contexts. The reason for the selection of three notions of "voice", "text", and "context" is their centrality to the construction of human discourse. What all the chapters do, essentially, is showcase uses of language, or perceptions of uses, and a wide range of messages enshrined therein. Where they differ from each other is in how their authors carry out their analysis and present the concept of voice.

VOICE

Grimes (1975), a pioneer in the field who declared the significance of discourse study to linguistics, took the position, then new, that there are relationships beyond the sentence that linguists cannot explain, precisely because "the organization of a text above the level of the sentence has more to it than can merely be extrapolated from relationships within sentences" (p. 7). *Voice* is one of the effects brought about by the presence of the relationships above the sentences. These relationships are subsumed under the overarching term *discourse*, whose basic definition is "actual instances of communication in the medium of language" (Johnstone, 2018, p. 2). In the present volume, voice is, in the first instance, language itself, something that speakers and writers employ as a tool to discuss a subject or express themselves. According to Elbow (1994), it is "the literal, physical voice". He adds that since such a literal voice may differ between individual speakers, it displays "enormous variation in how we speak from occasion to occasion" (p. 2). Needless to say, voice is not literal and physical at all times but can be understood along the lines of Bakhtin's (1953/1981) now classic, yet still influential, "dialogicality"—a term whose origins lie in literary criticism. The point is that the term espouses the perspective that language is never unitary. Stated differently, language cannot be interpreted on its own—without recourse to another world (that with which the speaker is associated), the otherness of the speaker's self, or the messages that linguistic forms carry with them. The essential factors that have an impact on the formation of voice are society, of which language users are an integral part, and culture, which coexists with society. Bakhtin (1953/1981) aptly explains the composite nature of language as follows:

> Language—like the living concrete environment in which the consciousness of the verbal artist lives—is never unitary. It is unitary only as an abstract grammatical system of normative forms, taken in isolation from the concrete, ideological conceptualizations that fill it, and in isolation from the uninterrupted process of historical becoming that is a characteristic of all living language. (p. 288)

Bakhtin refers specifically to language in literature:

> Literary language—both spoken and written—... is itself stratified and heteroglot in its aspect as an expressive system, that is, in the forms that carry its meanings. (1953/1981, p. 288)

And he adds the following in light of what he calls "genre":

> Certain features of language take on the specific flavor of a given genre: they knit together with specific points of view, specific approaches, forms of thinking, nuances and accents characteristic of the given genre. (1953/1981, p. 289)

While voice features, directly or indirectly, in the discussions of all the chapters, it is important to point out that scholars in general have been geared towards the "social constructivist" perspective of Bakhtinian voice (see Matsuda & Jeffery, 2012). In other words, voice is seen to encompass not merely individual perspectives, as in its traditional understanding, but to be an amalgamation of social and individual dimensions, since voice is, at bottom, a concept in which different qualities are interwoven and entangled. Here, Tardy's (2012) tripartite definition of voice comes to mind. Voice is understood as if it were a continuum, from individual to social and dialogic. When voice reaches its dialogic sphere, it features an interaction of some sort, combining social and individual imprints. According to Tardy, this interactive and thus dialogic perspective culminates in effects such as interpersonal relations or other qualities akin to them. In written discourse, Tardy continues, the reader's role, beside the writer's authorship and the text he/she constructs, is another important resource for voice construction. After all, "voice" is an elusive notion, impossible to ascribe to a single school of thought. Despite its elusiveness, it has been successful as it has served as a fundamental instrument for scholars within different disciplines to interpret human behaviour and the mind.

TEXT

Wales (2014, p. 419) includes in *A Dictionary of Stylistics* an entry on *text*, in which she explains that text comes from the Latin verb *textere*, "to weave". It refers to something interwoven in a sequence of sentences. Let us connect this to Halliday and Hasan's (1985) definition of text. They state that text is "language that is functional" (p. 10), and they mean by *function*, "language that does some job in some context" (p. 10). As such, words carrying functions are opposed to isolated words or sentences that are understood without recourse to the text into which they are to be placed. This definition of function tallies with the nature of voice, on the grounds that voice, in Halliday and Hasan's sense, is essentially a function emerging from language and text. For Halliday and Hasan, text does not live without context; texts coexist with contexts. This close correspondence between the two adds significance to the meaningfulness of the title of this volume.

The chapters in this volume present a fascinating repository of texts, from words to phrases to clauses. The types of texts considered as the objects of study include interviewees' responses (Chapters 2, 3 and 4), newspaper articles (Chapters 5, 6 and 10), political speeches (Chapter 9), news and its translation (Chapter 8), literary works and paintings (Chapter 7), and replies to a questionnaire (Chapter 4).

CONTEXT

The final term is *context*. Context plays a crucial part in interpreting human language and behaviour. Etymologically, the word *context* is derived from *text* and the prefix *com-*, from the Latin *cum*, meaning "with, together, jointly", which became *con-* before certain sounds such as the plosive /t/ (Oxford Dictionary of English, 2010, p. 359). As Halliday and Hasan (1985) rightly wrote, context is something "with the text", and they underscore its essentially physical and psychological nature. That is to say, context is, in their words, "the situation … in which texts unfold and in which they are to be interpreted" (Halliday & Hasan, 1985, p. 5).

Grundy (2008) apprehends the notion of context on the basis of two terms, *macro* and *micro*. The former is presumptive as it is determined by the cultural and/or encyclopaedic knowledge that we have at our disposal. Micro context contrasts with macro in that it is created directly by speakers or writers themselves in the process of text construction. The contexts dealt with in this volume are largely a blend of "macro" and "micro"—cases that cannot be defined by the separation of the two poles.

Another interesting point regarding context is that although none of the chapters make explicit reference to the notions of macro and micro context, their analyses tap them implicitly, to different degrees, to interpret their data and achieve their research objectives. In chapters taking up aspects of Malaysia, society surely represents a macro context, and some interpretations make implicit reference to micro context.

In the following section, I try to specify how voice, text, and context are demonstrated, combined, or negotiated in each chapter.

THIS VOLUME

Chapters 2 and 3 deal with voices of individuals, what Elbow (1994) classifies as "literal voice", which means both the sound and the style of what one says. Chapter 2, *Voices of Migrant Workers in a Community of Practice: A Study of Bangladeshi Migrants' Use of the Malay Language in Malaysia*, by Tanzeel Chowdhury and Lee Luan Ng, is based on interviews conducted by the authors. It discloses five migrants' voices as foreign workers and concludes that the most effective method of integrating blue-collar migrants into the community of practice in Malaysia is fluency in the target language, which might well improve their marginalised social status; although, importantly, this alone is unlikely to eliminate their social distance from the target community. Chowdhury and Ng suggest that specific training courses be offered to new migrants to help them join the target society successfully. Chapter 3, *Voices of Concern Amongst Teachers on the Academic Performance of Foster Children*, by Cherish How and Jariah Mohd Jan, also utilises interviews to collect data. "Voices" here refers to teachers' views on foster children at school. The major tool of analysis is the classification of teachers' expressions of concern by looking at certain linguistic usages (e.g. intensifiers and modal verbs). Adopting an approach informed by speech act theory, the authors find that the most salient strategy employed by the interviewed teachers is the representative act, constituting 81 per cent of all tokens. Since a representative act "represents" the speaker's inner mind, the discovery of such an act warrants the interpretation that teachers' responses correspond to the forces of otherness of Bakhtin's original thesis.

Chapter 4, *Understanding and Applying the Critical Academic Voice: Bridging Theory and Practice*, by Stephen J Hall, adopts a reflective approach to investigate how voice is integrated in academic written discourse in the Malaysian university context. Hall sources material from 20 respondents of a questionnaire as well as semi-structured interviews. He defines academic voice as "a series of complex choices needed to position oneself as both an authoritative writer and a critical scholar". In other words, academic voice is embodied in the construction of written discourse, often by means of manipulating metadiscourse strategies. Hall's study discloses that writing academic reports in academic voice poses more challenges than writing without it for users of English as an additional language.

Chapters 5 and 6 focus on major English-language newspapers in Malaysia as objects of study. In Chapter 5, *Multiethnic Voices in Loanwords in the Malaysian Dailies*, Manjit Kaur Balwant Singh seeks to explain how voices emerge in the usage of loanwords in newspaper articles in Malaysian English, particularly those derived from Sanskrit by way of Malay. By considering contrast as the realisation of dialogic voices, the chapter discloses the ways in which loanwords are adopted or their meanings expanded in response to Malaysian sociocultural contexts or, more technically, contrasting scenarios. This shows that usages of loanwords do not develop through simple contact between two languages but through conceptual dynamism, which is clearly evidenced in Malaysian print-media discourse. In Chapter 6, *Voices in the Naming of Disabled Persons in Print Media*, Pei Soo Ang and Siang Lee Yeo analyse examples taken from *The Star*, a mainstream English-language newspaper in Malaysia, and seek to identify how disabled people are named. Since the act of naming disabled people reveals the reality of a society in which such terms are used, as well as the linguistic reality, the authors categorise these "namers" as "social actors". These actors utilise lexical, structural, or euphemistic tools which are reflections of social rules and practices embedded in the Malaysian print media. Voices are claimed to be present in the ways social actors construct ideology in discourse, which are argued to represent the Bakhtinian view of heteroglossia.

Chapter 7, *Voices of Fear: Nightmare Landscapes in Western Fantasy Literature and Fantastic Painting*, by Elżbieta Chrzanowska-Kluczewska, analyses nightmarish landscapes in fantasy literature and painting in European and North American contexts. While poems, prose works and paintings are categorically distinct, the emotion of fear is a salient ingredient of nightmarish landscapes, shared by the three artistic genres. Chrzanowska-Kluczewska argues that the voice of fear, which is defined as a basic emotion, bears an ambiguity between displeasure and excitement, and that this is brought about when the writer/painter intends to impress the reader/viewer. This aspect of fear is found to have a parallel to Bakhtinian heteroglossia or, to use another word, intertextuality.

Chapter 8, *Translating English Political Discourse into Arabic: Roles of the Translator, Context, and Voice*, by Kais Amir Kadhim, tackles translation from English to Arabic based on extracts from BBC News as the source text and their Arabic translations, also offered by the BBC, as the target text, and considers translators' multiple voices. The translators often go beyond their role of transforming text from one language to another, particularly when they intend to transmit cultural or social information. This chapter shows effectively how translators take on the role of dominant writers and how they respond to their imaginary audience(s). The multiple roles played by the translators fit neatly into the notion of Bakhtinian dialogic voice.

Chapters 9 and 10 examine two different and distinct texts and contexts, but they share a similar standpoint in that they investigate their problems from a "critical" perspective of language use. In Chapter 9, *Investigating the Shift in Voice and Rhetoric of United States Administrations Regarding the Middle East 2001–2016* Mourhaf Kazzaz analyses key speeches given by US presidents George W Bush and Barack Obama, drawing upon the theoretical framework of critical discourse analysis, and reports two important findings that are apparently linked. First, there is a remarkable shift between the two administrations. Second, there is a marked contrast between Bush's and Obama's speech styles. The results are cogently reinterpreted by means of Bakhtinian multiple voices. Although character voice is present in both presidents' speeches, interlocutor voice is absent from Obama's. The reason Bush used interlocutor voice within the same genre of presidential speech is due to the "false solidarity" it allowed him to engender effectively with the audience. In Chapter 10, *Critically Negotiating British and American Englishes: Voices from Indonesia*, Ribut Wahyudi pursues the problematic issue of native speakerism in an Indonesian context. The chapter takes up articles posted by two Indonesian scholars, Rezia Usman and Nelly Martin, in a national English-language newspaper, *The Jakarta Post*. A critical analysis comes into play when the contents of the articles are regarded as "subjectivities" in the Foucauldian sense. Voice is conceived of by Wahyudi as a contrast between "self" as an Indonesian and "other" as someone who seeks to speak English like a native speaker. The chapter offers the important message that this attitudinal dialogism may not be an effect of problematisation of native speakerism in Indonesia alone but also in many other, if not all, Expanding Circle countries around the globe.

REFERENCES

Bakhtin, M. M. (1981). *The dialogic imagination: Four essays* (C. Emerson & M. Holquist, Trans.). University of Texas Press. (Original work published 1953)

Elbow, P. (1994). What do we mean when we talk about voice in writing? In K. Yancey (Ed.), *Voices on voice: Perspectives, definition, inquiry* (pp. 1–35). National Council of Teachers of English.

Grimes, J. E. (1975). *The thread of discourse.* Mouton.

Grundy, P. (2008). *Doing pragmatics* (3rd ed.). Arnold.

Halliday, M. A. K., & Hasan, R. (1985). *Language, context, and text: Aspects of language in a social-semiotic perspective.* Deakin University.

Johnstone, B. (2018). *Discourse analysis* (3rd ed.). John Wiley & Sons.

Matsuda, P. K., & Jeffery, J. V. (2012). Voice in student essays. In K. Hyland & C. S. Guinda (Eds.), *Stance and voice in academic genres* (pp. 151–165). Palgrave Macmillan.

Oxford Dictionary of English. (2010). Context. In A. Stevenson (Ed.), *Oxford dictionary of English* (3rd ed.). Oxford University Press.

Tardy, C. M. (2012). Current conceptions of voice. In K. Hyland & C. S. Guinda (Eds.), *Stance and voice in academic genres* (pp. 34–48). Palgrave Macmillan.

Wales, K. (2014). *A dictionary of stylistics* (3rd ed.). Pearson Education.

Chapter 2

Voices of Migrant Workers in a Community of Practice: A Study of Bangladeshi Migrants' Use of the Malay Language in Malaysia[1]

Tanzeel Chowdhury* & Lee Luan Ng‡

ABSTRACT

One of the major consequences of migration is the change in the migrants' language practices which is indirectly linked to their identity construction. Migrants usually strive to successfully blend into society to facilitate their adaptation to the new culture and language practice. The present study aims to explore the voices of a specific group of migrant workers by investigating how five Bangladeshi migrants have negotiated their identities in a specific community of practice. The results reveal that the language environment, investment in the language learning process, and the social distance between the interlocutors are some important aspects impacting the migration process. The implications of the study suggest that training in language for specific purposes along with employee orientation programmes may help migrants successfully blend into the target society.

Keywords Identity construction, social distance, migrant workers, community of practice

1 We would like to dedicate this chapter to the many migrant workers who are involved in many economic activities in Malaysia. We hope this chapter will contribute towards improving the relevant training for blue-collar migrant workers that is put in place by their local employers. This work was partially supported by Universiti Malaya Research Grants [UMRG: RP051C-17HTM].

* Independent scholar, Bangladesh

‡ Universiti Malaya, Malaysia

INTRODUCTION

Part of the impact of globalisation is the increase in human migration from one country to another in search of jobs. These individuals who migrate from one country to another intending to be employed, other than on their account, are called *migrant workers* (Usher, 2005). Migration for employment has become a global issue since it has affected most countries in recent years (International Labour Organization, 2006). According to the International Labour Organization's estimates, in 2017, migrant workers accounted for 164 million of the world's approximately 258 million international migrants. Twenty-point-four per cent of these migrants migrate to Asia and the Pacific region (International Labour Organization, 2015). Workers in these regions mainly migrate for elementary occupations and medium-skilled work. These migrant workers contribute to the host countries' economic development through skills, labour, services, and competitiveness. They also contribute to financial remittance and skill and knowledge development upon their return to their countries of origin. Many of these migrant workers fill labour market niches in destination countries by taking up jobs that nationals do not want or cannot fill. However, a number of these workers also experience labour exploitation and abuse during recruitment and employment (Kneebone, 2010), which relates to the issue of the well-being of the migrant workforce in the host country. This discrimination may create an imbalance in the overall workforce in the host country, which is a concern since tension in the workforce tends to create pressure in the economy.

Malaysia has one of the largest migrant worker populations among Asian countries, comprised of workers from different countries in the region. A substantial number of these migrant workers who work at restaurants, petrol stations, and in the manufacturing, construction, and plantation sectors come from Bangladesh. The majority of these migrant workers are low- or unskilled and migrate to Malaysia with no prior knowledge of the linguistic and cultural practices in the target communities. Moreover, they have limited command of lingua franca such as English which makes it difficult for them to adapt to the environment in the host country, which may be linked to the phenomena of exploitation and abuse mentioned earlier. Yet, some of these Bangladeshi migrant workers seem to be successful in different social activities as they adapt to the new social environment. It appears that language works as one of the main tools that present the voices of these workers and enable them to change their marginalised position. The community in which they work seems to affect this transition process too. The practices in the target community appear to cause a change in their language practices and subsequent identity construction.

Therefore, this study focuses on the experiences of blue-collar Bangladeshi migrant workers who are located in a specific community of practice (CofP) in Malaysia, specifically their struggles while trying to create a sense of belonging in the host community. It investigates the factors that impact identity negotiation by these low-skilled Bangladeshi migrant workers in Malaysia in terms of their language practices within a specific CofP. Hence, the study aims to explore two questions:

(1) What factors impact the identity construction of blue-collar Bangladeshi migrant workers in Malaysia in terms of their language practices in a particular CofP?

(2) What impact does this CofP have on the process of Bangladeshi migrant workers' identity negotiation?

The outcomes of the study will help researchers understand how the CofP can assist migrant workers in settling down in the target context. Additionally, the findings will prove to be relevant to Language for Specific Purpose training as part of employee orientation programmes for migrant workers.

LITERATURE REVIEW

> A community of practice is a set of relations among persons, activity and world, over time and in relation with other tangential and overlapping communities of practice. (Lave & Wenger, 2002, p. 115)

A CofP consists of social subgroups engaged in common activities. The focus of a CofP is the practice or activity of the members that indicates they belong to the group. The practice or activity includes global or specific aspects of language structure, discourse, and interaction patterns. The CofP framework explains the changing nature of identities and social relations that occur during socialisation (Lave & Wenger, 1991). Wenger (1998, as cited in Holmes & Meyerhoff, 1999) introduces three main dimensions as the basis for the creation of a CofP. First, *mutual engagement* refers to the regular interaction between speakers. Second is a *jointly negotiated enterprise* consisting of features such as shared goals, contributions from participants during ongoing processes of negotiation, an understanding of roles of individuals, and mutually defining identities. Finally, there is a *shared repertoire* developed by speakers: linguistic resources and routines that accumulate over time and are subject to negotiation. Therefore, according to these dimensions, speakers in a CofP develop a common sense of identity as they spend more time together sharing knowledge through interaction.

This interaction in a CofP creates changes in the language-related experiences of migrant workers and shapes their identities. This is because the interaction transforms who the workers are and what they can do in the community. Workers in a CofP are given different social roles with different responsibilities. While mastering those roles and interacting with other members, they acquire the new language and at the same time construct multiple identities. According to Wenger (1998, as cited in Holmes & Meyerhoff, 1999), "learning is a natural and inevitable aspect of life, and a fundamentally social process" (p. 174). Hence, the CofP perspective views the language acquisition process as a mode of participation in the social world rather than a simple acquisition of knowledge in isolation, and pays attention to the membership of the learners in the community rather than to the learners themselves (Haneda, 1997). Since individuals play different roles in different communities, they negotiate and develop their identities while playing these roles within and across communities.

A discussion of identity is important in this regard. Identity is "how a person understands his or her relationship to the world, how that relationship is constructed across time and space, and how the person understands possibilities for the future" (Norton, 2000, p. 5). It is an ever-evolving process that changes over time depending on the roles individuals play in different social settings. It informs social relationships and communicative exchanges which result in individuals having more than one identity in a given context (Block, 2006). Norton (1995) suggests that the power relationship between the language learner and the target language speakers is crucial. How much power the learner feels he or she has while speaking the language plays an important role in constructing his or her identity in the context. Hence, identity is also constructed based on the social relationships of the subjects, which change over time as the subjects take different positions in different social situations. Identities constructed in different social situations are termed the social identity of individuals. It is the sense of belonging to a particular social group and may be defined by ethnicity, language or any other group (Tajfel & Turner, 1979). According to Tajfel (1978, as cited in Holmes & Meyerhoff, 1999), social identity argues "... that individuals' social behaviour is a joint function of (a) their affiliation to a particular group identity that is salient at that moment in the interaction, and (b) their interpretation of the relationship of one's in-group to salient out-groups ..." (p. 177). These identities are abstract representations that are constructed over time through social processes.

Language learners' complex social identities are reproduced in their daily social interactions. Through language, learners negotiate a sense of self within and across different contexts and also gain or are denied access to powerful social networks (Norton, 1995). Thus, language is not only a medium of communication but also a way through which individuals gain access to a particular social context. Norton (2010) views language "not only as a linguistic system, but as a social practice in which experiences are organized and identities negotiated" (p. 364). Identity construction is related to language use and all kinds of interactions in an individual's daily life. The role of language in interaction is determined by the identity perceived by the participants. At the same time, the use of language helps speakers shape their identity in a particular context (Norton, 2000). Hence, there is an interrelationship between language and identity that is developed over time with the increased involvement in interactions.

Language and identity are combined through language choice and language practice to convey social roles and identities. Speakers may be considered "insiders" (in-group) by mirroring the language of the interlocutors or "outsiders" (out-group) when their language differs from members of the social group. Hence, speakers looking for positive social identity can modify their language or learn a new language to join a particular social group

(Gee, 2004). Therefore, language plays an important role in social identity construction and helps individuals understand their roles and positions in society.

In a similar way, the fluid nature of identity results in a shift in individuals' identities over time. Research on language socialisation demonstrates that when individuals participate in a particular social group, they display identity in new ways related to the linguistic conventions of the group (Vickers & Deckert, 2013). The CofP framework helps delineate the shifting of identities and the construction of relations that occur in the process of socialisation (Lave & Wenger, 1991). According to Lave and Wenger (1991):

> Moving toward full participation in practice involves not just a greater commitment of time, intensified effort, more and broader responsibilities within the community, and more difficult and risky tasks, but, more significantly, an increasing sense of identity as a master practitioner. (p. 110)

Therefore, according to the CofP framework, mastery of language is tied to a shift in identity. This framework helps us understand the movement of individual identity from novice to expert. The ways through which individuals display expert and novice identities are facilitated by group conformity. The change occurs when individuals develop skills within the CofP. Vickers and Deckert (2013) mention: "As participants move from novice to expert, they also move from the periphery of the community of practice to the core, thereby, shifting identity with relation to the group" (p. 120).

Vickers and Deckert (2013) in their study find that a shift in expertise from novice to expert coincides with multiple shifts in other aspects of the identity of a migrant worker participating in a CofP. Another result of the shift in identity is investment in the learning process. Liu and Xu's (2013) study indicates that new teachers joining a CofP shift their identities to adapt to the new work order in the workplace and the learning process is shaped as well as reshaped by various power relationships in the community. Lee's (2014) study also reveals that immigrants participate in different communities in the target context, creating several changes in their identities. They tailor their strategies to different problems while learning a language in order to become successful speakers of that language.

The present study makes use of the above-mentioned notion of identity shift in a CofP to investigate the shift of identity of the Bangladeshi migrant workers via their voices as the shift takes place within the bounds of a particular CofP. It also uses Mallinson and Childs's (2007) insight towards the end of the chapter.

METHODOLOGY

Based on pre-identified criteria, qualitative data were collected using a semi-structured interview with five Bangladeshi migrant workers working in multiple branches of KK Mart, a Malaysian grocery chain. The study employed random purposive sampling, in which participants were randomly selected based on the criteria set by the researchers: (a) Bangladeshi nationals, (b) blue-collar workers, and (c) working in Malaysia. The shops included in the study are located in KL Sentral, Kuala Lumpur. There is a community of workers who are employed in these shops in KL Sentral, to which the participants belong. However, they do not necessarily share similar repertoire in terms of their language practices. The following table presents the demographic profile of the participants.

Table 1 Demographic profile of migrants working at KK Mart, KL Sentral

Participants	P1	P2	P3	P4	P5
Duration of stay in Malaysia	4 years	5 years	6 months	8 months	3 months
Job responsibilities	Providing customer service	Providing customer service	Arranging products & customer service	Arranging products	Arranging products
Education	Secondary school certificate	Secondary school certificate	Higher secondary school certificate	Higher secondary school certificate	None
Proficiency in English	Elementary	Secondary	Secondary	Secondary	None

A semi-structured interview was used as the primary research instrument for data collection, whereby a set of self-prepared questions was used to guide the interview. Following Seidman's (1991) approach, a wide range of open-ended questions was asked to create an atmosphere of friendly conversation rather than that of a data-gathering interview, to help the respondents open up to the interviewer. The interviews were conducted in the participants' mother tongue, Bangla, to help respondents express their feelings and thoughts freely and create solidarity between the interlocutors. The data were collected over one week, with each conversation lasting from 30 to 40 minutes. The conversations were audio-recorded with the respondents' consent and later transcribed and translated for analysis.

The analysis of the data was conducted using Thematic Analysis (TA), a technique used as part of a systematic description of the content in semi-structured interviews (Kvale, 2007). The study employed the following six phases of TA introduced by Braun and Clarke (2006):

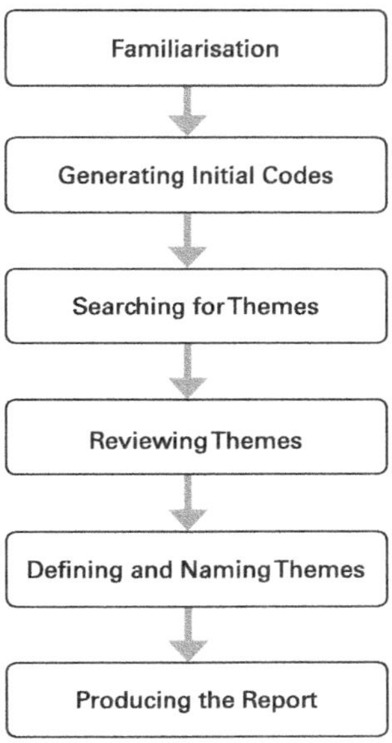

Figure 1 Phases of thematic analysis

The researchers first read and re-read the transcribed data to be familiar with their content. Then, the data were *coded* to identify important features relevant to the research questions. The codes were then examined and collated to *identify themes* which later were *reviewed* against the data set to determine their relevance. The next step involved developing a detailed analysis of each theme along with *deciding names* for them. Finally, a *coherent narrative* representing the voices of the Bangladeshi migrant workers was outlined to discuss the themes and describe the patterns.

ANALYSIS AND DISCUSSION

The study aimed to investigate the factors that affect the identity formation of Bangladeshi blue-collar migrant workers working in a specific CofP in Malaysia in terms of their language practices, as can be observed through their voices. After the data were collected, a qualitative analysis was conducted following Norton's (2000) approach to explore the relationship between identity and language learning. The analysis took into consideration the respondents' interpretations of needs in the target society, their relationships with other people, and their beliefs in social practices, to appropriately understand their identity formation in terms of language acquisition in that specific CofP. As discussed earlier, individual identity relates to an individual's perception of his or her roles in specific contexts in society, while social identity is the sense of belonging to a particular social group. Keeping this notion of identity in mind, the following sections present an analysis of the voices of Bangladeshi migrant workers in a specific CofP in Malaysia to determine the factors behind their identity formation in terms of their language practices and how the community affects their identity formation.

The qualitative analysis of data was conducted following Norton's (2000) approach to explore the relationship between identity and language learning. The analysis not only identified the respondents' choice of language for interaction in the target society and their reasons behind choosing that specific language, but also considered their interpretations of needs in the society, their relationships with people, and their beliefs in social practices to understand their identity formation. In line with that, the following sections present an analysis of the data to determine the relationship between language and identity among Bangladeshi migrant workers in Malaysia and how the community in which they work affects their language learning process.

The analysis of the data revealed three aspects that impact the identity negotiation of the migrant workers in the specific CofP. The following table briefly presents these aspects.

Table 2 Overall aspects based on the interview sessions

Aspects that Impact Identity Negotiation of Migrant Workers in CofP	Participants				
	P1	P2	P3	P4	P5
The language environment in the CofP	✓	✓	✓		
Investment in the language learning process			✓		
Social distance between the migrants and the locals	✓			✓	

As can be observed in Table 2, the first aspect, *the language environment in the CofP*, was detected during the interview sessions with P1, P2, and P3. The second aspect, *investment in the language learning process*, was extracted from P3's interview and the third aspect, *social distance between the migrants and the locals*, was identified from P1 and P4.

The next section presents a detailed discussion of how the aspects impact identity construction of Bangladeshi migrant workers working in a particular CofP in Malaysia in terms of their language practices.

The language environment in the CofP

The language environment in the workplace is an important factor that affects migrant workers' language choices. All the migrant workers stated that they needed to learn Malay because no one at their workplace preferred to speak in English. As P3 mentioned:

> If you need to order goods for the shop, you have to use Malay because otherwise, the people will not understand you. No one in this sector can speak in English properly. So, even if you know good English, learning Malay is 100% necessary. Also, all managers use Malay. English does not work with them. English can be used only for customer service.

P2 shared a similar experience:

> No one here in Malaysia wants to speak in English. They always prefer Malay over English. So you have to learn the language.

Hence, Malay is the dominant language in this particular CofP. The respondents mentioned that English is needed in Malaysia since one can encounter foreigners almost every day. However, they do not require a good command of English because they only need it to talk to foreign customers. On the other hand, being fluent in Malay is essential because they need to converse in it if they want to blend into the CofP.

All the respondents mentioned that they felt marginalised when they first came to Malaysia and joined their workplace since they could not speak the local language. Also, as can be observed in Table 1, all of them had to start with very basic work such as arranging products. They were not given important tasks even if they had the expertise, simply because they could not speak Malay. P1, P2 and P3 could upgrade their posts after having developed fluent Malay. P4 and P5, on the other hand, are still working at the basic level because they are not fluent in the language. P5 does not even express any hope of success in the future because he has given up hope of learning Malay. He believes that since he is not educated, he cannot learn a new language and hence will never be able to improve his position in society. He does not even attempt to communicate with any of the locals and has remained marginalised ever since he arrived in Malaysia.

Hence, expertise in Malay has helped at least three of these workers gain confidence as professionals in the community. They are observed to have overcome the marginalised position created by the language barrier by acquiring the local language. According to P1:

> I used to feel nervous all the time when I first came here because I did not know the language. After some months, I started to overcome this nervousness when I started to learn Malay. The Malay manager is very supportive.

Therefore, being fluent in Malay has enabled these migrants to take active part in community practices and overcome their marginalised position. It allows them to consider themselves legitimate professional members of the community. Therefore, the acquisition of the dominant language of the CofP is important for migrants to create a professional identity at their workplace.

According to Lave and Wenger (1991), language learning takes place as a result of participation in community practices. Since blue-collar migrants participate in common activities in the community with Malay-speaking locals, they learn the language in the process. Moreover, learners are given specific roles and responsibilities in the community. While fulfilling these roles, they learn the language and construct multiple identities associated with those roles (Lave & Wenger, 1991). They become successful speakers of Malay and at the same time gain expertise in their particular roles in the CofP. It enables them to create a professional identity in that particular CofP. Thus, becoming proficient speakers of Malay helps them create a professional identity as workers in that particular Malay-speaking CofP.

Investment in the language learning process

The notion of investment in the target language learning process "attempts to capture the relationship of the language learner to the changing social world" (Norton, 1995, p. 17). The migrants' investments in the language learning process can be understood through their expectations from the target CofPs and how they understand future possibilities in those specific communities. Blue-collar migrants in Malaysia can expect better job prospects if they can learn Malay since it is the dominant language spoken by the majority of the community. This is the reason why they invest in the language learning process and become successful speakers of Malay. For example, P3 mentioned:

> If I can speak in Malay, I will be able to provide better customer service. That will help me expand my scope of work here in this shop.

Therefore, the relatively higher investment in the language learning process among blue-collar workers is the result of a desire to have better prospects in the CofP. According to Norton (2000), "when learners invest in a second language, they do so with the understanding that they will acquire a wider range of symbolic and material resources, which will, in turn, increase the value of their cultural capital. Learners expect or hope to have a good return on that investment—a return that will give them access to hitherto unattainable resources" (p. 10). The responses suggest that Malay is the primary tool for the migrants that enables them to successfully blend into the target society. Acquisition of the language increases their linguistic capital which in turn gives them access to other resources such as better job prospects in the target community. This is the reason why there is great investment in Malay learning among these Bangladeshi migrant workers.

Moreover, the concept of investment suggested by Norton (1995) indicates the relationship of learners to the target language and their desire to learn and practise it. Their investment in the language learning process results in the investment of their changing identity (Norton, 2000). Most Bangladeshi blue-collar migrants migrate to Malaysia as expatriates with no prior knowledge of the culture and society. They are initially denied legitimate participation and membership in society because of the lack of communicative competence. However, they gradually identify their social roles in the CofP by applying strategies to learn Malay. This investment in the language learning process helps them shift their identity from novice speakers of the language to expert speakers.

Lave and Wenger (1991) mention that achieving full participation in practice does not only require a "greater commitment of time, intensified effort, more and broader responsibilities within the community, and more difficult and risky tasks but, more significantly, an increasing sense of identity as a master practitioner" (p. 110). The newly arrived blue-collar migrants learn Malay through "legitimate peripheral participation" from the "old-timers". To achieve participation, these migrants conceptualise themselves as members of that particular community, not just individuals who have come to Malaysia for work. From being peripheral members of these communities, these workers try and become successful Malay speakers and thus achieve full participation. Therefore progress towards mastery of the language is tied to a shift in identity for these blue-collar workers.

Social distance between the migrants and the locals

The aforementioned themes suggest that Bangladeshi migrants learn Malay very easily, which helps them create a professional and expert identity. However, expertise in this language does not help minimise the social distance between them and other people in the CofP. The participants reported that even though they can speak fluent Malay, they are not that successful in making local friends. The demanding job schedule is the first reason behind this social distance between these two groups. The migrant workers do not get the opportunity to use Malay in social interactions apart from those at their workplace because of their demanding work schedule: seven days per week and twelve hours per day. Hence, they do not get opportunities to go out and mingle with locals. The lack of opportunity to go out and spend time in the community creates social distance between migrants and locals. As a result of this, the desire to blend into the target society becomes challenging for migrants to fulfil. Even though it is easier for them to create a professional identity in the target CofP, the social distance makes it difficult for them to create social identity.

Another reason why these migrants cannot minimise social distance is that even if they can speak fluent Malay, the locals still identify them as expatriates. P1 mentioned:

> Even if I know Malay, I am still a foreigner. Locals also know this. They don't talk to us as their friends. They just say whatever is necessary.

Hence, the Malay-speaking locals do not seem comfortable socialising with migrants who join the community as new members. As a result, instead of trying to merge into the target society, they create a community with their fellow Bangladeshi workers outside of the community. They spend their free time together and also shop at Bangladeshi shops. For these migrants, it creates a sense of solidarity and nationalism, which indirectly influences the social distance between these migrant workers and the locals. P4 explained why he prefers to socialise with his countrymen as he views himself as a Bangladeshi and does not plan to stay in the host country for a long period:

> I don't want to stay here for long. My country is everything for me; it is my heaven. My future is there. Bangla is our main language because we are Bangladeshis.

Besides, competence in Malay does not provide these workers with freedom of speech. None of the blue-collar migrants reported initiating conversation in Malay with the native speakers. All of them mentioned that they only speak Malay when they are spoken to. Norton (2000) suggests that communicative competence in the target language gives speakers "the power to impose reception" (p. 8), enabling them to get access to the society. However, in this case, even though blue-collar migrants achieve communicative competence in Malay, they do not achieve the "right to speech" and remain marginalised in the community. Hence, expertise in Malay does not help them create a social identity in their CofP.

Cervatiuc (2009) finds that migrants who regard themselves to be incompetent speakers of the target language develop strategies to create opportunities to communicate. They look for situations in which they can speak and try to break the barriers of marginalisation. In this process, they create a social identity whereby they can finally identify themselves as members of the community. However, the Bangladeshi migrant workers in this study did not report developing any strategy to cope with their issue of creating social identity in Malaysia. They tend to accept their marginalised position in the society and prefer group identification with their fellow Bangladeshi migrants as expatriates, resulting in a strong sense of companionship, but not necessarily bridging their social distance from the local community.

CONCLUSION

The voices of these migrant workers suggest that the dominant language in the CofP plays a significant role in the way migrants perceive how language can help them achieve social power. Most of them learn Malay because this is the tool that can potentially help create solidarity with other members of the community. The success in learning Malay enables them to create a sense of professionalism in the CofP. The need to learn Malay makes these Bangladeshi migrant workers invest in the language learning process, and eventually aids them to master the language while shifting their identities from novice to expert members of the society. However, expertise in Malay does not necessarily aid them in creating legitimate social identities and minimising social distance.

The findings of the study suggest a few implications. First, learners invest in the target language learning process and learn better when the need to learn the language is great. Hence, identifying and addressing learners' language needs in their living context may help them become successful language learners and adapt to the work environment faster. This could be useful for language teachers and curriculum developers. Secondly, language learners need to use the target language in real situations to help them in the formation of social identity as legitimate speakers of the target language. Hence, it is important to provide learners with opportunities to practise the target language in real situations to enable them to gain confidence. Finally, CofPs play an important role in the natural language learning process of migrants.

The above-mentioned implications may provide some suggestions in developing strategies to include in the language courses designed for migrants travelling to a target country for the first time. These strategies can be included in Language for Specific Purpose courses for new migrants along with employee orientation programmes. First, course developers can identify the language needs of migrants in the target society. They can then develop language courses tailored to those specific needs to help individuals become successful language learners. Also, language courses can include activities during which learners will get opportunities to practise the target language in real-life situations. It will develop confidence in the learners to speak the target language. Furthermore, language teachers can create small communities of practice with language learners who share similar interests. Learners will learn the language in a natural setting while completing tasks in those communities. Supporting new migrants in such ways may help them overcome their marginalised position at an earlier stage of their migration.

Simultaneously, this study also poses a few limitations. The literature review drew attention to Mallinson and Childs's (2007) study in which they suggest that migrants may have differences in terms of their language practices even though they belong to similar CofPs or have similar demographic profiles. This is because several other factors such as structures of social class, gender, race and language also affect the process of language acquisition and identity construction. Similarly, in the present study there may have been other factors behind the Bangladeshi migrants' language acquisition and identity construction that were overlooked due to time constraints. Taking these factors into account may derive different results. Moreover, the study was conducted in an urban setting and did not consider the context of rural settings. In addition, only male blue-collar migrants participated in the interviews, while white-collar and female migrants were not included. Besides, the study managed to collect data from a limited sample size due to time constraints. Hence, further studies are advised to cover different contexts, such as rural areas and other areas in the urban context in Malaysia, to provide better and more detailed insight into this area of study. Finally, conducting further studies with bigger sample sizes consisting of different demographic profiles may provide more crucial findings that can be used to fortify the generalisation regarding this area of study.

Concluding remarks

Most Bangladeshi blue-collar migrants travel to Malaysia with no prior knowledge of the cultural and linguistic practices of the target context. Many mentioned that they have to deal with culture shock upon arriving in Malaysia, which makes the adaptation and integration process more challenging for them. Therefore, employers and foreign labour agencies should consider organising orientations for new migrants to help them familiarise themselves with the social and linguistic practices of the target context. It will facilitate their transition to the new society and help them play more effective roles as members of the Malaysian community.

REFERENCES

Block, D. (2006). Identity in applied linguistics. In T. Omoniyi & G. White (Eds.), *The Sociolinguistics of Identity* (pp. 34–49). Bloomsbury.

Braun, V., & Clarke, V. (2006). Using thematic analysis in psychology. *Qualitative Research in Psychology, 3*(2), 77–101.

Cervatiuc, A. (2009). Identity, good language learning, and adult immigrants in Canada. *Journal of Language, Identity, and Education, 8*(4), 254–271.

Gee, J. P. (2004). *Situated language and learning: A critique of traditional schooling.* Routledge.

Haneda, M. (1997). Second language learning in a 'Community of Practice': A case study of adult Japanese learners. *Canadian Modern Language Review, 54*(1), 11–27.

Holmes, J., & Meyerhoff, M. (1999). The Community of Practice: Theories and methodologies in language and gender research. *Language in Society, 28*(2), 173–183.

International Labour Organization. (2006). *ILO multilateral framework on labour migration: Non-binding principles and guidelines for a rights-based approach.* International Labour Office.

International Labour Organization. (2015). *ILO global estimates on migrant workers: Results and methodology.* International Labour Office.

Kneebone, S. (2010). The governance of labor migration in Southeast Asia. *Global Governance, 16*(3), 383–396.

Kvale, S. (2007). Analyzing interviews. In *Qualitative research kit: Doing interviews* (pp. 102–119). Sage Publications.

Lave, J., & Wenger, E. (1991). *Situated learning: Legitimate peripheral participation.* Cambridge University Press.

Lave, J., & Wenger, E. (2002). Legitimate peripheral participation in communities of practice. In R. Harrison, F. Reeve, A. Hanson & J. Clarke (Eds.), *Supporting lifelong learning volume 1: Perspectives on learning* (pp. 111–126). Routledge Falmer.

Lee, E. J. (2014). Motivation, investment, and identity in English language development: A longitudinal case study. *System, 42*, 440–450.

Liu, Y., & Xu, Y. (2013). The trajectory of learning in a teacher community of practice: A narrative inquiry of a language teacher's identity in the workplace. *Research Papers in Education, 28*(2), 176–195.

Mallinson, C., & Childs, B. (2007). Communities of practice in sociolinguistic description: Analyzing language and identity practices among black women in Appalachia. *Gender and Language, 1*(2), 173–206.

Norton, B. (1995). Social identity, investment, and language learning. *TESOL Quarterly, 29*(1), 9–31.

Norton, B. (2000). *Identity and language learning: Gender, ethnicity, and educational change.* Pearson.

Norton, B. (2010). Language and identity. In N. Hornberger & S. McKay (Eds.), *Sociolinguistics and language education* (pp. 349–369). Channel View Publications.

Pavlenko, A., & Norton, B. (2007). Imagined communities, identity, and English language learning. In J. Cummins & C. Davison (Eds.), *Springer international handbooks of education: International handbook of English language teaching* (Vol. 15, pp. 669–680). Springer.

Seidman, I. E. (1991). *Interviewing as qualitative research: A guide for researchers in education and the social sciences.* Teachers College Press.

Tajfel, H., & Turner, J. C. (1979). An integrative theory of intergroup conflict. In W. G. Austin & S. Worchel (Eds.), *The social psychology of intergroup relations* (pp. 33–47). Brooks Cole.

Usher, E. (Ed.). (2005). *Essentials of migration management: A guide for policy makers and practitioners* (Vol. 3). United Nations Publications.

Vickers, C. H., & Deckert, S. K. (2013). Sewing empowerment: Examining multiple identity shifts as a Mexican immigrant woman develops expertise in a sewing cooperative community of practice. *Journal of Language, Identity & Education, 12*(2), 116–135.

Chapter 3

Voices of Concern Amongst Teachers on the Academic Performance of Foster Children

Cherish How* & Jariah Mohd Jan*

ABSTRACT

Since foster children have to leave foster home once they turn 18, being financially independent is challenging, especially for those without good academic credentials. Hence, this qualitative study examines the voices of concerned teachers as they attend to the academic needs of foster children in Malaysia. Using Searle's (1976) speech act categories and Hall and Hord's (1987) stages of concern for analysis, findings reveal that the representative act is prominent in teachers' concern when they describe, demonstrate, state, and explain educational matters regarding foster children. More specifically, the teachers utilise linguistic features to intensify their concern. In doing so, the children's academic needs can be highlighted to social welfare agencies to provide better educational services for foster children.

Keywords Voices of concern, speech act theory, academic performance, teachers, foster children

* Universiti Malaya, Malaysia

INTRODUCTION

Children from foster homes attend public schools and undergo national examinations just like children from typical family backgrounds. Nevertheless, the majority of foster children do not perform well academically (Berger et al., 2015; Forsman et al., 2016; O'Higgins et al., 2017).

It has generally been reported that foster children often perform poorly in tests such as national reading and numeracy tests (Harvey & Testro, 2006; Segermark, 2017; Smithgall et al., 2004) as they are unable to attain the targets of national benchmarks (Evans et al., 2004; Merdinger et al., 2005; Sawyer & Dubowitz, 1994). In Malaysia, many foster children are weak in core subjects, namely English, Mathematics and Science (Chan, 2013). Studies also reveal that a third of current foster children and two-thirds of foster alumni drop out of high school; only 10 per cent of them manage to achieve a high school diploma (Courtney & Dworsky, 2005; Joiner, 2001).

In Malaysia, eradicating illiteracy is one of the main aims of the government. Thus, foster children's poor academic performance is indeed a barrier to fulfilling the national objective. Foster children who struggle academically do not have anyone to depend on when they leave foster home at the age of 18. Hence, it is challenging for those who have poor academic performance to pursue tertiary education and secure jobs that can make them financially independent (Ministry of Education, 2012). In turn, they will face difficulties in renting a house or purchasing health insurance due to the high cost of living (Emerson & Lovitt, 2003), leaving them vulnerable to life's misfortunes. In light of this, the academic performance of foster children is a grave concern as the number of these children is increasing (Daim, 2016).

While there are numerous and exhaustive studies on foster children's poor academic performance, the aforementioned studies do not analyse the voices of concern among school teachers despite them playing a vital role in the children's education. To close this gap, the present study takes a more specific approach in examining the voices of concern of teachers who specifically address the academic needs of foster children. This study also aims to examine the teachers' concern as very few teachers are actually familiar with the academic needs of said children, who are often assumed to have come from typical family backgrounds (Emerson & Lovitt, 2003) and are thus similar to other children. Moreover, studies on "concern" from a sociolinguistic perspective, particularly in a Malaysian foster home context, are scarce. Examining the voices of concern is therefore vital to inspect the extent of teachers' concern regarding the academic performance of foster children in Malaysia. Thus, these reasons warrant the conduct of this study as teachers' voices function as a starting point for addressing foster children's academic needs.

We draw on speech act categories and stages of concern to analyse the interview responses of school teachers in addressing the academic needs of foster children. Our analysis demonstrates how school teachers use speech acts to voice their concern. At the same time, we also evaluate the degree of school teachers' concern about the academic performance of foster children. The discussion covers the ways concern is voiced via linguistic features.

SPEECH ACT OF CONCERN

Before we proceed to explain the analytical framework of this study, we wish to explain speech act categories and stages of concern individually. Speech acts encompass five categories, namely representative, directive, commissive, expressive, and declarative acts.

Representative acts are often used by speakers to present their thoughts via stating, reporting, claiming, predicting, insisting, describing, or hypothesising (Cutting, 2002; Searle, 1976).

Directive acts are used by speakers to direct hearers via commands, requests, invitations, or suggestions (Cutting, 2002) in order to perform actions (Searle, 1976).

Commissive acts are used when speakers express commitment or obligation to fulfil their forthcoming actions via promises, threats, offers, refusals, vows, or volunteering (Cutting, 2002; Searle, 1976).

Expressive acts reflect speakers' feelings, attitudes, or psychological states via apologies, regrets, congratulations, compliments, or condolences (Cutting, 2002; Searle, 1976; Searle & Vanderveken, 1985).

Declarative acts are often employed by speakers who have certain authority in a specific context, for instance, a priest, prime minister, or king. Speakers use these acts to dismiss employees, declare war, or resign from jobs, for example (Cutting, 2002; Searle, 1976).

Speech acts such as refusals, complaints, condolences, congratulations, requests, and apologies have been well researched in the field of pragmatics. Yet, studies on speech act of concern are limited and researchers often categorise concern under "expressive acts". For instance, Carretero et al.'s (2015) study on online interaction among university students focuses on "self-centred" and "other-centred" types of expressive speech. According to their study, expression of concern or worry is considered a "self-centred" type of expressive speech (Carretero et al., 2015, p. 187). Besides Carretero et al. (2015), Kampf's (2016) study on sustaining solidarity in political discourse finds that politicians can be seen expressing concern towards the hearers' wellbeing. Although the aforementioned studies mainly classify concern under expressive acts, concern can also be classified under other categories of speech acts such as directives in some circumstances. To illustrate, Kuang's (2015) study on Malaysian text messages reveals that concern is also expressed through directives such as "be strong" or "take care" in expressing condolences, which simultaneously indicate concern and care for the recipients of the condolences. The vagueness of speech act categories under which "concern" falls and the limited studies on concern from a pragmatic perspective are reasons that prompt this study to examine speech act of concern.

Speech act of concern entails speech act categories and stages of concern (How, 2019). It refers to actions of concern performed through words, phrases, or utterances (Austin, 1962) that represent a speaker's "feelings, preoccupation, thought and consideration given to a particular issue or task" (Hall & Hord, 1987, p. 61) and "the mental activity composed of questioning, analysing, re-analysing, considering alternative actions and reactions and anticipating consequences" (Hall et al., 1979, p. 5).

Speech act categories per se are not sufficient to explore the extent of concern of teachers. Drawing from Hall and Hord's (1987) Concerns-Based Adoption Model (CBAM), this study additionally adopts and adapts seven stages of concern. Hall and Hord (1987) created CBAM to evaluate, describe, and explain teachers' concern about the transformation they undergo when new curriculum resources and teaching practices are implemented in school. This model consists of stages of concern, levels of use and innovation configurations as the key diagnostic tools. Of these three tools, the stages of concern are the most appropriate to be applied in this study to examine one's degree of concern.

The following table illustrates the original expressions of concern from the stages of concern derived from Hall and Hord (1987). The vertical arrows in the tables refer to the organisation of the stages of concern, from awareness (i.e. the lowest stage) to refocusing (i.e. the highest stage). Although there are seven stages, the highest stage is numbered as 6 and the lowest stage is 0 to designate little or no concern about an issue. Additionally, these stages are not hierarchical, as teachers' concern in a succeeding stage may not affect or be connected with the concern they voiced in a preceding stage (Anderson, 1997; Straub, 2009).

Table 1 Stages of concern (Hall & Hord, 1987)

Stage of Concern	Expression of Concern
6. Refocusing	I have some ideas about something that would work even better.
5. Collaboration	How can I relate what I am doing to what others are doing?
4. Consequence	How is my use affecting learners? How can I refine it to have more impact?
3. Management	I seem to be spending all my time getting materials ready.
2. Personal	How will using it affect me?
1. Informational	I would like to know more about it.
0. Awareness	I am not concerned about it.

This study adapts Hall and Hord's (1987) original expressions of concern to analyse the extent of concern of teachers towards the academic issues and needs of foster children (Table 2).

Table 2 Adaptation of Hall and Hord's (1987) stages of concern

Stage of Concern	Description	Example(s) of Expression
6. Refocusing	To identify the suggestions given or actions taken by teachers to address the academic needs of foster children	I think they need somebody to monitor them. We will try to solve their problems.
5. Collaboration	To investigate whether teachers collaborate with others to overcome the issues they encounter	We discussed with the Principal how to resolve the situation.
4. Consequence	To analyse the consequences of the barriers faced	I think that their lack of self-confidence maybe caused them to be in the bottom / lower classes.
3. Management	To explore the issues that may delay academic assistance from being rendered to foster children	Even though I'm a class teacher, I don't have a lot of time in the class.
2. Personal	To identify teachers' personal feelings when attending to the academic needs of foster children	I felt pity for them.
1. Informational	To identify teachers' willingness to learn more about foster children's issues	They need someone to talk to. If you don't talk to them, you won't know what is inside them. I always ask them.
0. Awareness	To identify teachers' awareness of foster children's problems	They don't understand a thing. It's like you're teaching a primary school.

Each degree of concern was analysed based on the emergence and salient patterns of concern which can be identified via lexical choice from the teachers' interview responses.

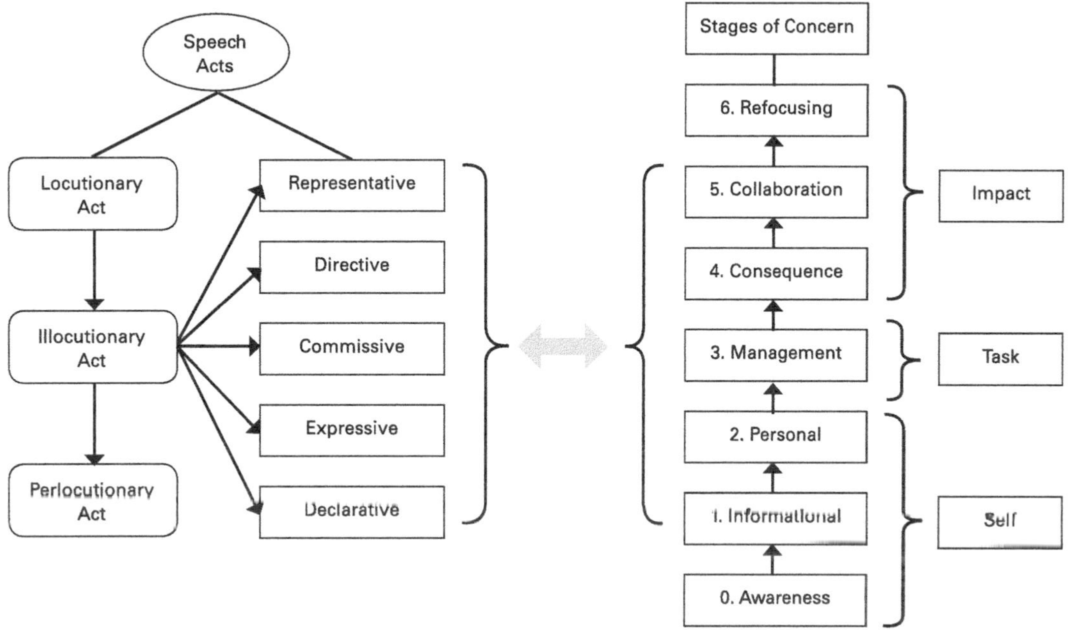

Figure 1 Representation of framework of analysis for speech acts (Searle, 1976) and stages of concern (Hall & Hord, 1987)

Figure 1 illustrates the combination of speech act theory and stages of concern as an analytical framework in this study to analyse the voices of concern amongst teachers.

The combination of speech act categories and stages of concern yields deeper understanding of how concern is voiced. Correspondingly, the realisation patterns of speech act of concern can be unveiled. Furthermore, the degrees of concern from teachers regarding the academic performance of foster children can be identified. Last but not least, academic issues that need immediate attention can be recognised through the language of concern. Hence, this analytical framework assists this study to meet the research aims.

DATA AND INSTRUMENTS

A total of 26 school teachers from a semi-urban secondary school in the Klang Valley participated in this study. Using the purposive sampling method, these teachers were selected because they have students from foster homes in their classes. The teachers in this study are the principal, assistant principals, form teachers, subject teachers, club teachers, physical education teachers, counsellors, discipline teachers, and Islamic study teachers.

The interviews with the teachers were conducted in a meeting room in the school. We employed open-ended interview questions to elicit more information from the teachers regarding how concerned they were about the foster children and the types of academic needs and issues of these children that needed immediate attention. Each interview took approximately 15 minutes. The overall duration of interview sessions with the teachers was approximately 8 hours and 19 minutes. The audio interview data were transcribed using the adaptation of Jefferson transcription conventions (1984, 2004) for analysis purposes (Table 3).

Excerpts of interviews in the Malay language were translated to English for non-native Malay speakers to comprehend the texts. Following Hepburn and Bolden's (2013) multi-linear transcription, the first line shows the original interview responses in Malay; the literal translation of the text is in the second line; and lastly, the intended meaning in English is in the third line.

Table 3 Adaptation of Jefferson transcription conventions (1984, 2004)

Notation	Name	Function
/	Slash	Indicates breaks between utterances
?	Question mark	Indicates rising pitch or intonation, used when speakers pose questions
underline	Underlined text	Indicates the emphasising of words, phrases or utterances
:::	Colon(s)	Indicates prolongation of a sound
(XXX)	Single parenthesis with triple X	Indicates unclear utterances
((*italic text*))	Double parentheses	Indicates non-verbal activity

VOICES OF CONCERN IN TEACHERS' INTERVIEWS

This section provides analysis of teachers' voices of concern about foster children's need for attention, with particular regard to monitoring the children's academic performance, as it is the most salient need raised by the teachers. While stages of concern are not hierarchical, this section is organised based on the lowest to the highest stage of concern to illustrate the language structure of concern at each stage.

Awareness: Employing intensifiers to reinforce the academic needs of foster children

At the awareness stage, the teachers employ representative acts to describe their awareness as well as intensifiers to emphasise their descriptions of the foster children's academic needs.

In Excerpt 1, T4 emphasises foster children's need for attention (*memerlukan perhatian* [line 2]). Within her emphasis, T4 uses the explicit intensifier *memang*, "really" (lines 2 and 3) and particle *lah* in line 2 as reinforcements that boost the verbs *memerlukan*, "need" (line 2), and *nak*, "want" (line 3).

Such usage of intensifiers in her response shows her awareness of the foster children's academic needs.

Excerpt 1

(1) T4: *Saya rasa kalau macam daripada rumah bakti ni / yang saya*
I think if like from home foster this / which I
I think regarding (a student) from a foster home / based on my

(2) *perhatikan dia* ***memang memerlukan perhatianlah*** */ selalunya /*
observe he/she indeed needs *kan* attention *lah* / always /
observation he/she really needs attention / always /

(3) *kadang dia* ***memang nak*** *menarik minat kita tu untuk bagi*
sometimes he/she indeed wants pull interest our that to give
sometimes he/she really wants to draw our interest so that we give

(4) *perhatian kepada dia /*
attention to him/her /
attention to him/her /

The need for attention among foster children is also brought up by T11 in Excerpt 2.

Excerpt 2

(1) T11: *Pertama /saya rasa mereka* ***sangat perlukan*** *perhatian /*
first / I think they very need *kan* attention /
firstly / I think they really need attention /

(2) ***sangat*** */* ***sangat perlukan perhatian*** */ er::: yang kedua /*
very / very need *kan* attention / the second /
really / really need attention / secondly /

(3) *hmm::: saya rasa IQ dia sama je / cuma perhatian tu lah*
I think his/her IQ same only / only attention that *lah*
I think his/her IQ is the same / it's only the need for attention

(4) *saya rasa yang* ***paling penting*** */*
I think the most important /
I think is the most important /

T11's awareness of foster children's need for attention is shown by the use of explicit intensifiers and a modal verb. To assert the importance of providing attention to these children, T11 repeatedly uses the explicit intensifier *sangat*, "really", and the modal verb *perlukan*, "need", as a means of reinforcement. Additionally, she further emphasises the importance of attention for these children with the explicit intensifier *paling*, "most", to strengthen the illocutionary force of the adjective *penting*, "important" (line 4).

Informational: Describing the way teachers address the academic needs of foster children

Being aware of the challenges foster children encounter in their studies is not enough. Thus, these teachers take the initiative to further understand foster children's academic issues, as at times these children do not reveal their predicaments to anyone. T24, in Excerpt 3, states that she helps foster children in her class by trying to be closer to them.

Excerpt 3

(1) T24: *Saya cuba rapatkan diri saya dengan dia dalam kelas* /
I try closer myself with him/her in class /
I will try to be close to him/her in class /

(2) ***saya bagi tumpuan*** / *apabila saya bagi kerja* / ***saya pergi***
I give attention / when I give tasks / I go
I give attention / when I give tasks / I go to

(3) ***tempat dia*** / *saya* ***tanya macam mana*** / ***boleh buatkah tak***
place his/her / I ask how / can do *kah* or cannot
his/her place / I ask him/her whether / he/she can do it

(4) ***boleh buat*** / *daripada situ dia akan mula minat untuk belajarlah* /
do / from there he/she will start interest to learn *lah* /
or not / from there he/she will be interested to learn /

T24 describes her willingness to learn more about the academic issues faced by foster children in her class when she exemplifies *saya bagi tumpuan*, "I give him/her attention", *saya pergi tempat dia*, "I go to his/her place", and *saya tanya macam mana boleh buatkah tak boleh buat,* "I ask whether he/she can do it or not", from lines 1 to 3. Such actions show her interest in the foster child's academic issue. When more attention is given to the child, he or she begins to show interest in learning.

Personal: Expressing feelings about foster children

During the interviews, teachers also expressed feelings about the challenges foster children face.

Excerpt 4

(1) T23: Since *saya kenal dua orang ni* ***memang*** *saya* ***kesianlah*** /
since I know two people this really I pity *lah* /
since I know these two foster children I really felt pity for them /

(2) *bagi saya* ***memang kesian*** / *jadi bila tanya banyak-banyak kali*
for me really pity / so when ask many times
for me I really felt pity / so even when they ask lots of questions

(3) *pun* / okay *betul* / ah *cantik* / *macam tu lah* / *saya rasa*
also / correct / beautiful / like that *lah* / I think
I will tell them it is correct or beautiful / just like that / I think

(4) *dia orang* ***memang memerlukan kita punya perhatianlah*** /
they really need our own attention *lah* /
they really need our attention /

In Excerpt 4, T23 highlights her feeling of *kesian,* "pity", with the personal pronoun *saya,* "I". T23's feeling of sympathy in lines 1 and 2 regarding the academic needs of foster children in her class is further reinforced by the frequent use of the explicit intensifier *memang,* "really" (lines 1 and 2) and particle *lah* (line 1). Besides expressing her feeling, she further justifies her sympathy by using the explicit intensifier *memang,* "really" (line 4) in the statement *dia orang memang memerlukan kita punya perhatianlah,* "they really need our attention", to accentuate the necessity of providing attention to foster children.

Management: Describing the challenges teachers encounter while attempting to address needs

Time constraints, large class sizes, and heavy workloads are the challenges many teachers encounter while trying to attend to the needs of foster children in school. These challenges may delay assistance from being rendered to foster children.

Excerpt 5

(1) T12: hmm::: er::: ***kekangan masa*** / erm::: *dengan::: er::: kuantiti*
constraints time / with quantity
time constraints / with quantity

(2) er ***nisbah guru dan pelajar*** / *sebab guru seorang / pelajar*
ratio teacher and student / because teacher one / student
teacher-student ratio / because for every teacher / there

(3) *ramai* / *so* ***kita*** *pun* ***banyak yang nak control***
many / so we also many that want control
are many students / so we also have many things to control

(4) ***dengan*** *yang* ***kerja-kerja yang sedia ada yang lain kan*** /
with work which available that others *kan* /
along with the existing work right? /

(5) ***payah*** *juga nak catch up tu* /
difficult also want catch up that /
It's also quite difficult to catch up /

In Excerpt 5, T12 represents teachers in general who encounter the same difficulties in school with the use of the personal pronoun *kita*, "we", in line 3. She also uses the adjective *payah*, "difficult", (line 4) to describe the tremendous effort needed to complete the work on time. T12's response may indicate time constraints are a plight in addressing the academic needs of foster children. Hence, teachers' time constraints can affect the academic performance of foster children as teachers may not be able to provide more attention to them.

Excerpt 6

(1) T9: *Sebenarnya dia orang ni* erm *memerlukan perhatian dan*
actually they this need attention and
actually they need more attention and

(2) *kasih sayang yang lebih* / *sebenarnya* / *tetapi* er::: *pandangan*
love which more / actually / but view
lots of love / actually / but my

(3) *peribadi saya lah* / *itu* ***sukar*** / ***sangat sukar*** *sebabnya*
personal my *lah* / that difficult / very difficult because
personal view / is that it is difficult / very difficult because

(4) ***dalam kelas kita nak jaga 38 orang*** /
in class we want take care 38 people /
in a class we have to manage 38 students /

Likewise, in Excerpt 6, T9 asserts that foster children need more attention in school (lines 1 and 2). However, due to the large number of students in a class, she is unable to address their needs (line 4). Additionally, T9 describes the difficulty in dealing with foster children when she repetitively employs the adjective *sukar*, "difficult", and explicitly intensifies with an adverb *sangat*, "very" (line 3), to reinforce her description. By describing her plights, the teacher is reaching out for support as it is beyond her capacity to provide more attention to foster children.

Consequence: Describing the way foster children react when their needs are not fulfilled

When the teachers describe the ways foster children behave in class via representative acts, their descriptions indicate awareness of the consequences of foster children not receiving enough attention. For instance, T1 in Excerpt 7 describes the way foster children react in the classroom when their academic needs are not fulfilled.

Excerpt 7

(1) T1: *kita* ***kena*** *pergi* personal / *maksudnya* / er::: *kalau*
we have to go personal / means / if
we have to go (to them) personally / which means / if

(2) *kita* er::: *mengajar satu-satu perkara tu* / dia ***lebih*** *kepada*
we teach one by one thing that / he/she more to
we teach a particular thing / they will more likely be

(3) *macam* / ***cikgu datanglah duduk saya sebelah ni*** /
like / teacher come *lah* sit me beside this /
like / teacher come and sit beside me /

(4) er::: *macam mana* / *dia* ***lebih*** *sentuhan peribadi tu lebih* /
how / he/she more touch personal that more /
how / they require more of a personal touch /

With the modal verb *kena,* "have to", in line 1, T1 emphasises the need to personally approach foster children in class. She then demonstrates the way a foster child in her class reacts by quoting her request for attention *datanglah duduk saya sebelah ni,* "come and sit beside me", in line 3. Her demonstration not only reflects the true condition of her response, but also acts to highlight the consequence of foster children not receiving adequate attention. Furthermore, T1's use of the adverb *lebih,* "more", in lines 2 and 4 also refers to the foster children's degree of preference regarding guidance from teachers. T1's emphasis and demonstration of foster children's need for attention represent her concern.

The consequence of a lack of attention is also illustrated in Excerpt 8 when T3 describes the way a foster child reacts in his class.

Excerpt 8

(1)	T3:	*Pelajar ni dia tak berapa minat* / *dia* ***memang selalulah***
		student this he not so interest / he indeed always *lah*
		this student is not so interested / indeed he is always
(2)		*tunjuk* **protest** / *macam tu lah* / ***protest*** *tu dia akan* er:::
		shows protest / like that *lah* / protest that he will
		protesting / something like that / when he protests he will
(3)		protest *muka dia* / ***expression muka dia*** / *dan* **kadang-kadang**
		protest face his / expression face his / and sometimes
		show it in his face / his facial expression / and sometimes
(4)		***dia bising*** /
		he noisy /
		he is noisy /

T3 describes and elaborates the way the foster child "protests" (line 2) during class via his facial expression, *muka dia,* and his action: *kadang-kadang dia bising,* "sometimes he is noisy", in lines 3 and 4. He also reinforces the verb "protest" via the multiple intensifiers *memang selalulah,* "indeed always" (line 1), and explicit intensifier particle *lah* while describing the child's behaviour to show his awareness of the consequence of a lack of attention given to the foster child.

Correspondingly, T26 also describes and exemplifies the rebellious characteristic of a foster child in her class.

Excerpt 9

(1) T26: ***macam*** *kalau* ***ada cikgu tu bagi tahu saya*** / *kerja*
like if got teacher that informed me / work
for example if there is a teacher who informed me / the work

(2) *tak siap* / *kalau cikgu tu* ***macam*** *bagi denda dia sikit* /
not complete / if teacher that like gives punishment him little /
is not completed / if the teacher punishes him /

(3) ***macam*** *dia memberontaklah dia* / ***tangan dia dia hempap atas***
like he rebel *lah* he / hand his he bangs on
like he will rebel / he bangs his hand on the

(4) ***meja*** / ***macam tu*** / *nampaklah tingkah laku dia* /
table / like that / seen *lah* attitudes his /
table / like that / that's where his attitude can be seen /

Although she did not witness the foster child's behavioural problem herself, T26 describes the type of rebellious behaviour displayed by the foster child that she heard about when she frequently employs the adverb *macam*, "like" (lines 1 to 4). She exemplifies with *tangan dia hempap atas meja*, "he bangs his hand on the table", in lines 3 and 4 to make her point and to provide the interviewer with a clearer picture of the child's behaviour in class. T26's description of her awareness from a second-party point of view when she states *ada cikgu tu bagi tahu saya*, "there is a teacher who informed me", in line 1 shows her concern as she does not ignore the consequences.

Collaboration: Describing collaboration and ensuring support

Despite the consequences of foster children lacking attention from teachers, the teachers describe their collaboration with others to try and address the need for attention among foster children. Excerpt 10 is an example of a teacher's response.

Excerpt 10

(1) T18: *Saya rasa pelajar-pelajar ni* ***perlukan*** *bimbingan daripada orang*
I think students these need guidance from people
I think these students need guidance from someone

(2) *selain daripada role dia di rumah / rumah anak yatim tersebut /*
other from role his/her in house / home orphanage that is /
other than their role in the house / the foster home /

(3) *dia* ***perlukan*** *orang lain / terutamanya guru untuk membantu*
he/she needs people other / especially teacher for helping
they need others / especially teachers to help

(4) *mereka / dan* ***kita*** *memang kita bercadanglah*
them / and we indeed we suggest *lah*
them / and we actually suggested to our

(5) *pihak-pihak sekolah / pihak PIBG baru ni* ***bermesyuarat*** */*
parties school / party PIBG just this meeting /
school community / at a recent parent-teacher association meeting /

(6) ***kita*** *bercadang untuk mengadakan konsep mentor-mentee /*
we plan to have concept mentor-mentee /
we planned to have a mentor-mentee concept /

(7) *dan Insha'Allah pelajar-pelajar ini* ***kita*** *akan kekalkan /*
and Godwilling students these we will be retained /
and Godwilling these students will be retained /

(8) ***kita akan*** *tetapkan ibubapa angkat di sekolah /*
we will set parents foster in school /
we will set foster parents in school /

T18 employs a commissive act in line 7 to ensure that the foster children's need for attention is fulfilled. He highlights the necessity for foster children to be monitored via the modal verb *perlukan,* "need" (lines 1 and 3). In his assurance *kita akan tetapkan ibubapa angkat di sekolah,* "we will set foster parents in school", the commissive element can be seen in the use of the modal verb *akan,* "will" (line 7). He gives assurance of establishing a mentor-mentee system for foster children in order for them to obtain more attention and monitoring in school. Instead of *saya,* "I", he employs the personal pronoun *kita,* "we", in lines 4 to 7 to represent the school committee as a whole. He states the collaboration of the school and parent-teacher committee through the verb *bermesyuarat,* "meeting", in line 5 to indicate their act of working together to attend to foster children's academic needs.

Refocusing: Giving suggestions

When teachers have some ideas to help foster children but such ideas are beyond their capacity, they reach out for assistance from higher authorities and give suggestions. In Excerpt 11, T12 provides suggestions to eradicate the difficulty in providing attention to foster children in class.

Excerpt 11

(1) T12: *Kalau dari segi pembelajaran /* ***saya rasa*** *kalau macam*
if in terms of learning / I think if like
if in terms of studying / I think if

(2) *dia orang dekat sekolah ni / sebab macam cikgu satu kelas*
them at school this / because like teacher one class
they are in the school / because like a teacher in a class

(3) *macam* ***kena kawal ramai pelajar kan*** */ so saya rasa*
like has to control many students right? / so I think
has to control a large number of students right? / so I think

(4) ***dia orang lebih kepada*** er::: *sesuai dalam kumpulan kecil kut* /
they more to suitable in group small perhaps /
they are more suitable to be in a small group perhaps /

Before providing her suggestion, T12 describes the problem encountered by teachers in line 3, *kena kawal ramai pelajar,* "has to control a large number of students". Herein lies the modal verb *kena,* "has to", which serves to indicate the obligation of a teacher in managing a large number of students in a class. In order to overcome such an issue, T12 suggests *saya rasa dia orang lebih kepada* er::: *sesuai dalam kumpulan kecil kut,* "I think they are more er::: suitable to be in a small group perhaps", in lines 3 and 4. In her suggestion, she mitigates with the hedge *saya rasa,* "I think" (line 3), the particle *kut,* "perhaps" (line 4), and prolongs the pause filler /er:::/ (line 4). Perhaps T12 is cautious about sharing her opinion during an interview as her social position of a teacher plays a part in her response. Nevertheless, her suggestion indicates her aspiration to provide a better and more effective learning environment for foster children.

Excerpt 12

(1) T9: *Saya rasa **mesti** buat satu test / guru-gurulah **mesti** ada*
I feel must do one test / teachers *lah* must have
I think there must be a test / the teachers must have

(2) *satu standard standard test yang kita boleh bagi pada students*
one standard standard test that we could give to students
a standard test that we can use on these students

(3) ***supaya kita boleh kenal pasti dia*** /
so that we could identify him/her /
so that we can identify their weakness /

Similar to T12, T9 in Excerpt 12 also uses the hedge *saya rasa,* "I think", to begin her suggestion *saya rasa mesti buat satu* test, "I think there must be a test", in line 1. She suggests the need to create a standardised test in order to identify foster children's weaknesses. The frequent use of the modal verb *mesti,* "must", in line 1 serves to strengthen the absolute necessity of recognising the weaknesses of foster children before assessing them.

Moreover, T9's suggestion is further supported by the reason *supaya kita boleh kenal pasti dia,* "so that we can identify their weakness", in line 3. Additionally, she highlights in the interview that there is no standard test thus far. Hence, the teacher's suggestion indicates the need for standard assessment tests in schools to identify students' proficiency, knowledge, and skills. Similar to the expression of concern in the previous excerpt, the teacher's concern and aspiration to provide foster children with a better learning environment can be identified through her suggestion.

Refocusing: Giving suggestions and demonstrations

Not only do teachers give suggestions, but their concern can also be identified when they demonstrate the way they assist foster children in their classes. For example, T10 in Excerpt 13 gives a suggestion and demonstration of how foster children should be treated in school in an attempt to address the academic needs of these children.

Excerpt 13

(1) T10: ***Kita perlu memberi orang kata penekananlah pada mereka***
we need to give people say emphasis *lah* to them
we need to give more emphasis to them

(2) ***ni*** / *fokus lebih sikit pada mereka* / er *dari segi*
this / focus more little on them / in terms of
focus more on them / in terms of

(3) *latihannya kebiasaannya* ***saya memang panggil dua orang ni***
tasks usually I indeed call two people this
tasks usually I indeed call both of them

(4) ***untuk ke depan*** / *duduk di meja saya / jadi pada masa tu saya*
for to front / sit at table my / so at time I
to come to the front / sit at my table / so that's when I

(5) ***akan monitorlah di mana kesilapan dan kekurangan mereka*** /
will monitor *lah* where mistakes and weaknesses their /
will monitor them in terms of their mistakes and weaknesses /

T10 employs the modal verb *perlu*, "need to", to accentuate the need to focus more on the foster children. However, unlike T12 and T9's responses in Excerpts 11 and 12, T10 not only suggests how to address the academic needs of the foster children in her class (line 1), but also demonstrates the way she monitors these children in order to reinforce her suggestion. She demonstrates by exemplifying the way she handles these children in the utterances *saya memang panggil dua orang ini untuk ke depan,* "I indeed call both of them to come to the front", in lines 3 and 4, and *saya akan monitorlah di mana kesilapan dan kekurangan mereka,* "I will monitor them in terms of their mistakes and weaknesses", in lines 4 and 5. She emphasises the effort she puts in when attending to foster children's academic needs by employing the adverb *memang,* "indeed" (line 8). T10's suggestion and demonstration show her sense of concern as a teacher for the foster children in her class.

DISCUSSION AND FINAL REMARKS

Our findings demonstrate that "concern" can be expressed not only via expressive acts, but also representative acts, directive acts, and commissive acts. To put it in another way, concern is an expression or feeling which involves thought and consideration of a particular issue. Thus, our findings defy Carretero et al.'s (2015) and Kampf's (2016) studies which classify "concern" as an expressive act.

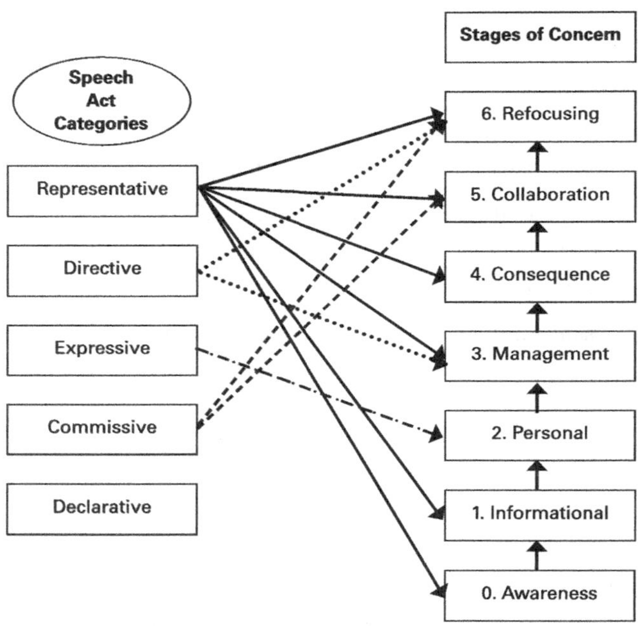

Figure 2 Results of speech act categories and stages of concern

The value of each type of arrow in Figure 2 is illustrated in the following.

———	Representative act
··········	Directive act
—·—·—·—	Expressive act
- - - - - -	Commissive act

Figure 2 shows that representative acts are salient in the awareness stage, followed by the management, refocusing, consequence, informational, and collaboration stages. There are three categories of speech act in the refocusing stage, namely representative, directive, and commissive, while one category of speech act is found in the awareness, informational, personal, and consequence stages (How, 2019; How & Mohd Jan, 2019). Figure 2 also shows that more categories of speech act are found at higher stages as teachers try to express their concern for the academic needs of foster children.

Table 4 Percentages of speech act categories in teachers' concern

Speech Act Category	**Percentage**
Representative acts	81%
Directive acts	46%
Expressive acts	27%
Commissive acts	8%

Table 4 shows that most of the interview responses were reflective of representative acts. During the interviews, teachers employed representative acts to describe, assert, explain, justify, and state their awareness of the consequences of a lack of attention given to foster children. Most importantly, the teachers frequently employed multiple intensifiers such as *memang selalulah*, "indeed always", *memang sangat*, "indeed really", or the explicit intensifier *sangat*, "really", as well as the modal verb *perlukan* or "need" in order to reinforce the necessity of providing attention to foster children. The use of intensifiers and modal verbs serves to indicate that immediate attention is needed to address the highlighted issue.

Besides being aware, teachers claimed to have delved into the academic issues of foster children as described by the way they offer attention to them via the verb *tanya*, "ask", and the first-person pronoun *saya*, "I". Such acts fall into the informational stage as they indicate the teachers' enthusiasm to overcome attention-seeking and behavioural problems exhibited by foster children.

Additionally, the teachers employed expressive acts to express their feelings of sympathy regarding the foster children's lack of attention, which falls into the personal stage. They also utilised the particle *–lah* in *kesianlah* to reinforce their feeling of sympathy. Such a particle, according to Alfred et al. (2013), is a possessive adjective that serves to strengthen the lexical item that can be regarded as "emphatic in meaning" (Goddard, 1994, p. 151), for instance *kesianlah* (pity + *lah*). The teachers' sympathy led them to provide foster children with more attention and monitoring in school.

Despite feeling sympathetic, the teachers were hindered by a lack of time to fully attend to the foster children's academic needs. At the management stage, they revealed their predicaments by using the adjectives *sukar* and *payah*, both of which mean "difficult". To further strengthen the adjectives, the use of the adverb *sangat*, "very", was also present. Hall and Hord's (1987) study shares similar findings of expression of concern, whereby time constraints appear to be one of the obstacles that delay assistance from being rendered by teachers to make a situation better.

As a consequence of the teachers' lack of time with foster children, they revealed their concern at the consequence stage that foster children have behavioural problems in school, as these children try to get attention from teachers during class. The teachers described and demonstrated the way foster children behave or react in class when their needs are not fulfilled to indicate their concern about what affects these children.

Aware of the consequences, the teachers work together and improvise or adapt to situations in order to address the foster children's needs. They described their collaborations with others using the personal pronoun *kita*, "we", to represent the school community as a whole and ensured help would be given when the modal verb *akan*, "will", was used.

At the final stage (i.e. refocusing), teachers reached out by suggesting ways to identify foster children's academic weaknesses such as creating a standardised test. They also suggested forming smaller groups of students in a class so that it would be easier for them to focus on the foster children. In a sense, the researchers and interviewers act as the transmitters of suggestions made by the teachers because the targets of the messages are not physically present to hear their predicaments (Mauri & Sansò, 2011). Furthermore, the teachers tended to mitigate their suggestions with the hedge *saya rasa,* "I think". The act of mitigation could suggest the teachers' preference to safeguard their academic position in order to sustain social harmony in their workplace (Gom et al., 2015). Although the teachers mitigated, they also emphasised the importance of their suggestions with the modal verbs *kena,* "have to", *mesti,* "must", and *perlu,* "need to". From giving suggestions to describing the ways they attend to foster children's needs, the teachers shifted the use of the personal pronoun *kita,* "we", to the use of the personal pronoun *saya,* "I", to indicate their enthusiasm in providing academic assistance to these children in class.

Before we end this chapter, we would like to make two final points. First, by revealing school teachers' voices of concern about foster children's academic performance, the voices can raise awareness of academic constraints and needs that require immediate attention. Such awareness could assist schools and social welfare agencies in mending educational services for these children.

Secondly, this study demonstrates that the benefit of combining Searle's (1976) speech act categories with Hall and Hord's (1987) stages of concern is the potential to allow a more comprehensive analysis of teachers' voices of concern. Language, particularly linguistic features from teachers' interview responses, can be analysed via Searle's (1976) categories of speech acts, while the teachers' degrees of concern can be identified through Hall and Hord's (1987) stages of concern. Without a doubt, such a combination contributes to the existing body of literature on speech act of concern.

REFERENCES

Alfred, R., Mujat, A., & Obit, J. H. (2013). A ruled-based part of speech (RPOS) tagger for Malay text articles. In *Asian Conference on Intelligent Information and Database Systems* (pp. 50–59). Springer.

Anderson, S. E. (1997). Understanding teacher change: Revisiting the concerns based adoption model. *Curriculum Inquiry, 27*(3), 331–367.

Austin, J. L. (1962). *How to do things with words.* Harvard University Press.

Berger, L. M., Cancian, M., Han, E., Noyes, J., & Rios-Salas, V. (2015). Children's academic achievement and foster care. *Pediatrics, 135*(1), 109–116.

Carretero, M., Maíz-Arévalo, C., & Martínez, M. Á. (2015). An analysis of expressive speech acts in online task-oriented interaction by university students. *Procedia-Social and Behavioural Sciences, 173*, 186–190.

Chan, C. C. (2013). *A comparative study on rumah kanak-kanak (children residential home) and rumah tunas harapan (foster home) in Malaysia: A child-centric perspective* [Doctoral dissertation, National University of Singapore, Singapore]. Retrieved from https://core.ac.uk/download/pdf/48732415.pdf

Courtney, M. E., & Dworsky, A. (2005). *Midwest evaluation of the adult functioning of former foster youth: Outcomes at age 19.* Chapin Hall Center for Children at the University of Chicago.

Cutting, J. (2002). *Pragmatics and discourse: A resource book for students.* Routledge.

Daim, N. (2016, May 5). 209 children successfully placed among foster families since 2014. *New Straits Times.* https://www.nst.com.my/news/2016/05/143714/209-children-successfully-placed-among-foster-families-2014

Emerson, J., & Lovitt, T. (2003). Educational plight of foster children and what can be done about it. *Remedial and Special Education, 24*, 199–203.

Evans, L. D., Scott, S. S., & Schulz, E. G. (2004). The need for educational assessment of children entering foster care. *Child Welfare, 83*(6), 565–580.

Forsman, H., Brännström, L., Vinnerljung, B., & Hjern, A. (2016). Does poor school performance cause later psychosocial problems among children in foster care? Evidence from national longitudinal registry data. *Child Abuse & Neglect, 57*, 61–71.

Goddard, C. (1994). The meaning of lah: Understanding emphasis in Malay (Bahasa Melayu). *Oceanic Linguistics, 33*(1), 145–165.

Gom, D., Jiony, M. M., Tanakinjal, G. H., & Siganul, R. S. (2015). Understanding cultural differences in ethnic employees' work values: A literature review. *American Journal of Economics, 5*(2), 112–118.

Hall, G., George, A., & Rutherford, W. (1979). *Research & Development* (Report No. 3032). University of Texas, Research and Development Center for Teacher Education.

Hall, G., & Hord, S. (1987). *Change in schools: Facilitating the process.* State University of New York Press.

Harvey, J., & Testro, P. (2006). *Report card on education of Australian children and young people in care.* CREATE Foundation.

Hepburn, A., & Bolden, G. B. (2013). The conversation analytic approach to transcription. In J. Sidnell & T. Stivers (Eds.), *The handbook of conversation analysis* (pp. 57–76). Blackwell.

How, C. (2019). *Language of concern on the academic performance of Malaysian children in foster care* [Unpublished doctoral thesis]. Universiti Malaya.

How, C. & Mohd Jan, J. (2019). Speech act of concern on the academic performance of Malaysian foster children. *GEMA Online® Journal of Language Studies, 19*(3), 88–108.

Jefferson, G. (1984). Transcript notation. In J. Heritage (Ed.), *Structures of social interaction* (pp. 346–369). Cambridge University Press.

Jefferson, G. (2004). Glossary of transcript symbols with an introduction. *Pragmatics and Beyond New Series, 125,* 13–34.

Joiner, L. L. (2001). Reaching out to foster children. *American School Board Journal, 188*(5), 30–34.

Kampf, Z. (2016). All the best! Performing solidarity in political discourse. *Journal of Pragmatics, 93,* 47–60.

Kuang, C. H. (2015). Functions of Malaysian condolences written in text messages. *Social Sciences and Humanities, 23*(1), 1–19.

Mauri, C., & Sansò, A. (2011). How directive constructions emerge: Grammaticalization, constructionalization, cooptation. *Journal of Pragmatics, 43*(14), 3489–3521.

Merdinger, J. M., Hines, A. M., Osterling, K. L., & Wyatt, P. (2005). Pathways to college for former foster youth: Understanding factors that contribute to educational success. *Child Welfare, 84*(6), 867–896.

Ministry of Education. (2012). *Malaysian education blueprint 2013–2025.* Ministry of Education, Malaysia.

O'Higgins, A., Sebba, J., & Gardner, F. (2017). What are the factors associated with educational achievement for children in kinship or foster care: A systematic review. *Children and Youth Services Review, 79,* 198–220.

Sawyer, R. J., & Dubowitz, H. (1994). School performance of children in kinship care. *Child Abuse and Neglect, 18*(7), 587–597.

Searle, J. R. (1976). A classification of illocutionary acts. *Language in Society, 5*(1), 1–23.

Searle, J. R., & Vanderveken, D. (1985). *Foundations of illocutionary logic.* Cambridge University Press Archive.

Segermark, D. R. (2017). *Students in foster care at risk of school failure: Addressing multiple needs* [Master's thesis, St Cloud State University]. Retrieved from http://repository.stcloudstate.edu/cgi/viewcontent.cgi?article=1058&context=sped_etds

Smithgall, C., Gladden, R. M., Howard, E., George, R. M., & Courtney, M. E. (2004). *Educational experiences of children in out-of-home care.* Chapin Hall Center for Children. Retrieved from https://www.chapinhall.org/wp-content/uploads/Smithgall_Educational-Experiences-Children-Out-of-Home_Report_2004.pdf

Straub, E. T. (2009). Understanding technology adoption: Theory and future directions for informal learning. *Review of Educational Research, 79*(2), 625–649.

Chapter 4

Understanding and Applying the Critical Academic Voice: Bridging Theory and Practice

Stephen J Hall*

ABSTRACT

As novice academic writers venture into academic discourse, the multiplicity of voices which Bakhtin (1953/1981) termed "heteroglossia" may be a series of complex choices needed to position oneself as both an authoritative writer and a critical scholar. A necessary reflective awareness of positioning one's academic voice involves diverse discourse choices. Critical theory and research into the author's voice also argue for an authorial positioning to create a reader/writer negotiated understanding. Within this complexity, there is little research into reflective approaches which develop the academic writer's voice, although studies of hedging are numerous. This paper draws on earlier research and reflective data from novice academic writers, many venturing from the workplace into a Malaysian university, to focus on ways of developing the individual voice as an authoritative academic writer.

Keywords Academic voice, authoritative voice, hedging, metadiscourse strategies, novice academic writers

* Sunway University, Malaysia

INTRODUCTION

Novice academic writers are often challenged by the rigours of academic writing in which both non-discursive and discursive features require mastery, as one builds an authoritative and critical academic voice. The form of an academic writer's text is highly prescribed for particular disciplines and publications, in terms of layout, fonts, quotations and numerous other gatekeeping norms, which standardise the form of the writing. Such non-discursive features have long been codified in many systems with increasing complexity, as can be seen in the widely used American Psychological Association (APA) Sixth and Seventh Edition Publication Manuals which have mushroomed in size, along with other systems, of which six are in use in United Kingdom universities alone. Neville (2010) in his guide to referencing states that the judicious use of non-discoursal features, such as paragraphing and referencing, can help student writers "find their own voice" (p. vii), yet the challenge is greater than the choice of formatting, as the writer crafts his or her individual voice.

An encompassing definition of voice in written discourse is that of Matsuda (2001), who argues for the co-constructed definition for second language writers as follows: "Voice is the amalgamative effect of the use of discursive and non-discursive features that language users choose, deliberately or otherwise, from socially available yet ever-changing repertoires" (p. 40). In later work, it is argued that "voice is not a set of certain discursive features; rather, voice is the reader's impression derived from the particular combination of the ways in which both discursive and non-discursive features are used" (Matsuda & Tardy, 2007, p. 237). The researchers note that the notion of voice as an individualistic statement of self should be clarified, as voice reflects a socially driven act that is the result of interactions and choices. Drawing on earlier work (Bakhtin, 1953/1981; Fairclough, 1992; Ivanic, 1998), Matsuda and Tardy (2007) describe "a growing awareness of identity in discourse as an expression not only of the individual but also the surrounding social relations" (p. 237). This position can be seen in their study of academic reviewers assessing Rhetoric papers, a defined interaction with closely defined discourse expectations. One reviewer problematises a paper as "agnostic positioning" (Matsuda & Tardy, 2007, p. 244), suggesting that the student writer is a relative newcomer to the very specific expectations of academic writing as he or she does not establish a confident critical stance. Nelson and Castelló (2012) make this process explicit:

> [A] writer's voice is inferred from textual cues by those who read the text; it is manifested in the social relation between writer and reader in a particular context. A writer may seek to project a certain kind of voice and make choices for writing that seem associated with that kind of voice, but voice is not realized until perceived by a reader. (p. 40)

The broader challenge which may cause more reflection and internal questioning is how to gain entry into the particular community of academic readers and writers as an authoritative voice, with an identity based on a linguistically well-supported critical stance. Many novice writers are unsure of how their own voices can be heard and unclear about how to empower themselves in a field in which others are more experienced, known or published.

The process of creating a scholarly voice in the prescribed discourse community of an academic text involves understanding one's identity in academic writing and the route to becoming an accepted member of the academic writing community (Hyland, 2002), through a well-crafted writer's voice and the construction of one's own identity and voice within the "community of practice" (Wenger, 1998).

This paper will present an overview of earlier research on the authoritative, academic writer's voice, augmented by a report on a piece of small-scale qualitative research of novice writers for a Master's course for working adults within a Malaysian private university. The content focus of the participants' writing was sustainable development and management. Within this context, I will argue that identifying, self-reflecting and applying one's own academic voice within written text plays an important role in positioning a writer as a critical scholar with authority, authenticity and appeal.

To unpack the cacophony of voices in academic text, I will use an overview of voice in academic writing, as well as the views of some research report writers, many of whom had been away from academia for some years. In this paper I do not use Bahktin's 1981 definition of the *authoritative* voice in which he described "authoritative discourse" as discourse that does not enter into dialogue (p. 344). This paper uses the terms *authority* and *authoritative voice* as often applied in prescriptive texts and writing research as projecting competence and credibility, which create for a reader a sense of engagement with a voice which has academic authority. This process is indeed a social interaction between an academic writer and a reading audience, as will be explored. The focus of this paper will be on the author's voice and building stance and criticality through "metadiscourse" (Hyland, 2005, p. 1), as academic papers are persuasive and argumentative by nature (Hyland, 2012; Swales, 2004).

It will be suggested that there are processes for crafting an academic writer's voice with authority, while maintaining criticality through discoursal means, for example hedging. These processes are experienced by novice writers who may benefit from a reflective approach and the process of *voicing* the evolving development of the academic voice. It is useful to begin by specifying the concept of the academic voice.

HEARING AND USING THE ACADEMIC VOICE

Early research into the individual author's voice involved calls for listening inwardly and exploring the individuality of one's own voice, as described in the expressivist traditions of the 1960s and 1970s. Elbow (1973) wrote that "In your natural way of producing words there is a sound, a texture, a rhythm … a voice … the main source of power in your writing … [T]his voice is the force that will make a reader listen to you, the energy that drives the meaning" (p. 7) (cited in Nelson & Castelló, 2012, p. 1). Elbow (1994, p. xx) moved beyond the obvious physical voice and the individualist persona aspects to list five meanings of voice which are relevant to written text in general:

(1) Audible voice or intonation (sound with a text);
(2) Dramatic voice (the character or implied author in a text);
(3) Recognisable or distinctive voice;
(4) Voice with authority;
(5) Resonant voice or presence.

As we have noted earlier, the recognisable voice and the voice with authority (points 3 and 4 above) in academic writing need to involve the content of the written text (discursive features) and the form of the written presentation (non-discursive features) as described earlier (Matsuda & Tardy, 2007).

It could be argued that non-discursive features are easier to use and construct than discursive ones, particularly when voice in academic writing involves elements of persuasion, as writers are expected to craft writing with reader expectations of much more than referential knowledge (Hyland, 2005). This requires a writer's stance in order to build an authorial voice within a well-defined genre. Finding that stance obliges a writer to understand not just the topic, but also themselves within the target audience, which is the reading community of the chosen discipline.

All writers are advised to consider the target audience and expectations of the readers as they grapple with understanding the particularities of the writer as an individual. Such a writer's voice has been characterised as being in three general dimensions: the individual, social and dialogical (Tardy, 2012), with the individual aspect being a discernible mark of the writer as a presence or an informed critical voice. The social dimension describes the voice as being within a social context, and in the case of academic writers this may require an imagining of the reader and reflection on the vocabulary, grammar and textual organisation of particular disciplines (Krause, 2014). This dialogical dimension has a framework drawn from well-established theorising and is an area which is perhaps under-rated in prescriptive approaches to writing. Bakhtin (1953/1981) sees voice as an utterance which is

> always a two-sided act. In this moment of its use, at one and at the same time, it responds to what preceded it and anticipates what is to come. When we speak, then, we do two things: (a) we create the contexts of use to which our utterances typically belong and, at the same time, (b) we create a space for our own voice. (Cited in Bucholtz & Hall, 2005, p. 586)

If one broadens one's scope beyond the spoken voice to academic written text, it is clear that the dialogic interaction is with a reader who is usually experienced in the topic being described, analysed and perhaps critiqued.

Yet any awareness and application of the desired academic voice begin with the writer's perception of himself or herself and his or her self-reflectivity, to which we now turn.

SELF-PERCEPTIONS OF NOVICE WRITERS AND BUILDING THE AUTHORIAL VOICE

The novice writer's perception of self involves not just linguistic identity but also a knowledge of how to craft his or her presence in a text. Many statements of what an authorial voice is and how it can be created can be found in a variety of "how-to" texts on the craft of academic writing, from the early work of Arnaduet and Barrett (1984) to more contemporary guides (Corbyn, 2020; Swales & Feak, 2012). Some texts and studies argue that one's sense of identity and confidence as a beginning academic are vital for crafting the individual academic voice (Cheng & Steffensen, 1996; Livytska, 2019). Writing as a librarian and a trainer in academic writing, Wilson (2019) selected four prominent guides to the skills and attitudes involved in crafting an effective academic voice. Her view of a self-aware and effective writer is one which includes the person sharing his or her own viewpoint through stance and persuasive use of language to establish presence and authority within the text.

The fourth of the texts which Wilson analysed was a qualitative study of 100 successful academic writers, for whom publication outcomes and reputation in a variety of fields were used as measures to determine that effective writers were skilled users of the authorial voice. When describing the differences between articulate writers and novice writers, Wilson argues that self-perception plays a large part in being a confident voice, and suggests that construction of an evolving identity as a professional in one's chosen field requires reflection and greater self-awareness. In other words, the voice of an effective academic writer includes an awareness of the readership and the norms of the "community of practice" (Wenger, 1998) to which the writer is seeking admission through publication acceptance.

Perception of oneself as entitled to an individual voice acceptable to an experienced group of readers may be impeded by what Jensen (2017) terms the neophyte academic writer's "demons" and "myths" (p. 36). In particular, as post-graduate students of this writer have reported, there is often the belief that one must create a ground-breaking, utterly novel piece of writing to fill the much talked-about "research gap" (Bagheri, 2020). Jensen sees this desire for the "magnum opus" as a stumbling block in the evolution of a novice writer's confidence in the crafting of his or her own voice. This may also relate to another hurdle which academic writers may create for themselves: procrastination. Boice (1990, p. 10) attributes this to self-imposed setting of "individual standards that may exceed one's energy or capacity". Other examples of how self-perception blocks working as a confident authoritative writer can be found in studies of the role of identity as a speaker of another language writing in English, a common factor in the context of this paper.

Identity and English as second language academic writers

Identity and multiple identities have been widely researched concepts in the last two decades and are often linked to the concept of voice in second language academic writing (Almudaffari et al., 2019). After Belcher and Hirvela (2001) edited a special thematic issue of the Journal of Second Language Writing on the varied dimensions of voice in second language writing, voice, in this context, became a more widely used yet contested concept in terms of being linked to notions of identity and individualism as a dominant cultural value. This is well described by Matsuda and Tardy (2007, p. 236), who contend that the notion of voice and the writer's own identity "[have] often been related to the realm of the personal and individual, whereas academic writing has been characterized as relatively impersonal—if not objective or neutral—and therefore voiceless". If we add the notions of individualism versus collectivity (Hofstede, 2001) and the contestation of excessive individualism in personalised writing, a space of uncertainty may be created for many novice writers working in their additional language of English. This notion of individualism and collectivist thinking and its impact on the transition from inner social voice to written expression remains contested (Vande Kopple, 2012) and, arguably, under-researched. However, it has been well established that an individual's voice, especially for those writing from a bilingual or multilingual perspective, involves the social aspect. There is a dialogic series of choices in which the key to success involves acceptance by the specific English language academic readership. The role of this *context* in terms of the dialogic relationship with the target readership and acceptance into the community of academic practitioners within one's chosen field is central to choices which academic writers need to make. This includes discipline-specific issues:

> Broadly, writers in the hard sciences and engineering prefer to downplay their personal role to highlight the issue under study, while a stronger identity is claimed in the humanities and social science papers. (Hyland, 2002, p. 352)

The researcher continues by suggesting that academic writing is indeed not uniform and that second language writers face very specific discourse choices to meet their particular readers' needs. These differ from their other writing or personal communication approaches and include an evolving sense of identity, as one becomes accepted as part of an academic community which will have differences of style, dependent on discipline. The scope of the academic voice within discipline specific contexts (Krause, 2014) is an area of continuing research, but a topic beyond the scope of this paper, so we will look to broader concerns. Hyland (2002) does this by suggesting that the craft requires changes from academe as mentors of novice writers beyond producing only impersonal statements to providing options with an "awareness of the effects of self-mention and enabling them [the learners] to recognise both the choices available to them and their impact ... [so as] to meet the considerable challenges of academic writing in a second language" (p. 357). This is the context of the small study, described later in this paper.

Cultural variation, positioning and hedging

It has been suggested that authorial presence and clarity in a writer's stance may be linked to cultural variation in rhetorical strategies, especially when academic writing may be a recently acquired skill set. From within Arabic culture, some writers writing in English do attempt persuasive exaggeration and overemphasis in a way that can be perceived as overly certain and overly generalised. In the experience of this writer, L2 (learners of English as a second language) Arab speakers mark the certainty of claims with an abundance of emphatics, which may undercut claims and positive acceptance of a writer as an authoritative voice, an observation shared by others (Hinkel, 2003; Hyland, 2005). Other studies note that Iranian and Turkish post-graduate writers use less hedging and more boosters than their counterparts writing in English as their first language (Abdollahzadeh, 2011).

A working definition of hedging was first suggested by Lakoff (1972, p. 175) as "words whose job is to make things fuzzy". Writers often use hedges with a range of modal verbs, such as "seems", "suggests" and "opines", and also employ modifiers such as "may", "probably" and "perhaps" to withhold commitment, present assertions with precision and "give deference and recognition to the reader and avoid unacceptable over-confidence" (Hyland, 1996, p. 449). Crompton (1997, p. 281) used a functionally based definition of hedges, stating that "a hedge is an item of language which a speaker uses to explicitly qualify his/her commitment to the truth of a proposition he/she utters". Introducing a cross-cultural study of Malay users hedging in Malay contrasted with English academic articles, Loi and Lim (2019) suggest that:

> As more non-native English speakers are communicating in written academic English, more also tend to use discoursal patterns typical of their own tongue but alien to English ... The problem faced by second language learners (L2) is that they are not only learning a foreign or second language, but also acquiring cross-cultural competence in the use of hedges. (p. 37)

The researchers concur with others working with Chinese first language speakers (Ho & Li, 2018) that higher-rated essays in English involve wider use of hedging and metadiscourse (MD) strategies, a term used by Hyland after his work on the academic voice (Hyland, 1995). The Chinese researchers found that the use of hedges and a wider range of expressions which modify statements of certainty gained wider acceptance for first-year Chinese-speaking academic writers. In the Malaysian context, Loi and Lim (2019) found a wider use of hedges in English than in Malay academic discussion sections. They suggest that there are cultural influences when writing bilingually. Furthermore, Nivales (2011) asserts that students trying to write effective English language texts must learn to use hedges in order for their ideas to be "taken seriously" by the academic community (p. 43). Yet for second language writers it appears that a holistic approach to the academic voice needs not only the use of hedging, but also the application of MD strategies.

MD STRATEGIES

Creating audience engagement in academic writing requires a range of techniques which are presented in some, but not all, academic writing courses as ways of establishing a cohesive author's voice. Along with the establishing of an author's stance is the important role of MD. Crismore et al. (1993) defined MD as linguistic material that does not add to the propositional content of the text but "is intended to help the listener or reader organise, interpret, and evaluate the information given" (p. 40). When a writer is establishing his or her stance it is clear that there is much more involved than the use of the personal pronoun "I", for, as Hyland (2005) points out, expressing authorial stance and one's critical positioning is usually realised through interactional MD strategies.

Hyland's (2005) widely used model of MD distinguishes *interactive* from *interactional* resources (terms borrowed from Thompson, 2001, p. 58). Interactive features are concerned with ways of organising discourse to help readers recover a writer's intentions. Interactional features signal more explicitly the presence of the writer and his or her attitudes, commitments and assessments of material (cited in Hyland & Jiang, 2020). The presence of the writer through the use of these resources may help build a clear position or voice.

Almudhaffari et al. (2019) note that "an effective use of interactional MD strategies creates a rhetorical effect on the audience which could probably lead to a convincing academic argument" (p. 17). These multilingual researchers include hedging as part of metadiscoursal strategies. It is useful to consider MD markers as they have been assessed as being an effective part of authors establishing stance and individual interpretation. This is also an area which some English second language academic writers find challenging (Aitchison & Lee, 2006). In Hyland's model (2005, pp. 50–52) these interactive features (with examples from their 1965 corpus) comprise the following:

- ***Transitions*** comprise an array of devices, mainly conjunctions, used to mark additive, contrastive, and consequential connections between clauses, as opposed to events in the external world.
  1. By contrast, the weight of the hair was raised in the cold by from 9 to 29%. Accordingly, the total insulation conferred by skin plus hair was slightly higher in the cold than at 21°C. (Biology)

- ***Frame markers*** are references to rhetorical elements of text structure, used to sequence, [to] label text stages, to announce discourse goals and to indicate topic shifts.
  2. In the next section we elaborate these objections further. (Sociology)

- ***Endophoric markers*** make additional material salient and available to the reader in recovering the writer's intentions by referring to tables, diagrams or other parts of the text.
  3. As noted above, a small dc offset may be applied here for balancing purposes. (Electronic Engineering)

- ***Evidentials*** indicate textual information which originates from outside the current text, mainly consisting of citations ([e.g.] Smith argues that) and explicit evidential markers ([e.g.] according to).
  4. According to Florey (1961), evidence of cholinesterase activity does not necessarily imply that acetylcholine is the transmitter. (Biology)

- ***Code glosses*** restate, reword or illustrate ideational information for greater clarity.
  5. In other words, practical difficulties are one thing and theoretical limitations are quite another. (Applied linguistics)

These resources assist with managing the dialogic relationship with the reader and signal the author's views, his or her voice, by highlighting what the writer sees as salient or less weighty. In recent work on MD and cohesion, Hyland and Jiang (2020, p. 138) state, "there is broad agreement that texts demonstrate both the writer's stance on something and an awareness of readers". Yet the question remains as to how novice writers establishing themselves when English is their second or additional language develop awareness of these skills. One suggestion is to incorporate reflective practice to raise writers' awareness when crafting an effective author's voice.

THE REFLECTIVE APPROACH TO BUILDING THE WRITER'S VOICE

Reflective practice has been widely applied in English language teaching and learning with various techniques for identifying problems and solving them through self-analysis in supportive settings, as Farrell (2018) details in a broad summary. Schon (1983) in his pioneering work in this area describes the importance of problem identification as one becomes part of an academic community, through the ongoing challenge of refining practice through self-inquiry for professional development. Richards describes reflection as "an activity or process in which experience is recalled, considered, usually in relation to a broader purpose" (1990, p. 5).

In the widely used reflective approach within teaching and learning, described in various terms such as critical reflection and reflective practice (Roulston et al., 2008), it is acknowledged that academic practice, which can include developing one's academic writing, depends on several processes linked to how one sees oneself. Changes come about as previous practices, for example personal learning or writing approaches, are brought under a lens of self-questioning in a facilitative setting (Hall, 2013). The reflective approach involves self-analysis and finding one's own voice. It is part of the Master's programme in the Malaysian private university mentioned in the Introduction, within the academic writing component, and also features a reflective journal as part of another subject within the same programme. The semi-structured discussion part of this research was therefore facilitated as a familiar, reflective developmental activity.

METHODOLOGY FOR SMALL-SCALE ACTION RESEARCH

This qualitative action research involved gathering information on the specific areas which concern postgraduate academic writers as they develop skills in crafting an effective academic voice. The context of this study is such that the data gathering was dual-purpose, as it addressed action-research information gathering and was also intended to contribute to the course refinement process, within a relatively new Master's programme.

The research participants were three cohorts of part-time Master's adult students with class sizes ranging from six to 14 per cohort. The first cohort were part of a blended learning delivery course, while the other two were parts of fully online courses. Of a total of 20 respondents to the questionnaire, four were international students: two from Yemen, one from China and one from Thailand. The remaining participants, all Malaysian, were all multilingual, with four having Chinese secondary school backgrounds. The age range was 24 to 40, with 12 female participants and eight males. All but two of the participants had had 3–15 years' work experience before coming back to academic study, which meant that academic writing was not a skill which had been recently applied.

Research questions

The research questions, shown below, addressed the notion and practice of positioning the author's voice through a dual-purpose questionnaire and the later verbal discussion:

(1) Which features of the author's voice in an academic report do you find most difficult?
(2) Which features of constructing your author's voice do you perceive as requiring further learning?
(3) If need be, what do you plan to do to develop an authoritative and/or critical voice within writing for your field of study?

Research setting

The setting of the small-scale study was academic writing workshops within the aforementioned Master's programme. The first of the three-hour interactive lecture cum workshop sessions conducted by this writer focused on Summarising, Paraphrasing, Quoting and Beginning the Literature Search. This half-day programme was conducted early in the Master's programme, meaning that the researcher had met the participants before engaging in any research activity linked to the later session. The focus of both workshops was to develop awareness and skills for "academic authorship" (Dysthe, 1996, p. 396) and introduce the notions of the author as a user of academic norms through skills related to avoiding plagiarism and expressing an individual author's voice. The researcher met the same group three months later for a further interactive half-day workshop on "Using the Academic Voice", a more in-depth course developed by the researcher from much earlier Doctoral work with Leicester University. The voluntary research was conducted after this second session with an online survey and recording of the semi-structured interviews, serving as platforms for participants' reflections in small-group discussion, predominantly online also. This process involved all three cohorts of students, so the responses ranged across the small and diverse adult learner groups with a total of 70 minutes of discussion. The purpose was to yield qualitative data on the academic voice through analysing the novice writers' perceptions and needs in the area of academic research report writing. The researcher had no involvement in assessment of the participants' writing output, and all participation in the questionnaires and recording of reflective feedback within the semi-structured interviews was voluntary.

After re-introducing the notion of reflective practice (Farrell, 2018) as a means of developing oneself in learning and academic work, the purpose and the links to the online questionnaire were shared. Participants had encountered reflective learning in a related course to which this writer contributed. The questionnaire was followed by recording of group discussion, using semi-structured interview protocols (Carspecken, 1996) as prompts. Carspecken describes the importance of providing a safe "space" of maximum flexibility so that interviewees can reflect and share their own voices in a dialogic exchange. For turn-taking there was an open approach, and interaction was facilitated by offering open general questions as prompts, without any judgemental comments (see Appendix B). In the second and third of the three sessions, this also meant all cameras were turned on, so as to stimulate greater interaction during the Zoom online sessions, the platform for the last two recordings.

The video recordings were examined and emergent themes were identified based on recurring utterances, using the utterance as the basic unit of analysis (Crookes, 1990; Hall, 1991). Stressed syllables were also considered as signalling importance in the discourse. Content analysis using recurrent key words led to categorisation and subsequent select transcription of the discussion sessions focused on the dominant areas of participants' concerns. A brief analysis of questionnaire ranking and samples of participants' conceptions of using the academic voice follows.

RESULTS: VOICES OF THE NOVICE WRITERS

Participants were given an online form in which 15 items were scored on a Likert scale from *challenging* to *easy*. These scores were totalled to produce the ranking list below, which gives indicative data of the 20 participants' perceptions of the difficulty of the aspects of academic writing which were taught. With the small sample size this only provides an indication of what is viewed by participants as areas of greater difficulty in their particular contexts.

Ranking list from most difficult to least:

(1) Expressing one's opinion in an authoritative way
(2) Expressing a critical voice and judgements
(3) Hedging and using guarded language to avoid generalisation
(4) Arguing one's own idea in a paragraph or chapter (tied with point 5)
(5) Ensuring a cohesive line of argument
(6) Differentiating between description and analysis
(7) Using unsourced statements based on the understanding that readers view these as one's views
(8) Using tenses in academic writing
(9) Presenting voices of research participants
(10) Paraphrasing and using appropriate words
(11) Summarising and grammar changes
(12) Referencing
(13) Using and choosing quotations
(14) Concluding and linking sections to ensure continuity
(15) Reading academic articles in one's field

This list suggests that expressions of the author's voice and hedging pose greater difficulties than paraphrasing, summarising and quoting. The largest numerical differences occurred between the ranking of using unsourced statements and using tenses in academic writing. This suggests that the use of the academic voice poses greater challenges than the more grammatically direct areas of paraphrasing, summarising and so on. This indicative information is reinforced in greater depth by the reflections of the novice writers themselves.

The voices of novice academic writers

The select transcriptions below, derived from content-driven data, are samples of participants' answers to the semi-structured prompts used in post-course discussion over three time periods. The transcriptions are almost completely verbatim, with minor editing for clarity. Of the 20 participants, two did not contribute to discussion. The participants are identified P1–20 and the primary language of the respondents is identified in the case of the comments related to English as an additional language influence.

Role of meta-discourse, tenses and signalling a writer's position

The fewest comments related to the items listed 8–15 above, and these may be seen to be issues of cohesion, as with:

> The way we join up ideas and mix in my own voice, my being me the researcher has meant lots to learn. I think because of my biology background where we were taught be objective. No ["I", or "myself"]. Always told ["]be objective["]. But now I am looking at the social issue side and not experiments. I have to think differently ... oh, and write differently too. A change, maybe it's making a view, opinions can go in. Like you say, a voice. (P12)

For many of the participants, four of whom came from "hard science" backgrounds, there were questions about using tenses and signalling through MD. As one (P20) said, "We are used to using experimental sequencing and [there is] no 'I' in there". She continued:

> It's all new, this idea of the academic voice, so I have to look at when things are real for all using the present tense and all the linking things. The grammar of academic voice is so different from a presentation. Ah ... I see how I can use the joining back and forward links. I need to write more using those. Then, yes, more practice, then maybe I feel confident in really putting me into the research—my voice.

When answering the first prompt about the academic voice one participant (P8) said:

> It's [a] mix of things to use, I think. The signals are not like speech. More formal and kind of guarded, tentative. Cannot be just "wow wow wow"... like a talk. It's the joining it all up, then I find I go back and weigh up more and rewrite and then look at details and think about my ideas, position. Voice [blah blah]. It's not easy making it all hang together—as we learnt, cohesion, and then putting myself and ideas into it.

Hedging and avoiding over-generalisation

The balance between hedging and appearing authoritative did prompt considerable questioning during the workshop and concerns were expressed about the balance between asserting oneself and over-generalising, as the following show:

> I want to be seen as knowing what I say. Yes. Ah ... I think I overgeneralise. That's what Prof. ___ said in my first assignment. So now I use more modal verbs and that list we got was useful. (P1)

Comments also mentioned the role of the writer's first language, as in one of several examples quoted below.

> I am really not sure about how to moderate certainty. We are not used to so many of those modal verbs and ... how [to state] the degree of certainty. ["]Possible["] and ["]probable["] and all that. I have had to learn to be not so certain. Sometimes us Yemeni, we like to be very certain. I know my friends tell me that. But this academic writing style is very different with this hedging and all. (P5)

On the other hand, the influence of other languages (Malaysian Chinese) produced the opposite response:

> P3: The big question is when to sound certain? When can I know that I should be authoritative? The know it all ... ha ha.
>
> Interviewer: We have talked about the role of evidence and building the argument up over the paragraph or section.
>
> P3: I guess it's when I think I have built up supporting details, then, and then [show] evidence. Details, ah, then those signalling things, then the bigger point. That takes time and writing, huh?

Expressing authority in the author's voice

Self-perception and establishing oneself in the academic field was expressed as a process needing much learning, as follows:

> I feel insecure as the readers all know the field and I am like a baby learning to walk. (P8)
>
> We should be told more about how to get in the network. Once we know more in our field[,] I guess we would get more sure about, well, our own voice in that academic place. (P8)
>
> I do not know when I kind of get entitled to my own opinion, my own thinking, but I already have it from my work experience, maybe. So maybe my experience goes into the voice of me. Myself, I mean. (P7)
>
> Interviewer: How would you like to be seen in the community of academic writing?
>
> P7: As having something original to share. I guess I have to make my argument evidence-based and hanging together, then readers will believe me. Yes, believable and different. Still learning how to put it all together. We need more training.

Being a writer in English as an additional language

All but three of the participants indicated that English was an additional language for them, and these three, like all the other participants, were acquiring the conventions of the academic voice, hedging and MD after some time away from academic writing. In the last cohort, which was fully online, there were a number of cross-cultural points shared. Three examples follow:

> I am not used to talking about myself as we tend to downplay that side of things like, well, even accepting compliments. You know, Prof ... the brand-new dress is just ... an old thing I found. So I was taught ["]do not project yourself["] and I have had to change that. As you say, reflect and change with, with ... this academic voice thing in writing (P12, Malaysian Chinese speaker)

> We always avoid conflict, so we are experts in not putting the I up there. Especially when I was taught earlier, be objective in research, and now the academic voice. I know I have to have my say, as I have things to say for sustainability (P18, Thai speaker)

> I think that we may [see it] as less easy[,] this type of writing. I have learnt that the use of that academic voice is also like a second language ... for the English first language speakers too. We talk, right guys, and it's not so easy to write. So it does not really matter how you speak [because] this writing is a whole new game. (P19, Malaysian Tamil speaker)

Academic writing does involve a particular voice with techniques which take time to master. It seems that the first language of an academic writer impacts not just the style of writing but also a writer's self-perception of how much he or she can foreground his or her own individual voice. The use of the academic voice and its development through courses is an area worthy of further research, particularly with the complexity of increasing internationalisation.

CONCLUSION

When embarking on teaching the academic voice and the inclusion of the researcher as an active voice in this very formalised genre, one encounters a variety of learner responses to foregrounding the authoritative voice. The development of an academic voice involves a stance, and this is signalled by balancing hedging and certainty with a supportive structure of MD. Those writers changing from hard science disciplines, with the lesser presence of the researcher, debate how objective one can be in social science approaches while presenting the researcher's voice, an area worthy of further research. There remains much to explore when working with the English language academic voice as used by speakers of English as an additional language.

Of more immediate concern are novice writers' needs, which can be as specific as understanding the degrees of certainty in modal verbs and hedging, to wider issues such as the need for explicit development of techniques which build an understanding of academic readers' expectations. It is suggested that academic writing courses include ways of building "young" researchers' confidence through reflective activities and academic networking techniques, so as to develop authoritative, dialogic academic voices.

REFERENCES

Abdollahzadeh, E. (2011). Poring over the findings: Interpersonal authorial engagement in applied linguistics papers. *Journal of Pragmatics, 43*(1), 288–297.

Aitchison, C., & Lee, A. (2006). Research writing: Problems and pedagogies. *Teaching in Higher Education, 11*(3), 265–278.

Almudaffari, M., Supayan, H., & Ho, I. A. (2019). Interaction in academic L2 writing: An analysis of interactional metadiscourse strategies in applied linguistics research articles. *The Southeast Asian Journal of English Language Studies, 25*(3), 16–32. DOI:10.17576/3L-2019-2503-02

Arnaudet, M., & Barrett, M. (1984). *Approaches to academic reading and writing.* Prentice Hall.

Bagheri, M. (2020). Disruptive technologies or big-bang disruption: A research gap in marketing studies. In Á. Rocha, J. Reis, M. Peter & Z. Bogdanović (Eds.), *Marketing and smart technologies: Proceedings of ICMarkTech 2019*, pp. 229–241. Singapore. DOI:10.1007/978-981-15-1564-4_22

Bakhtin, M. M. (1981). *The dialogic imagination: Four essays* (C. Emerson & M. Holquist, Trans.). University of Texas Press. (Original work published 1953)

Belcher, D., & Hirvela, A. (Eds.). (2001). Voice in L2 Writing. *Journal of Second Language Writing, 10*(1–2).

Boice, R. (1990). *Professors as writers: A self-help guide to productive writing.* New Forums Press.

Bucholtz, M., & Hall, K. (2005). Identity and interaction: A sociocultural linguistic approach. *Discourse Studies, 7*(4–5), 585–614.

Carspecken, P. (1996). *Critical ethnography in educational research: A theoretical and practical guide.* Academic Press.

Cheng, X., & Steffensen, M. S. (1996). Metadiscourse: A technique for improving student writing. *Research in the Teaching of English, 30*(2), 149–181.

Chu, R. H., & Xiaowen, W. (2020). From faithfulness to information quality: On 信 in translation studies. In L. Lim & D. Li (Eds.), *Key issues in translation studies in China: New frontiers in translation studies*, pp. 111–142. DOI:10.1007/978-981-15-5865-8_6

Corbyn, J. (2020). *How to improve your writing: A guide to using the snowflake method in academic work.* Independent publisher.

Crismore, A., Markkanen, R., & Steffensen, M. S. (1993). Metadiscourse in persuasive writing: A study of texts written by American and Finnish university students. *Written Communication, 10*(1), 39–71.

Crompton, P. (1997). Hedging in academic writing: Some theoretical problems. *English for Specific Purposes, 16*(4), 271–287.

Crookes, G. (1990). The utterance, and other basic units for second language discourse analysis. *Applied Linguistics, 11*(2), 183–189.

Dysthe, O. (1996).The multivoiced classroom: Interaction of writing and classroom discourse. *Written Communication, 13*(3), 385–425.

Elbow, P. (1994). Introduction. In P. Elbow (Ed.), *Landmark essays on voice and writing.* (pp. xi–xvii). Hermagoras Press.

Fairclough, N. (1992). *Discourse and social change.* Polity Press.

Farrell, T. S. C. (2018). Reflective practice for language teachers and learners. In J. I. Liontas & M. DelliCarpini (Eds.), *The TESOL encyclopedia of English language teaching.* John Wiley & Sons. DOI: 10.1002/9781118784235.eelt0873

Hall, S. J. (1991). *The effect of split information tasks on the acquisition of mathematics vocabulary.* [Unpublished master's thesis]. Victoria University of Wellington.

Hall, S. J. (2013). Deconstructing aspects of native speakerism: Reflections from in-service teacher education. *Journal of Asia TEFL, 9*(3),107–130.

Hinkel, E. (2003). *Teaching academic ESL writing: Practical techniques in vocabulary and grammar.* Routledge.

Ho, V., & Li, C. (2018). The use of metadiscourse and persuasion: An analysis of first year university students' timed argumentative essays. *Journal of English for Academic Purposes, 33, 53–68.*

Hofstede, G. (2001). *Culture's consequences: Comparing values, behaviors, institutions, and organizations across nations.* Sage Publications.

Hyland, K. (1995). The author in the text: Hedging in scientific writing. *Hong Kong Papers in Linguistics and Language Teaching, 18*, 33–42.

Hyland, K. (1996). Writing without conviction? Hedging in science research articles. *Applied Linguistics, 17*(4), 433–454. DOI:10.1093/applin/17.4.433

Hyland, K. (2002). Options of identity in academic writing. *ELT Journal, 56*(4), 351–358.

Hyland, K. (2005). *Metadiscourse*. Continuum.

Hyland, K. (2012). Undergraduate understandings: Stance and voice in final year reports. In *Stance and voice in written academic genres* (pp. 134–150). Palgrave Macmillian.

Hyland, K., & Jiang, F. K. (2020). Text-organizing metadiscourse: Tracking changes in rhetorical persuasion. *Journal of Historical Pragmatics, 21*(1), 137–164. DOI:10.1075/jhp.00039.hyl

Ivanic, R. (1998). *Writing and identity: The discoursal identity in academic writing*. John Benjamins Publishing.

Jensen, J. (2017). *Write no matter what: Advice for academics*. The University of Chicago Press.

Korthagen, F. (1993). Two modes of reflection. *Teaching and Teacher Education, 9*, 317–326.

Krause, K. L. D. (2014). Challenging perspectives on learning and teaching in the disciplines: The academic voice. *Studies in Higher Education, 39*(1), 2–19. DOI: 10.1080/03075079.2012.690730

Lakoff, G. (1972). Hedges: A study in meaning criteria and the logic of fuzzy concepts. *Chicago Linguistic Society Papers, 8*, 183–228.

Livytska, I. (2019). The use of hedging in research articles on applied linguistics. *Journal of Language and Cultural Education, 7*, 35–53.

Loi, C. K., & Lim, J. M. H. (2019). Hedging in the discussion sections of English and Malay research articles. *GEMA Online Journal of Language Studies, 19*(1), 36–61. DOI: 10.17576/gema- 2019-1901-03

Matsuda, P. K. (2001). Voice in Japanese written discourse: Implications for second language writing. *Journal of Second Language Writing, 10*(1–2), 35–53.

Matsuda, P. K., & Tardy, C. M. (2007). Voice in academic writing: The rhetorical construction of author identity in blind manuscript review. *English for Specific Purposes, 26*, 235–249.

Nelson, N., & Castelló, M. (2012). Academic writing and authorial voice. *Studies in Writing, 24*, 33–51. DOI: 10.1108/S1572-6304(2012)0000024007

Neville, C. (2010). *The complete guide to referencing and avoiding plagiarism.* Berkshire.

Nivales, M. L. M. (2011). Hedging in college research papers: Implications for language instruction. *Asian EFL Journal, 52,* 35–45.

Richards, J. C. (1990). Beyond training: Approaches to teacher education in language teaching. *The Language Teacher, 14,* 3–8.

Roulston, K., McClendon, V. J., Thomas, A., Tuff, R., Williams, G., & Healy, M. F. (2008). Developing reflective interviewers and reflective researchers. *Reflective Practice, 9*(3), 231–243.

Schon, D. A. (1983). *The reflective practitioner: How professionals think in action.* Basic Books.

Swales, J. (2004). *Research genres: Exploration and applications.* Cambridge University Press.

Swales, J., & Feak, C. P. (2012). *Academic writing for graduate students: Essential tasks and skills.* Michigan Series in English for Academic and Professional Purposes.

Tardy, C. M. (2012). Current conceptions of voice. In K. Hyland & C. S. Guinda (Eds.), *Stance and voice in written academic genres.* Palgrave Macmillan. DOI:10.1057/9781137030825_3

Thompson, G. (2001). Interaction in academic writing: Learning to argue with the reader. *Applied Linguistics, 22*(1), 58–78.

Vande Kopple, W. J. (2012). The importance of studying metadiscourse. *Applied Research in English, 1*(2), 37–44. DOI:10.1111/j.1530-2415.2011.01276.x

Wenger, E. (1998). *Communities of practice: Learning, meaning, and identity.* Cambridge University Press.

Wilson, E. (2019). On academic writing. *Journal of New Librarianship, 4,* 193–207.

Appendix A: Google Form—Ranking academic writing challenges

Thank you for consenting to take part in this online Google Forms questionnaire. The information collected is for research and course development purposes and will be treated as anonymous and confidential. Please identify the language you consider as your first language.

Please rank each item below. The Rankings range from 1 from challenging to 5 for easy. Your comments in the last open box are valued. Thank you for taking part.

(1) Using tenses in academic writing
(2) Referencing
(3) Using and choosing quotations
(4) Paraphrasing and using appropriate words
(5) Summarising and grammar changes
(6) Expressing a critical voice and judgements
(7) Hedging and using guarded language to avoid generalisation
(8) Differentiating between description and analysis
(9) Arguing one's own idea in a paragraph or chapter
(10) Ensuring a cohesive line of argument
(11) Expressing one's opinion in an authoritative way
(12) Presenting the voices of research participants
(13) Using unsourced statements based on the understanding that readers view these as one's views
(14) Concluding and linking sections to ensure continuity
(15) Reading academic articles in one's field

Appendix B: Semi-structured focus group discussion

These open-ended prompts are to stimulate discussion. They will be used in the discussion session following the course. As discussed and agreed earlier, your consent to being recorded implies that the transcription may be used for research purposes and to improve the workshops. All information is treated as anonymous and none of the discussion has any impact on assessment. Please take time to reflect on these questions before the discussion.

Your active participation is much appreciated. Many thanks.

(1) What is your idea of the academic voice?
(2) How would you like to be seen in the community of academic writing?
(3) What ideas do you have for improving as an academic voice?
(4) What would you like to know more about regarding academic voice?
(5) Any other comments?

Chapter 5

Multi-Ethnic Voices of Loanwords in the Malaysian Dailies[1]

Manjit Kaur Balwant Singh*

ABSTRACT

The social creativity of the multi-ethnic community in Malaysia is exploited in the current prime Malaysian dailies which target the processes that take place within the Self and the inclusive society-of-selves, succinctly espousing the Bakhtinian dialogical theory of language. The society-of-selves are the selves in the social structure that make up the multi-ethnic society. The data for this study consist of loanwords of Sanskrit origin borrowed into Malay and are hence found in the Malaysian English newspapers *The Star* and *New Straits Times*. The Sanskrit word *maharddhika*, "great prosperity", borrowed as *merdeka*, "independence", expresses the collective voices in Malay; yet, Malaysian English users voice themselves idiosyncratically by coining phrases like *Merdeka cheer*, *Merdeka festival* and *Merdeka celebrations*. These newly coined terms are undoubtedly due to the combined quality of the author's inner-Others that creates a variety of contrasting relationships of voice in loanwords. The inner-Others are voices of the Others within ourselves and, in this case, they are the voices of the community.

Keywords Malaysian English, multivoicedness, dialogical Self, voice, contrast, author, reader

[1] My heartfelt appreciation goes out to my mentor, Dr Toshiko Yamaguchi, for presenting me with this opportunity to further my research by writing a chapter and rendering her patient support and expert guidance at all stages of my pioneering adventure. Without her insightful feedback, this would not have been possible.

* Independent scholar, Malaysia

INTRODUCTION

The multifaceted voices of the community in Malaysia that exist within the Self and the inclusive society-of-selves succinctly combine the concept of a dialogical Self, whereby the Self is considered an intrinsic part of the community, bringing together the multiplicity of interacting voices. The concept of "dialogic" (meaning social) nature of language was established by the renowned Russian philosopher and literary critic, Mikhail Mikhailovich Bakhtin (1895–1975). From the perspective of the dialogic theory, there is a dialectic relationship between an individual and the society he or she lives in, reflecting life as a shared event of human systems. This association is often constituted by tensions as we constantly participate in dialogue, which is one way of acquiring knowledge through communicative interactions. However, as Bakhtin (1953/1981) retorts, "[L]anguage is not a neutral medium that passes freely and easily into private property of the speaker's intentions; it is populated—overpopulated—with the intentions of others" (p. 208), thus requiring the commitment of working with the complexity of others. As such, "othering" represents each group's social dichotomies that are embodied in their discourse, and the linguistic choices they make inevitably encode their semantic stance.

This concept of voice which relates to a word being both unique and shared implies the "Self-in-relation-to-Others" which, as Aveling et al. (2015) explain, is imbedded in the "interdisciplinary tradition of dialogism" (p. 673). Their qualitative method of unpacking the voices of the Self and others and their interactions was instrumental in mapping the meanings and inferences that authors give to their experiences through "multivoicedness", which, as explicated by Yamaguchi (2004), originates from one's conscious experiences that are subtly related to the background or the context of use. While Bakhtin assents that all languages are socially shaped with embedded meanings and definitions, most significant, however, is that "these meanings and definitions can repeatedly be changed—or (re)produced, or (re)generated—through the process of dialogism" (Bakhtin, 1953/1981, p. 294), and this concept resonates in the loanwords explored in this study.

The Malaysian setting

The local population in Malaysia largely consists of Malays, Chinese, and Indians, and though Malay is the national language of the country, the influence of the ancestral languages of this community is very much intertwined with the second language of Malaysia, referred to as Malaysian English (ME). It has become a medium of expression for multi-ethnic speakers in Malaysia, "an interethnic link language in multilingual countries" (Lowenberg, 1986, p. 2), and is "appropriated by local speakers, and in that process it is diversifying and developing new dialects" (Schneider, 2003, p. 233). These distinct New Englishes have been born in postcolonial settings under idiosyncratic historical conditions (Schneider, 2003) and not by choice of the nations in the Outer Circle where English is not the native language of the society. According to Kachru (1990), the dissemination of English is viewed in three concentric circles: in the Inner Circle, English is the native or first language and in the Outer Circle, English is regarded as a second language, while in the Expanding Circle, English is learnt as a foreign language.

So, when a non-native language is "appropriated" by multi-ethnic speakers, collective voices play a crucial role in the dialogical Self, creating "positive or negative meanings in fields of uncertainty" (Hermans & Hermans-Konopka, 2010, p. 30).

Overview of data

The concept of "other-voicedness", also referred to as "multiple-voiced" language change, is analysed in this study with the coexistence of varieties, an important stylistic feature found in the linguistically representative code of newspapers. The online versions of major newspapers *The Star* and *New Straits Times* have a considerably large audience and the language used is often assumed, as Rademann (1998, p. 49) reports, "to be characteristic of the respective period and society they are published in", bringing together the linguistic influence of the country's multi-faceted diversity. This allows the exploration of Sanskrit loanwords that are historically rooted and socially shared, to examine "how far a given linguistic feature has changed over time"

(Rademann, 1998, p. 49) and what meanings speakers ascribe to sustain their social asymmetries through the conditioned discourse of the newspapers. Remarkably, the meanings acquired through these social interactions often voice an ideological struggle or hegemony within a society, providing the methodological means to scrutinise the relationships between voice, text, and the social world.

Background of loanwords

The loanwords in question are related to the Indian community speaking Indic languages like Punjabi, Hindi, Gujerati, Sindhi, and Bengali under the Sanskrit umbrella. In this community, Malaysian Sikh Punjabis form the largest number (David, 2013) and have rarely been researched in ME studies. Ironically, this elusive manifestation of Sanskrit loanwords has existed since the seventh century in the Malay language, which is famed for its overriding influence on ME (Morais, 2001). The old Malay language was heavily influenced by Sanskrit around the seventh century (de Casparis, 1997), and this indirect route of loanwords through Malay as the intermediary language delivers an incredible variation to voice in terms of heteroglossia, or "other-voicedness".

METHODOLOGY

The theoretical tools employed were based on a mixture of analysing the multivoiced Self which, as Aveling et al. (2015) perceive, "links the 'micro' to the 'macro' by examining the dialogical dynamics that structure knowledge, society and subjectivity through the 'society of mind'" (p. 674). This, Aveling et al. (2015) further explain, is based on the fact that in dialogism, "selves are co-constituted in micro- and macro-social relations" (p. 674). The three steps Aveling et al. (2015) propose focus on "identifying the voices of I-positions within the Self's talk (or text), identifying the voices of 'inner-Others', and examining the dialogue and relationships between the different voices" (p. 670).

To scrutinise multivoicedness in newspaper "dialogues" which, as Yamaguchi (2004) asserts "represent two different but interrelated aspects of the author's inner world" (p. 482), the concept of contrast, researched by her, was adopted. The study was on the postpositional particle *wa* in Japanese that is characterised to express literal contrast, as in "John ate a pizza, but Mary didn't" (p. 467). From the dialogical viewpoint, Yamaguchi claims that the contrastive *wa* "manifests itself as the expression of the author's multivoicedness" (p. 467), and these social alternatives, she perceives, originate from the conscious experiences of the author and are realised through the contrast of association, evaluation, and conflict. This premise was instrumental in decoding the relationships between the dialogical voices and examining the dialogue in the context of the word to complement meaning-making.

The patterns of linguistic variation of loanwords as a result of the media meeting the voices of the local multi-ethnic society, the classification of semantic change, followed the four different categories found in this study. The first were words with exactly the same meaning followed by words with partly the same meaning, then words with new meaning added, and finally words with the meaning reduced in ME. Loanwords whose meanings deviate or contrast could well be due to the author's conscious experiences or intentions as Yamaguchi (2004) claims in line with what Bakhtin referred to as the "author's dialogical voices" (1953/1981). The loanwords were analysed in the context of use, which is pivotal, as Yamaguchi (2004) emphasises that "the context is certainly the world we as author or reader inhabit" (p. 480). Further, citing Halliday and Hasan (1985, p. 5), there is a need to include the context of use as it "serves to make a bridge between the text and the situation in which texts actually occur". Undeniably, the context of use is the meeting point for analysing ethnic identity, and "to consider language use as meaning-making in a context makes it possible to explore the socially shared and historically rooted significations that are present in discourses" (Pietikäinen & Dufva, 2006, p. 207). With the aim of making explicit this existing link between dialogism, text, and context, the study elaborates on the dialogical voices through the concept of contrast, drawing on texts in news media.

ANALYSIS OF LOANWORDS

In Excerpt 1 below, the Sanskrit loanword *maharddhika* meaning "great prosperity" is borrowed as *merdeka*, "independence", into Malay and hence to ME with partly the same meaning. Gaining independence would have meant freedom from the shackles of colonial power for the people of Malaya. As Hermans (2003) relates: "Voices from the culture of origin do not simply disappear when people are involved in an acculturation process" (p. 95). Cultures bear collective voices which occupy social positions in the Self and such voices resonate their historically situated selves. These voices include their language, such as the colossal amount of borrowing of Sanskrit words into Old Malay which occurred around the seventh century during the Sriwijayaan Empire (de Casparis, 1997). Thus, while interacting with different cultures, this influence radiates the dialogical relationships with other voices. The dynamically related multivoiced users of the educated variety of ME, however, take it one step further in voicing themselves distinctively by coining phrases like *Merdeka cheer*, *Merdeka festival* and *Merdeka celebrations* which are aptly associated with prosperity, as in Excerpt 1 below.

Excerpt 1

> The Merdeka spirit was palpable throughout the country, with people coming out in force to mark the 60th National Day at the respective state-level celebrations. ("People from various states", 2017)

Firstly, based on the "Other is not in opposition to Self, but part of Self" (Bakhtin, 1953/1981, p. 354), this relatedness has to be accompanied by the notion of language that highlights performance. In addition, while discourse has the potential, as Pietikäinen and Dufva (2006) assert, "to capture the socially constructed", voice offers the platform to "inner thoughts and experiences" (p. 212). According to Excerpt 1, the 60th National Day celebrations were held nationwide, yet each reader related to the author's voice differently as he or she had diverse memories of the past and expectations for the future. The reporting phrases "was palpable throughout" and "people coming out" signal that a community event was relayed, seeking the readers' participation to identify themselves with the familiar text. The readers became the "imagined Others or generalised Others" (Aveling et al., 2015, p. 673) of the community in the author's dialogical Self, with whom he or she intends to share the spirit of freedom. The emphasis here is on the intercultural processes of shared assumptions; as Thompson (1996) suggests, "we need to appeal to the concept of shared knowledge" (p. 510). Examining how this shared knowledge is communicated rests solely on the context in which the author's dialogical voices are evoked.

Contrast by associating statements

In the dialogicality of contrast, Yamaguchi (2004) explains that the "author's dialogical voices are evoked when two situations or entities are associated with each other"; that is, "the author correlates information provided by the first clause with the information contained in the second clause" (p. 472). The word "contrast" can be misleading but, as Yamaguchi (2004) explains, contrast is not only realised in opposite poles; "the concept of positive vs. negative polarity" (p. 472), it can also be voiced in association of two entities. Based on this premise, in the first line of the excerpt, the author establishes the fact that the spirit of independence was profound with the words "The Merdeka spirit was palpable throughout the country", and in the second line he or she supplies further information, "with people coming out in force to mark the 60th National Day", associating both entities to amplify the message. The author engenders the "Merdeka spirit" in the minds of the readers so they can visualise the intensity of the celebrations and the spirit of independence by connecting with the author's inner-Others, the people who came out in force to mark the 60th National Day. Aveling et al. (2015) postulate that the "[i] nner-Others are rarely physically present ... rather they are given voice within and alongside the 'I', shaping and colouring the meaning of utterances" (p. 677). The background of the context of the words "Merdeka spirit" and "60th National Day" convey an irrepressible sense of history, as voice captures the strong connotations of loyalty and inclusivity that local speakers apprehend and the ideological sign behind the use of the words is undeniable.

In Excerpt 2 on the next page, the Sanskrit loanword *bhu-mi,* "earth" or "of land", borrowed into Malay as *bumi,* "earth", has been appropriated with another loanword *putra,* "son", to form the word *bumiputra,* "son of the soil". This loanword has become specialised in its usage with the restricted meaning of "native" in ME, along with abundant variations created by its users such as the short form *Bumi*, as in *Bumi firms, Bumi quota, Bumi vendors,*

Bumi concerns, Bumi power and *Bumi discount*. The plural form *Bumiputeras* is created very much like English plural forms by simply adding an "s", as can be seen below. Most creative, however, is the prefix non- which is attached to the loanword to imply non-native status, such as non-*bumiputera* or non-*bumis,* thus creating new forms.

Excerpt 2

> RM300m Teras Fund a success in helping Bumi firms (headline)
> Bumiputera businesses often find it difficult to get loans from banks. The government has offered credit guarantees under the Credit Guarantee Corporation (CGC) and other schemes, yet a lot of funds reserved for Bumiputeras are not used up. (Salleh, 2016)

Here, the author's voice is not referring to any "unspecified Others" (Thompson, 1996, p. 507) as in reported speech but the inner-Others, the potential *Bumiputera businesspeople,* based on Bakhtin's (1986) notion of addressivity in which he explains there is a shared responsibility between both parties to arrive at the projected meaning. In this case it is the author's voice and his or her inner-Others.

Contrast by opposing statements

To examine the manifestation of the author's multivoicedness, the text showing the author's attitude towards *Bumiputeras* acquiring loans displays contrast by these opposing statements being associated, namely "difficult to get loans" vs "government has offered" vs "yet a lot of funds ... not used up". Firstly, the author makes the supposition that "Bumiputera businesses often find it difficult to get loans from banks", followed by the opposing statement that "The government has offered credit guarantees", and finally the author's emotions of regret and disappointment are voiced in the concluding statement, "yet a lot of funds reserved for *Bumiputeras* are not used up". The theme of the excerpt does not suggest polarity between loans provided by banks and the government's schemes but the *Bumiputera* businesspeople who did not explore possibilities provided by the government in the face of difficulty, evidenced by a surplus of funds not taken up. This is the straightforward premise anyone would extract from the excerpt, but the headline suggests otherwise. Apparently the RM300m fund set up to help "Bumiputera businesses" was a success, meaning businesspeople were benefitting, but for reasons unknown not many took up the offer, thus the surplus funds. An author's dialogism is, as Bakhtin (1953/1981) explains, "made up of contradictory opinions, points of view and value judgments" (p. 281), which very often obscure the comprehension of the intended meaning.

In the next loanword, a new meaning not found in Sanskrit has been coined in ME. The loanword *upavasa*, "fast", borrowed into Malay as *puasa*, "fast", has been appropriated to *buka puasa*, "breaking of fast", which has none of the attributes of fasting. Instead, it is all about feasts, buffets, receptions, and events that promote breaking-of-fast meals, not abstaining from food. How voice relates this divergent meaning is investigated in Excerpt 3 below.

Excerpt 3

> Some hotels and restaurants in the state capital are cashing in on the fasting month by promoting buka puasa buffets for Ramadan despite not obtaining ... "halal" certificates. (Alagesh, 2015)

In this excerpt, the author is not making a supposition, nor is there any indication as to whose voice it is; but when unpacking voices, especially in newspaper reporting, it is important to look at the linguistic significance of the report against the background of language (Thompson, 1996). Meanwhile, the true meaning, Bakhtin (1953/1981) narrates, is "understood against the background of other concrete utterances on the same theme" (p. 281). This is also proposed by the semantic field theory, that the meaning of a word cannot be derived from the individual word in isolation, but in relation to its neighbouring words that articulate the content field and "stand in the relation of affinity and contrast to the word(s) in question" (Lehrer et al., 2012, pp. 3–4). The word "halal" in Excerpt 3 is in inverted commas, which is the author's way of signalling that it comes from a different language, but appears as a "more or less distinct, identifiable voice" (Thompson, 1996, p. 506). *Halal* is a Malay word used to designate food seen as permissible according to Islamic law by a recognised authority that issues a corresponding certificate, and the author voices this as shared knowledge of the Muslim community.

Contrast by evaluating opposing statements

To realise the author's dialogical voice, readers must comprehend the contrast of the two opposing statements that some hotels and restaurants were making money by promoting *buka puasa* buffets without "halal" certificates, and that too during the holy month of Ramadan. By evaluating the two statements, the author's implicit attitude surfaces, and though it is not stated openly, it is easy to recognise his or her inner voice that says these were unlawful acts and some decree was required to address this problem. The reporter's evaluation of what he or she is reporting is a crucial aspect of language reports (Thompson, 1996), as it serves the purpose of encompassing the inner-Others, the readers, in his or her manipulative voice which is directed towards the authorities. The author reiterates that the offenders were making money despite not having the permissible order of "halal" certificates, which was under the jurisdiction of the relevant authority that was apparently unaware. In this way, he or she is able to express the voices of the inner-Others, the readers and the local Muslim community as well. By analysing relationships with the multivoiced Self, one can accomplish the task of linking the "micro" to the "macro", as dialogism relates the selves to be "co-constituted in micro- and macro-social relations" (Aveling et al., 2015, p. 684). Here, the author has managed to encompass the entire local Muslim community by way of his or her manipulative voice.

Another loanword related to food is the good old *roti,* "flat bread", as borrowed from Sanskrit, but which has become famous for describing many varieties of bread like *roti jala,* "bread cooked like a net", *roti canai,* "bread ground down", *roti kaya,* "bread with coconut jam", *roti benggali,* "authentic homemade Benggali bread", *roti ayam,* "bread with chicken filling", *roti prate,* "bread made with ghee", *roti John,* "omelette bread", and *roti bakar,* "toasted bread", and even the seller of bread is referred to as the *roti* man. The following excerpt is one such example of loanwords being appropriated by local speakers, in which multiple different "I-positions" (Hermans & Gieser, 2011) play a crucial role in the dialogical Self.

Excerpt 4

> Craving for a hot *teh tarik* and crispy *roti canai* for breakfast? If you happen to be at the Putra World Trade Centre ..., you can get them for free from today until the end of the Umno General Assembly 2016 this Saturday. (Mohd, 2016)

The excerpt starts with a question and answer section in which the craving for *teh tarik*, "hot pulled tea", and crispy *roti canai*, "ground bread", is the topic of inquiry. This sort of reporting mimics the face-to-face interaction of a colloquial conversation and readers do recognise the familiar words used in the linguistic background (Thompson, 1996). Based on the assumption of shared knowledge, it signals that there is more than one voice involved, as the dialogical Self uses the voice of a typical food lover who craves such food and then shares the information of a familiar place where it can be had for free. Thompson (1996) proposes that in such a situation, "the voice must remain unspecified, since each reader is in fact being implicitly encouraged to accept it as his own voice" (p. 510). The author has taken the prerogative of speaking from multiple different "I-positions" (Hermans & Gieser, 2011) and this can take place within one text; or, as Aveling et al. (2015) word it, "within one context or even one utterance the Self may move between I-positions or voices" (p. 673). This manipulative aspect of reporting, Thompson (1996) divulges, "leads the writer to voice the reader's reactions (inducing the reader to accept him as his mouthpiece)" (p. 510).

Contrast by associating question-answer interaction

How the author's dialogical voice is evoked lies in the contrast of associating the question-answer interaction, whereby the author first asks who is craving a hot *teh tarik* and *roti canai* and in the second sentence suggests going to the Putra World Trade Centre to fulfil this craving. The conflicting roles of both asking a question and giving the answer reveal the author's subtle attitude towards what he or she is reporting. As Hermans (2004) writes, "[In] Bakhtin's (1929/1973) view, the relation of agreement and disagreement are, like question and answer, basic dialogical forms" (p. 302), while Bakhtin (1953/1981) further says, "[E]very word is directed toward an answer and cannot escape the profound influence of the answering word it anticipates" (p. 280).

The answering word, then, must exist in the author's subtle intentions. As Yamaguchi (2004) argues, "[T]he author's presumed intention should be the trigger of oppositions" (p. 468), which readers are unable to detect from the question and answer routine. However, they do recognise the voice is not the author's, as Thompson (1996) explains that a normal reporting voice does not involve any question and answer regimen and so this sort of frontal intrusion signals a different voice in language reports. He further elaborates why the manipulative sense must remain implicit, as "the manipulative purpose which leads the writer to voice the reader's reactions (inducing the reader to accept him as his mouthpiece) would be less effective—more open to contestation—if the attribution were explicit" (p. 510).

In the next excerpt, identifying the voice is, again, not such an easy task. The loanword *akasa*, "sky", is borrowed with the same meaning as *angkasa*, "sky", in Malay and teamed with the possessive suffix *-vant* from Sanskrit to make the Malay word *angkasawan*, "astronaut". It is constructed on the same basis as the Sanskrit word *antariksavant*, "sky", and possessive suffix *-vant*, literally meaning "astronaut", and further modified to be a countable noun in ME (e.g. "first *angkasawan*"), insomuch that it does not look like a loanword any more. The overall structure in ME is quite reasonable as the numerical value is added before the word *angkasawan* just like in standard English and is easily understood. In Malay, however, the numerical value is inserted after the word: *angkasawan pertama*, meaning "first astronaut", and so on. The word is used interchangeably as *angkasawan* and astronaut in the excerpt below.

Excerpt 5

> Angkasawan wants woman in space next (headline)
> National astronaut Datuk Dr Sheikh Muszaphar Shukor said it should be a woman who next makes the foray into space. ("*Angkasawan* wants woman in space", 2015)

Apart from the headlines the rest of the text after the word "said" looks much like a direct quote and it should be easy to identify the voice in a precise quotation in reported speech, but the inverted commas are missing. Also, if it is indirect speech, the word "said" should be followed by "that", but the word is omitted as well. Thompson (1996) regards direct and indirect (reported) speech as clear linguistic categories that require no definition, but he also reveals that while most examples fit easily into this traditional category, there are many more in which reporting someone else's dialogue fails to follow this tradition, just like in Excerpt 5. In this situation, language has to be treated as a meaning-making resource, and a move away from the structural angle is required, as Vološinov (1973) affirms that treating indirect speech merely in terms of inflexible alterations is likely to obscure the picture. It makes sense to follow Thompson's (1996) astuteness that if "mechanical transformations of direct to indirect speech" are side-lined, there is "a greater focus on the range of possibilities for talking about what other people say" (p. 525).

Contrast by conflicting oppositions

To unveil the dialogical dynamics involved, then, reported speech has to be treated as a response to a probable question by the author on who the next *angkasawan* should be. Working on the angle of contrast by conflicting opposition, the first part is verbalised explicitly while the unexpressed second half can be inferred from the cultural dichotomies involved, as the collective voices of culture portray the Self's social attitudes (Hermans, 2003). In such a situation, Yamaguchi (2004) affirms that the author expresses "various internal emotions, judgments, or attitudes in the face of a given context in which only one opposition is verbalized explicitly" (p. 470). In Excerpt 5, the positive attitude of the astronaut is stated in the headline "*Angkasawan* wants woman in space next", and this is followed by the dominant reporting signal by the author with the reporting noun in the main clause, after which there is the reporting message as the subordinate clause in the sentence "National astronaut Datuk Dr Sheikh Muszaphar Shukor said it should be a woman who next makes the foray into space". The choice of the reporting verb "said" without the distancing factor "that" signals a supportive response and endorses the inner-Other in the author, reflecting the evaluative manner of the voice from the perspective of the "I" (Burkitt, 2010).

However, conflict arises from the implicit contrast of the socio-cultural normalities which might not have been in favour of sending a woman into space, or other people who were sceptical. This is not verbalised explicitly, but on the contrary, the author voices the possibility of sending a woman into space. Hermans (2004) remarks that when partaking in the collective voice of the community or culture, "some voices have more social power than others, with the result that some voices are neglected, suppressed, or just not heard" (p. 303). Ironically, it was a woman who headed the project *Angkasawan* to successfully launch the country's first astronaut, Datuk Dr Sheikh Muszaphar, into space in 2007. Professor Emeritus Datuk Dr Mazlan Othman was the first director of Malaysia's National Space Agency, *Angkasa,* and also the first Malaysian to serve as director of the United Nations Office for Outer Space Affairs in Vienna (Sani, 2016). Perhaps this influenced the first *angkasawan* to voice his opinion.

Here, Raggatt's (2015) work clearly points to the primary source of meaning-making as "the rights, duties, and sanctions (e.g., based on status, or again, gender)", and the author's positioning and positions are "both driven by, and constrained by, social contracts". Thus the subject positions are "taken up from a palette defined by the culture, according to its rules" (p. 778).

DISCUSSION

The analysis of the excerpts above is scaffolded on the important theoretical concepts of multivoicedness and the "multivoiced Self", while the synthesising thread is the "dialogical Self". The dialogical Self is in fact a view from the other side, a look at things from the perspective of the Other. In the loanwords mentioned earlier, a multiplicity of voices can be gathered from the all-important context of use. As Yamaguchi (2004) emphasises, "[T] he author is committed to getting the reader to decipher his/her ways of using the language in different contexts", further edifying that the "effect of dialogicality would only be half the story" (p. 481) if context were not taken into account. Context-dependent meaning change, Traugott (2017) explains, is remarkable in the loanword *sanction*, the verb borrowed from French in the 18th century to mean "ratify, confirm", but since the second half of the 20th century, it has come to be used as "impose a penalty", bearing a negative meaning. Since both meanings are now in use, the intended meaning has to be resolved in the context. This is how important the context of a word is to meaning change, and thus shifting the focus from analysing voices in individual loanwords to the context of words in ME reveals the assimilation of the shared traditions of the various ethnic groups residing in Malaysia—the social facts comprising the status of the community, their roles, cultural beliefs, and facets of shared assumptions among local speakers.

In Excerpt 1, the multivoiced Self manifests in the many different inner voices of "I" as the reporter, "I" as the reader, "I" as the "people coming out in force" and as a member of a multi-ethnic society. These collective voices are based on the shared assumption of achieving *merdeka*, "independence", together, and the palpable spirit is meant to be celebrated by all: "Community voices necessarily involve a fused signal" (Thompson, 1996, p. 527). Similarly in Excerpt 4, the loanword *roti* is in every way common to the entire multi-ethnic population and the multivoicedness belongs to all food lovers craving crispy *roti canai*. The same applies to Excerpt 5 in which the interplay between active and passive voice carries explicit and implicit messages subjecting the inner-Others to the controversy of sending a woman into space and reaching out to their knowledge of cultural norms or impartiality, as they deem fit. The shared knowledge of cultural norms "is likely to draw more on the broader socio-cultural context of situation" (Thompson, 1996, p. 511), as readers are aware that an implicit message cannot be expressed in this particular context. Even regarding the concept of contrast, Yamaguchi (2004, p. 480) insists that "understanding of words necessarily involves an implicit dialogue". However, in Excerpts 2 and 3, the voice is clearly directed to the whole Muslim community in particular, though the generalised Others do relate to the messages as they have been exposed to the loanwords and are aware of the commonness. The loanword *bumiputra/bumiputera* is shaped from the loanwords *bumi*, "land", and *putra*, "son", but this creation does not exist in Sanskrit and was only coined in Malay. In contrast, the loanword *puasa* in Excerpt 3 is structured from *upavasa,* "fast", whereby the Old Malay language practised the deletion of the initial "u" to retain the word *puasa* (Poedjosoedarmo, 1982). The many variations in spelling are due to Old Malay having a less distributed phonemic inventory, as de Casparis (1997) discovered in his research to compile an Indonesian etymological dictionary, attesting that the modern Indonesian forms and the earlier ones in Malay were borrowed from Sanskrit and other Indian languages. While these linguistic features are underlined by vocabulary and grammatical choices of a language known as the background of language, the meaning-making formations provide the background to unveiling voice in varied social contexts. Also, voice is realised in context by contrast, utilising the subdivisions of "association, evaluation, and conflict, all of which possess, in effect, the form of coordinateness" (Yamaguchi, 2004, p. 482). This is further elucidated by Hermans (2004): "[W]hen the two phrases are taken as utterances from two different speakers, a dialogical relation of disagreement can be seen to exist" (p. 302), and a dialogue in a newspaper does represent two different but interrelated traits of an author's inner Self.

CONCLUSION

This chapter has analysed Sanskrit loanwords borrowed into Malay in the seventh century which now appear in ME, to scrutinise the meanings multicultural speakers ascribe to sustain their social asymmetries through the concept of "other-voicedness", also referred to as "multiple-voiced" language change with the coexistence of varieties, an important stylistic feature found in the linguistically representative code of newspapers. The loanwords were divided according to their degree of similarity of meaning into four different categories of exactly the same meaning in ME, partly the same meaning, new added meaning and finally meaning reduced in ME. The analysis used Aveling et al.'s (2015) method for identifying the voice in the multivoiced Self, while Yamaguchi's (2004) dialogicality of contrast reveals the processes involved to detect the intentions of the authors' multivoicedness. Employing just a rigid method, conversely, may simplify the complexity of the multivoiced Self.

These concepts provide useful methodological tools for analysing the multivoiced Self, detecting the voices of I-positions within a text, and identifying the voices of "inner-Others" and the community at large. The concept of dialogicality of contrast helped scrutinise the dialogue to unveil the manipulative aspects of reporting and arrive at reporters' implicit attitudes towards the reports. Also, as Aveling et al. (2015) propose, the analysis of multivoicedness is essentially done in the context of the word and the social field where the Self meets the inner-Others in the concept of dialogism, while suggesting that in being open to interpretation we must also be content that any final interpretation is never truly conclusive. Finally, it is this unfinalisability of the word that enables people to be divided from others as well as from within the Self (Burkitt, 2010). In the dialogical sense, this means that there is always a possibility to alter the ultimate or final meaning of the words one utters.

The inference of this study reveals the premise that multi-ethnic voices play a major role in keeping loanwords from ancient languages relevant, breathing new life into them to keep these languages alive. Voice helps create the intended meanings of loanwords borrowed from as long ago as the seventh century which still prevail today, as it provides the platform to multi-ethnic users to coin practical variations that keep the loanwords relevant in ME, based on shared assumptions of the Malaysian community. It is found that the loanwords have traversed or crossed over into their patriotism as in Excerpt 1, helped establish their identity as in Excerpt 2, and reinforced their cultural beliefs as in Excerpt 3. Even Malaysians' favourite food bears traces of these loanwords, such as an all-time favourite variety of *roti* as in Excerpt 4, and so too their space adventures as per *angkasawan* in Excerpt 5.

This research has revealed that when loanwords become appropriated, voice plays a crucial and decisive role bridged by language and the context of use explorations; as Yamaguchi (2004) reiterates, it is "the context in which we are expected to perceive that the author describes" (p. 481). Mastery of the symbolic tools allows ME users as social beings to ingeniously take up multiple positions and distance themselves from the Self in Bakhtinian terms and address the Self as the other, thus voicing themselves idiosyncratically by coining new words. This "ideological sign", Vološinov (1929/1973) insists, must remain living and "must ring with subjective tones in order to remain a living sign and not be relegated to the honorary status of an incomprehensible museum piece" (p. 39). Perhaps for a language to stay alive, it must loan its words to "voice", or suffer the fate of becoming a dead language.

REFERENCES

Alagesh, T. N. (2015, June 28). Some hotel operators offering Ramadan buffet without halal certificate. *New Straits Times*. https://www.nst.com.my/news/2015/09/some-hotel-operators-offering-ramadan-buffet-without-halal-certificate

Angkasawan wants woman in space next. (2015, March 20). *The Star*. https://www.thestar.com.my/news/nation/2015/03/20/angkasawan-wants-woman-in-space-next

Aveling, E. L., Gillespie, A., & Cornish, F. (2015). A qualitative method for analysing multivoicedness. *Qualitative Research, 15*(6), 670–687.

Bakhtin, M. M. (1981). *The dialogic imagination: Four essays* (C. Emerson & M. Holquist, Trans.). University of Texas Press. (Original work published 1953)

Bakhtin, M. M. (1984). *Problems of Dostoevsky's poetics* (M. Holquist, Trans.). University of Minnesota Press.

Bakhtin, M. (1986). In C. Emerson & M. Holquist (Eds.), *Speech genres and other late essays* (V. W. McGee, Trans.). University of Texas Press.

Burkitt, I. (2010). *Dialogues with self and others: Communication, miscommunication, and the dialogical unconscious.* Theory & Psychology, *20*, 305–321. doi: 10.1177/0959354310362826

de Casparis, J. G. (1997). *Sanskrit loan-words in Indonesian: An annotated check-list of words from Sanskrit in Indonesian and traditional Malay.* Universitas Katolik Indonesia Atma Jaya.

David, M. K. (2013). Roles of Sindhi grandparents in Malaysia. In *Indian Diaspora* (pp. 125–137). Brill Sense.

Halliday, M. A. K., & Hasan, R. (1985). *Language, context, and text: Aspects of language in a social-semiotic perspective.* Deakin University Press.

Hermans, H. J. (2003). The construction and reconstruction of a dialogical self. *Journal of Constructivist Psychology, 16*(2), 89–130.

Hermans, H. J. (2004). Introduction: The dialogical self in a global and digital age. *Identity, 4*(4), 297–320.

Hermans, H., & Hermans-Konopka, A. (2010). *Dialogical self theory: Positioning and counter-positioning in a globalizing society.* Cambridge University Press.

Hermans, H. J., & Gieser, T. (Eds.). (2011). *Handbook of dialogical self theory.* Cambridge University Press.

Kachru, B. B. (1990). World Englishes and applied linguistics. *World Englishes, 9*(1), 3–20.

Lehrer, A., Kittay, E. F., & Lehrer, R. (Eds.). (2012). *Frames, fields, and contrasts: New essays in semantic and lexical organization.* Routledge.

Lowenberg, P. H. (1986). Non-native varieties of English: Nativization, norms, and implications. *Studies in Second Language Acquisition, 8*(1), 1–18.

Mohd, H. (2016, November 30). Free teh tarik, roti canai from today till Saturday at PWTC. *New Straits Times.* https://www.nst.com.my/news/2016/11/193122/free-teh-tarik-roti-canai-today-till-saturday-pwtc

Morais, E. (2001). Lectal varieties of Malaysian English. In V. B. Y. Ooi (Ed.), *Evolving identities: The English language in Singapore and Malaysia* (pp. 33–52). Times Academic Press.

People from various states come out in droves to celebrate National Day (2017, September 1). *The Star.* https://www.thestar.com.my/news/nation/2017/09/01/colourful-fiesta-throughout-the-country-people-from-various-states-come-out-in-droves-to-celebrate-n

Pietikäinen, S., & Dufva, H. (2006). Voices in discourses: Dialogism, critical discourse analysis and ethnic identity. *Journal of Sociolinguistics, 10*(2), 205–224.

Poedjosoedarmo, S. (1982). *Javanese influence on Indonesian.* Department of Linguistics, Research School of Pacific Studies, The Australian National University.

Rademann, T. (1998). Using online electronic newspapers in modern English-language press corpora: Benefits and pitfalls. *ICAME Journal, 22,* 49–72.

Raggatt, P. T. (2015). Positioning: Dialogical voice in mind and culture. *Theory & Psychology, 25*(6), 775–797.

Salleh, H. (2016, July 25). RM300m Teras Fund a success in helping Bumi firms. *New Straits Times.* https://www.nst.com.my/news/2016/07/160502/rm300m-teras-fund-success-helping-bumi-firms

Sani, R. (2016, November 7). Leading women in science. *New Straits Times.* https://www.nst.com.my/news/2017/03/186532/leading-women-science

Schneider, E.W. (2003). The dynamics of new Englishes: From identity construction to dialect birth. *Language,* 233–281.

Traugott, E. C. (2017). Semantic change. *Oxford Research Encyclopedia of Linguistics.*

Thompson, G. (1996). Voices in the text: Discourse perspectives on language reports. *Applied Linguistics, 17*(4), 501–530.

Yamaguchi, T. (2004). Contrastive wa in Japanese: The author's dialogical voices and pragmatic acts. *Language Sciences, 26,* 467–483.

Vološinov, V. N. (1973). *Marxism and the philosophy of language* (L. Matejka & I. R. Titunik, Trans.). Harvard University Press.

Chapter 6

Voices in the Naming of Disabled Persons in Print Media

Pei Soo Ang* & Siang Lee Yeo*

ABSTRACT

This study engages a multi-perspectival inquiry into terms used to name or refer to disabled persons. The primary dataset is taken from 863 articles from *The Star*, a Malaysian mainstream newspaper. The types and frequencies of the perceived discriminatory and non-discriminatory references were tagged with the reported voices who employed them in the news reporting. These were then triangulated with 46 interviews with disabled persons, professionals, and non-professionals. Findings reveal that while non-discriminatory labels serve their practical purposes, their use is a paternalistic practice which emphasises the powerlessness of disabled persons. The debates in naming also suggest that what is deemed appropriate lies in the intention of a particular voice. This echoes the Bakhtinian view of "heteroglossia" whereby each voice represents a world view with its own values.

Keywords Voice, euphemism, media discourse, critical discourse analysis, critical disability studies

* Universiti Malaya, Malaysia

INTRODUCTION

Names are attributes, roles, and qualities of groups or their members both in "credited" or "discredited" forms (Reah, 2002, p. 62). They are surrounded by social rules and practices and have become a means of expressing attitudes towards certain groups. The naming of disabled persons[1] has been a highly contested issue as naming strategies carry ramifications that affect the self-perception of disabled persons and how the public perceives them (Haller, 2010; Haller et al., 2006). As a group, disabled persons are traditionally referred to as "disabled", "handicapped", "crippled", "moron[s]" or "retard[s]" (Ang, 2015). These terms suggest a negative tone underlying the discourses of deficit and shame. They influence identity categorisation and subsequently social positioning of disabled persons. With such implications, the practices of naming groups of disabled persons ought to be investigated.

Related to this is Goffman's (1963) proposition of stigma and bodily signs. In the area of critical disability studies, disability is perceived as a "sign system" that marks "bodies and minds" (Garland-Thomson, 2002, p. 5). An impairment or a condition, be it congenital or acquired, is perceived as an anatomical or pathological lack, loss or deficit (Ang & Yeo, 2018) which is socially interpreted as a personal tragedy, misery, and weakness (Zola, 1993). The term "stigma" was originally used to refer to bodily signs and designed to "expose something unusual and bad about the moral status of the signifier" (Goffman, 1963, p. 10). However, "stigma" is now seen more as a disgrace than as bodily evidence. The label of a stigma creates bias and influences expectations of and reactions towards disabled persons. Consequently, people are socially named based on their disabilities and how deviant they are from the so-called "norm" (Campbell, 2009; Goodley, 2014).

Naming is also associated with the phenomenon of labelling. Darrow and White (1998) defined labelling as "a process of creating descriptors to identify persons who differ from the norm" (p. 81). Labels are influenced by perspectives on a particular concept, roles played by social actors, and

1 The term "disabled person(s)" will be used in this chapter to refer to people with disability and "non-disabled" to those without disability, based on findings from a larger study by Ang (2015).

what a particular discourse aims to achieve. It is crucial to understand the choices of names and the voices that employ the labels in order to tease out who are using which terms or references, how naming is done and what these strategies imply. This is particularly so in the context of media and news reporting. In Monitoring the Convention on the Rights of Persons with Disabilities (United Nations, 2010), the United Nations acknowledges the role of the media in reflecting, influencing, and monitoring society's attitudes toward disabled persons. How the media use these naming strategies in their news dissemination can influence how these terms are interpreted.

Voice is a versatile term which can be defined differently in various contexts. In research, it is used to depict the agency and rights of individuals to enable their views, positions, needs, and feelings to be known, heard, and fronted (Coghlan & Brydon-Miller, 2014). If a voice is acknowledged, it receives power to negotiate and interact with other voices; the stronger the voice, the bigger the power in controlling, undermining, or silencing other voices. This can bracket people into hierarchies in society, creating unequal positioning (Fairclough, 2003). In this study, "voices" refers to the identified speakers or social actors in the data examined who employ certain labels to name or make references to individuals or groups of people who have impairments or disabilities. The identified actors are not merely the quoted speakers or "sayers" in systemic functional linguistic terms, but are argued as entities or agencies carrying different world views. The discursive choices when performing or realising the naming practice can be conscious or unconscious decisions. Hence, here the quoted social actors in the data sets analysed are argued as "voices" who are capable of shaping and influencing the discourse, not merely speakers who make the utterances.

With that in mind, this study aims to unpack the multiplicity of voices that utilise various phrases in naming disabled persons as represented in a Malaysian English language newspaper, *The Star*. The research questions asked are: (1) What are the terms used to refer to disabled persons by the represented social actors in the print medium?, and (2) What do they suggest about the voices behind the terms and about social practice? Candlin and Crichton's (2011) multi-perspectival approach will be adopted to elicit the multiple voices from semiotic resources (a newspaper) and triangulated with participants' perspectives (interviews with disabled persons, and professional and non-professional carers) as well as institutional voices (interviews with news editors and representatives from the World Health Organisation [WHO]). This affords the unpacking of preferred terms by each of the represented voices in the discourse.

DEBATES IN NAMING AND IDEOLOGICAL POTENTIAL

There are conflicting views between those who are comfortable with certain names or references and those who are not. The disputes predominantly surround the choices between euphemistic and non-euphemistic references (lexical choices) as well as between *person-first* and *disability-first* phrases (structural choices). Lexical choices refer to the selection of vocabulary which includes non-euphemistic terms such as "handicapped" and "retard", more neutral terms like "impairment" and "condition", and the euphemistic "special needs" and "differently abled". As exemplified earlier, the concern is a semantic one. What social and connotational meanings the lexical items carry will affect the identity and dignity of disabled persons. Structural choices point to the order of words in phrases, primarily fronting the person, such as "people (living) with ...", or fronting the disability, as in "a disabled person".

Euphemism is employed to conceal any form of expression considered too explicit, unpleasant, disagreeable, or offensive (Burridge, 2017). It is a linguistic strategy used for limiting the loss of face based on politeness or tact theory (Kasper, 1990), thus rendering respect and dignity, in this case to disabled persons. Disability has been euphemised as having special needs. "Special needs" morphed from the terms "Special Olympics" and "special education" established in the 1960s, and since then the term "special" has been loosely used in conjunction with disabilities (Gernsbacher et al., 2016). However, euphemism also receives disapproval. It is criticised as saving the producer's face rather than the recipient's (Gernsbacher et al., 2016). Terms such as "special", "physically challenged", "handicapable", and "differently abled" are regarded as condescending, making it seem as if people cannot deal with their disabilities, hence the sugar-coated references. Euphemisms can also be ineffective from a medical viewpoint (Gernsbacher, 2017) because they are imprecise, hide disability, and hinder accurate intervention. "Special needs", which is promoted by paternalistic "do-gooders", is also deemed offensive, patronising, distancing, and an encouragement of segregation rather than inclusiveness (Linton, 1998; Woodward, 1997).

In terms of phrase structure, the deliberation is between the *person-first* and *disability-first* structures. The *disability-first* structure positions a condition in an adjectival form (e.g. "disabled people" and "autistic children"). Media style guidelines generally characterise the disability-first language as depersonalising, since by fronting an impairment, a disability comes before a person (Commonwealth Style Manual, 1994). Disability-first also includes descriptions of people by their impairments such as an "epileptic" or "autistic person". It can degrade people and present them only in terms of their disabilities (Haller et al., 2006). Stereotyped phrases such as "wheelchair bound" and "confined to a wheelchair" may be inappropriate as they grant more power to the tool rather than the person using it. Collective terms such as "the disabled", "the blind" and "the Deaf" are also considered inappropriate by American media guidelines.

Despite this, there are certain disability groups, notably the blind, Deaf, and autistic communities, who prefer disability-first language to the person-first variety. Blind persons believe that it is respectable to be blind, without taking any pride or shame in it (Corbett, 1996; Jernigan, 2005). Deaf people take pride in being part of a linguistic minority, and autistic communities claim that autism is an inherent part of their identity, similar to other markers such as ethnicity, religion, and citizenship (Ang, 2015). With a social constructionist view, also known as a social model in disability studies, disability advocates in the United Kingdom and Malaysia prefer the term "disabled people" as they assert that people have been disabled by attitudinal and environmental barriers rather than their own physiological conditions.

In response to disability-first language, the *person-first* mode of expression is propagated. It imposes a phrase structure that names a person first, followed by the condition (e.g. "people with disability", "persons with autism" and "persons who have a learning disability"). This person-first mode of expression was first suggested by advocacy groups in the United States and officially adopted by the American Psychological Association. It purports that people should be regarded first as persons with feelings, emotions, desires, aspirations, and frustrations, rather than be defined by their diagnoses (NSW Physical Disability Council, 2010). Their disability is perceived as a secondary attribute and is not characteristic of identity. Focusing on persons first and then indicating their impairments will give respect and dignity to disabled persons (CT State Department of Education, 2007) and increase sensitivity to the needs of these citizens (Ohio Coalition for the Education of Children with Disabilities, 2015).

Critics of person-first language claim that in terms of language use, the structure is awkward and repetitive and causes tiresome reading and writing (National Federation of the Blind US, 1993). Kelman and Stough (2015) allege that the person-first structure is a hypocrisy, a fear of difference or fear of offence by the non-disabled. Penn and Nowlin-Drummond (2001) conducted a quantitative study on 90 participants regarding the use of three terms—"person with schizophrenia", "person with severe mental illness", and "schizophrenic". They found that effects of these terms were similar and the attitudes to stigma against the person diagnosed with schizophrenia did not change. A study on scholarly writing published on the Web of Science observed writers' differential application of person-first to children rather than adults and to children with more severe disabilities (Gernsbacher et al., 2016). As numerous disability scholars have argued, person-first language may be overused, so much so that it further stigmatises disability (Andrews et al., 2019). There is also no evidence that person-first terminology enhances sensitivity or reduces insensitivity (Collier, 2012).

The debates between the proponents and opponents of both person- and disability-first phrases are grounded in the Whorfian notion of "linguistic relativism" (Whorf, 1956), which presumes that language restricts our thinking and that when language changes, a desired outcome will follow. However, Leech (1981) claims that even with the introduction of new words to old concepts, associations would still be made to the referents intended to be hidden. Halmari (2011, p. 839) considers this view altruistic but "semantically naïve". Social views and perceptions of disabled persons will remain the same despite the change in naming strategies. In fact, naming will continue to evolve as each social actor has a different motivation in name choices within the contexts they operate in, be they personal, authorial, professional, or institutional voices. This can be reaffirmed by the Bakhtinian "heteroglossia" which is defined as "another's speech in another's language, serving to express authorial intentions but in a retracted way" (Bakhtin, 1953/1981, p. 324). Each voice represents a distinct point of view about the world, characterised by its own meaning and values, and thus words are not neutral. For Bakhtin, language and thought are dialogical; each utterance is a response to a prior utterance and is inhabited by the voices of others. What determine values are social attitudes or conventions, whereas political correctness is but a discoursal product of cultural politics (Fairclough, 2003).

In postmodernist literature, following Bakhtin, utterances are not seen as individual creations. For Pêcheux (1982), discourse is the platform upon which language and ideology merge. Adoption of words and their meanings varies according to the class position from which they are used, and according to the "discursive formation" they are located within. Pêcheux defines a discursive formation as "that which in a given ideological formation, i.e. from a particular position in a given conjuncture determined by the state of the class struggle, determines 'what can and should be said'" (Pêcheux, 1982, p. 111). For instance, the word *struggle* itself is a political term of the working class but may have a different meaning in another discourse. Similarly, in the context under study, *stroke survivor* suggests the narrative of a life ordeal and past suffering, rather than a positive connotation of overcoming something successfully.

Pêcheux emphasises the ideological consequences of discursive formations in positioning people as social subjects. Echoing Althusser's (1971) idea of ideological formation, Pêcheux suggests that people are placed in the imaginary position of sources of their discourse, but their discourse and they themselves are outcomes of their ideological positioning. This also reflects Fairclough's (2013) claim that texts have dialectical relationship with social practices. People are positioned and are themselves shaped by the "complex whole in dominance" of discursive formations (Pêcheux, 1982, p. 113). People's voices shape discourse and reciprocally, discourse determines the ideological or hegemonic view of a voice.

In sum, the Bakhtinian "heteroglossia" and Pêcheux's "discursive formation" as well as Althusser's "ideological formation" compel a discourse analysis of voices in naming disabled persons through a critical lens, as the language of ideology can be manifested through naming strategies.

METHODOLOGY

This study adapts Candlin and Crichton's (2011) multi-perspectival approach to uncover the complexity and multiplicity of voices involved in the naming practices of disabled persons. Figure 1 shows the adoption of three out of five perspectives from the original ontology, which are the semiotic resources perspective (a newspaper), discourse participants' (disabled persons', as well as professional and non-professional carers') perspective, and institutional perspective (news editors and officers from WHO).

Each circle or perspective within Figure 1 evokes different ways of understanding, investigating, perceiving, and representing, but the whole operates as a dynamic combination. The multi-perspectival approach affords the triangulation of perspectives to understand the intertwining relationship between the voices that determines the ways naming practices are negotiated. The multi-perspectival approach also provides grounded explanations, rather than superficial descriptions or interpretations in Fairclough's (2003) terms. Therefore, the method of inquiry in this research is designed with a critical analysis in mind.

The primary dataset was sourced from 863 news articles (an 832,000-word corpus) in *The Star*, a Malaysian mainstream newspaper, from July 2008 to December 2012. *The Star* was chosen as the key data resource as it was the leading English periodical with the highest circulation in print and online platforms (Audit Bureau of Circulations, 2018). Interviews were also

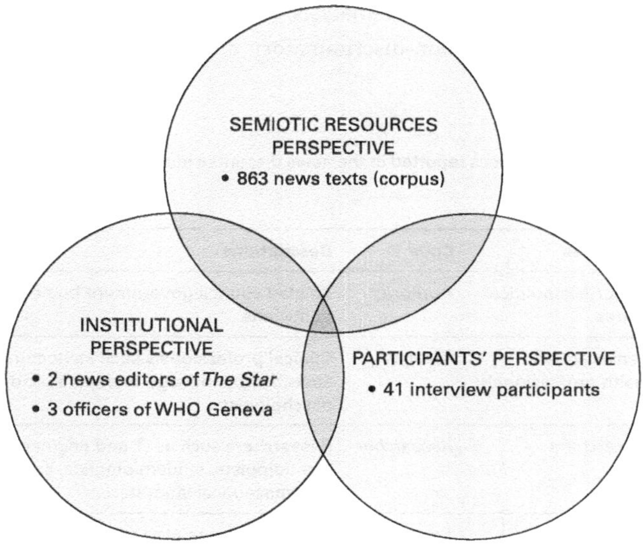

Figure 1 Adapted multi-perspectival ontology from Candlin and Crichton (2011)

conducted with 41 participants comprising disabled persons, parents, non-governmental representatives and professionals, two news editors of *The Star*, and three officers from WHO Geneva representing institutional voices. Assisted by a qualitative analytical software programme, Nvivo12, the types and frequencies of discriminatory and non-discriminatory terms were tagged with the reported voices of social actors in the news as seen in Table 1. To identify the represented voices in the news discourse, the corpus was parsed through the automatic semantic tagging available in the WMatrix4 concordancer under the function of "role". The various roles were then re-grouped as 15 categories of voice as exhibited in Table 1.

As presented in the literature, the debates on naming surround English lexical and structural choices with no consensus on what is considered appropriate or inappropriate. However, it is certain that the main argument centres on practicality, i.e. who is doing the naming, in what contexts, and what each voice perceives as non-condescending and polite. Therefore, based on the literature and for the purpose of analysis, the names have been grouped into two broad categories of non-discriminatory and discriminatory references (Tables 2 and 3).

Table 1 Categories of voices reported in the news discourse identified through the WMatrix4 concordancer

No.	Categories	Code	Descriptions
A	Authorities/political figures	*Authority*	Related council/government bodies and politicians
B	Medical/allied health professionals	*Medical*	Clinical professionals such as doctors, speech and language therapists, and clinical psychologists
C	Researchers	*Researcher*	Researchers such as IT and engineering technologists, epidemiologists, and those in pharmaceutical laboratories
D	Educators/trainers	*Educator*	Academicians related to education, teachers and trainers of educational programmes (non-profit bodies)
E	Business/private service providers	*Private service*	Business or private entities providing services for disabled persons such as early intervention and rehabilitation programmes (profit-making bodies)
F	NGOs/advocates	*NGO*	Personnel representing non-governmental organisations and disability advocates
G	Family members	*Family*	Immediate family members
H	Carers/volunteers	*Carer*	Carers at home who are non-family members, unpaid staff volunteering at intervention and rehabilitation centres
I	Charity sponsors/ donors	*Charity*	Personnel representing sponsors and donors to charities for disabled persons
J	Disabled persons	*Disabled person*	Disabled children, teens, and adults
K	Disabled columnists	*Disabled columnist*	References to Anthony Thanasayan and Ida Nerina as two frequent article contributors in *The Star*. Both are wheelchair users who write from the perspective of disabled persons
L	Journalists	*Journalist*	Journalists and editors of *The Star*
M	Public	*Public*	The general public

Table 2 Structures of non-discriminatory name phrases

Non-discriminatory references		
Grammatical Structure	**Name Structure**	**Type**
Head noun + prepositional phrase	People + with (condition)	Person-first
	People + on (autism spectrum disorder)	
Head noun + relative clause	People + who have (condition)	
Head noun + participial	People + having/living with (condition)	
Attributive adjectival	Intellectually/physically challenged + people	Euphemistic
	Special + people/noun	
Nominal adjectival	The + visually/intellectually impaired	
Lexicon	(Condition) + survivors	

Table 3 Structures of discriminatory name phrases

Discriminatory references		
Grammatical Structure	**Name Structure**	**Type**
Attributive adjective	(Condition) + people	Disability-first
Nominal adjectival	The + (condition)	
Lexicon	(Condition) + sufferers/victims/patients	
	Person/patient + afflicted with (condition)	Person-first but with non-euphemistic lexicon
	Person/patient + stricken with (condition)	
	Person/patient + suffering from (condition)	
	Person/patient + who suffer(s) from (condition)	
	Strokee/amputee/midget/dwarf/ handicapped/retard	Non-euphemistic lexicon

The following section will present the analyses of terms together with the represented voices.

ANALYSIS

Newspaper: Semiotic resource perspective

A total of 219 unique name phrases with an overall frequency of 4028 occurrences were associated with naming of disabled persons (see Appendix for an overview and Figure 2 for trends of use).

Overall, there were more uses of discriminatory phrases (N=2282) compared to non-discriminatory ones (N=1746). In the non-discriminatory category, the table in the Appendix suggests that person-first structure, which was most popularly used (N=1404), features the "people with ..." (N=1366), "people who have ..." (N=27) and "people having/living with ..." (N=11) variants. For discriminatory references, the attributive form "(condition) + people" had the highest frequency count (N=1225), followed by the adjectival "the + (condition)" and negative lexicons (N=226).

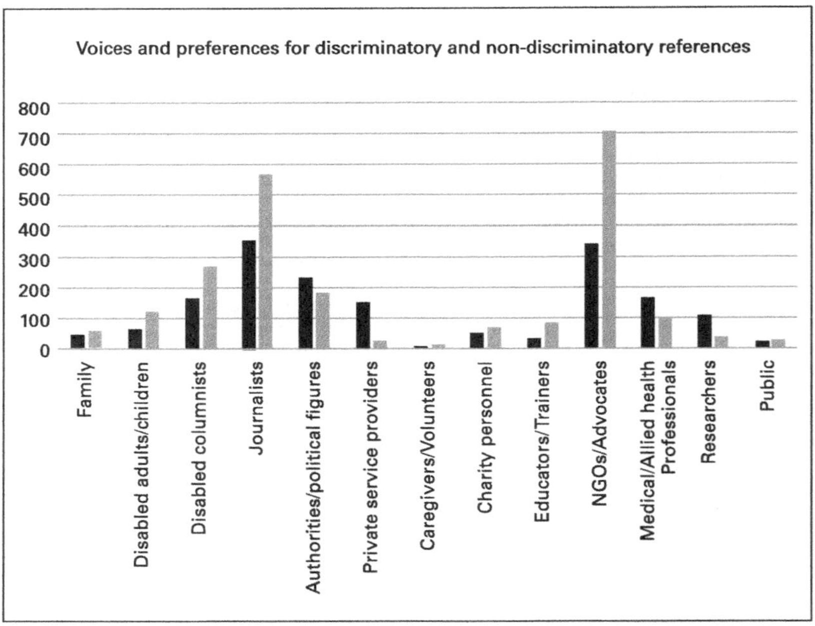

Figure 2 Overall trends on the use of discriminatory and non-discriminatory references by various social actors

In terms of voices, Figure 2 shows that in general, the most common voices in the news discourse were of NGOs (N=1056), followed by journalists/writers (N=626), and disabled newspaper columnists (N=437). This suggests that NGOs and those involved in journalistic writing have an immense influence on shaping naming.

Apart from the two predominant voices, the second observation is that institutional voices (presented in the following list) demonstrate preferences for non-discriminatory or euphemistic references (see Figure 2):

(1) Authorities/political figures
(2) Private service providers: intervention programme teachers, care centres, sexual assistants[2], accessible gadget distributors
(3) Medical/allied health professionals: consultants, speech therapists, clinical psychologists
(4) Researchers: biomedical and pharmaceutical researchers
(5) Charity sponsors/personnel/donors

It appears that these "external" parties opt for so-called more polite non-discriminatory terms. Perceived as being practically appropriate, this is a technique of showing respect to disabled persons who are their "clients" in this context. These parties ought to portray themselves as caring, people-friendly and sensitive towards the social group. For service providers and medical/allied health practitioners, good communication is key and a way to secure clientele. For researchers, euphemism is preferred most likely to maintain objectivity in reporting. As for charity personnel, non-discriminatory language is a gesture of goodwill, which is crucial for maintaining a good reputation.

Regarding preferences for discriminatory or non-euphemistic references, they were extensively used by the following:

(1) People who have direct contact with disabled persons (family, disabled persons themselves, disabled columnists, educators, trainers, NGOs)

2 A sexual assistant is defined as "any person who provides sexual assistance to physically and/or intellectually disabled people" including physical activities and discussions related to sexuality and contraception (Limoncin et al., 2014, p. 2)

(2) Journalists—high occurrence, but the non-euphemistic choices were used in reported speech or quotes, echoing terms used by the original sources. This is also confirmed by evidence from interview data with media personnel.

People who have direct contact with disabled persons tend to use so-called discriminatory references more frequently. This reflects an honest attitude which disregards the need to be politically correct. Journalists also recorded a high frequency of non-euphemistic references but they echoed such terms which came from the sources they reported. Staying truthful to the original sources is either a way of honouring them or avoiding the consequences of being perceived as impolite. All these reflect the argument against the euphemistic view, as it represents an altruistic perception but a semantically naïve view of disability (Halmari, 2011).

In terms of lexical choices, a significant pattern observed is the overuse of the term "special". For the attributive "special" (N=34), more than half of the occurrences took the form of "special people(/person)" (N=23) followed by "special needs child(ren)/kid(s)" (N=5) and "special child(ren)" (N=5). "Special" had a high co-occurrence with "children" and was primarily utilised to express endearment. The attribute "special", though not exhibiting a high frequency of occurrence when referring to people, is widely used with other lexical items not usually collocational with special needs (e.g. "special programme", "special school", "special attention"). A total of 26 phrases with a total frequency of N=1896 of these "offshoot" phrases was found. This was observed largely in the voices of journalists, followed by NGOs, authorities, and charity providers. The corpus suggests that "special" is overgeneralised to refer to any contexts or notions related to disabled persons. While this evokes a "nice" and "kind" tone, the question is to what extent this helps improve the lives of disabled persons.

The above-mentioned patterns observed from the semiotic resources' perspective will be triangulated next with data from the interviews.

Interviews: Participants' perspectives

Data from the participants' perspectives were obtained from 41 interviewees in Malaysia and coded as I-01 to I-41. As for the institutional perspective, the two news editors of *The Star* were I-42 and I-43. The three personnel of WHO Geneva were coded as I-44 to I-46. The semi-structured interviews covered three main questions on the acceptance of the person-first phrase "specific impairments" and the euphemistic "special".

On being questioned regarding person-first language for disabled persons, I-40 pointed out that this structure was only appropriate for specific reference to an impairment. He said it should be "people with impairment, not [people] with disability". Otherwise, the general reference should be "disabled people/persons" in the disability-first form as disabled persons are disabled by social, attitudinal, and environmental barriers. His view affirmed the social model of disability and WHO's definition whereby disability arises from the participation of an impairment in society; an impairment on its own may not cause disability.

On the acceptance of the general term "people with disability(ies)", only six interviewees (I-01, I-15, I-32, I-34, I-37, and I-39) gave a definite answer. I-34 and I-37 added that since "people with disabilities" and the abbreviation of "PWD" had been internationally accepted, they should be accepted locally too. However, most of the disabled persons interviewed were not inclined towards this term. For instance, I-08 felt that the meaning was different; I-37 said it was "funny" and "too mouthful [*sic*] to say". Another three participants (I-11, I-21, and I-26) highlighted that the phrase "differently abled" had also been used, but this was inaccurate. It was also criticised as being "too confusing" (I-32) and "too general", and needed to be more specific (I-02 and I-20). Interviewees also cautioned that they had been labelled as "less able" (I-01), a "deficit", a "lack" (I-02, I-20, I-38 and I-40), and persons who could "not do anything" (I-39). Disabled persons, even if they were called "differently abled", would not be able to solve the problem of discrimination they faced. Besides, there was no denial about their disabilities (I-14). Interviewees I-28 and I-34 opined that no label was "really needed" to name people with or without impairments and that disabled persons should just be known by their personal names (I-41). I-33 and I-14 admitted that naming depended on the relationship of the interactants, but it should be about gaining acceptance rather than naming conditions.

To the non-disabled professionals (I-15 and I-12), different terms made no difference and "differently abled" was a "matter of masking". Indeed, I-26 thought this was a term to please the non-disabled, better than using "handicapped". All these views point to the disabled interviewees being more comfortable with the disability-first rather than person-first references. Further, for professional caregivers working with children with intellectual and learning disabilities, 12 out of 14 expressed preference for the person-first structure in naming "children with autism", "children with dyslexia", and "children with Down Syndrome". Again, this suggests that the person-first structure was a choice only when referring to children. Interviewee I-04 (a physiotherapist) indicated that the person-first structure was preferable because children did "not understand language" and as also asserted by I-25, "Polite terms should be used at all times to be respectful though a child may not know [their meaning]". This echoed some similarities with the term *special* as the person-first structures were used with children but not with disabled adults. In short, when children were involved, others referred to them with terms of endearment.

For a head of a Parkinson's Disease NGO who was also a caregiver (I-26), euphemism was necessary because the use of terms like "Parkinson's sufferer", "patient" and "disease" is demotivating, insensitive, and inconsiderate. She said it is a fact that people suffer from the condition, but labelling them as "sufferers" is uncalled for because it would hurt the feelings of not only the persons with the condition but also their family members. Therefore, the person-first structure of "people (living) with Parkinson's" was preferred. For I-26, words defined a person as well as how that person with disability was viewed.

The group of five blind interviewees were unanimous about referring to themselves as "the blind". According to I-06 and I-09, it was the public who were not comfortable using the term "blind" and wrongly euphemised it as "visually impaired". Blindness is total loss of vision while "visual impairment" means different degrees of visual clarity in medical terms (I-08). Calling a blind person "visually impaired" is misleading even though it is intended to be a polite term by altruistic others.

The deaf community, however, rejected the euphemism of "hearing-impaired" for different reasons. A deaf linguist (I-11) felt that "hearing-impaired" categorises them as disabled. They do not see themselves as having a disability but instead embrace deafness as an identity of a linguistic minority. The contrast is clear: the blind want to be called blind because it is what it is; the deaf want to be called deaf because they perceive it as their identity and not a disability.

Parents with disabled children were not too concerned about terms used on their children. Other than for medical and diagnostic purposes, parents generally dissented when asked about specific terms for their children's conditions. They regarded their children as special as any parents would, not because of their impairment (I-20 and I-27). Specifically, I-12 accepted the name of her child's medical condition but felt that the public must recognise the condition and render assistance instead of pity. Another parent (I-17) jokingly commented that she wished Down Syndrome was "Up Syndrome" due to stigmatisation.

Further on the euphemism *special*, it was disapproved of by an occupational therapist (I-04) and an NGO head (I-23), who felt that calling someone "special" might be mistaken for ridiculing the person. Another five participants (I-09, I-17, I-19, I-21, and I-29) commented that "special" was a term "associated" only with children and not adults. This concurs with the corpus finding of "special" collocating with children. Disabled adults expressed stronger unease over "special" (I-07, I-33, I-36, I-37, and I-41). "Special" was "used to underestimate the expectation for success", thus lowering the expectation of a disabled person succeeding, or underestimating one's capability (I-10).

These show the varying perspectives of the interviewees. Generally, disabled persons were comfortable with terms such as "disabled", acknowledging some forms of lack or deficit in them, but detested any form of "special" identification. The more polite forms were employed by the non-disabled more frequently.

Interviews: Institutional perspective

Interviews were conducted with a news editor and a deputy chief editor of *The Star* to understand their journalistic policies and practices, as well as three officers responsible for handling issues of disability at the WHO headquarters in Geneva.

The news editor (I-43) confirmed that *The Star* had no "advocacy practice" for terms related to disabled persons but generally observed "politically correct terms" using qualifiers such as "living with" or "has" and avoiding certain terms such as "normal" and "able-bodied". When there were terms to be avoided, generally writers and editors would "work around the terms" or "reconstruct sentences". However, as a caregiver herself, I-43 felt that names for certain conditions ought to be made more specific in order for the public to better understand the specificity of each condition.

The other editor interviewed (I-44) explained that in her professional practice, choice of terminology was situational, dependent on context and flow of ideas, while judgement of correctness was based on experience. This suggests that news personnel rely heavily on their experience and ongoing on-the-job training to decide what is suitable for dissemination.

Moving on to terms used by WHO, all three interviews conveyed the policy of the institution. There is a requirement for WHO to be politically correct, maintain an internationally neutral perspective, respect client relationships, and focus on a positive vision. As such, polite language such as person-first language is often chosen for these purposes. I-45 also revealed that all WHO representatives are trained in communication, particularly the standard ways of referring to health issues. Similarly, another officer, I-46, clarified that the abbreviation of PWD and "people with disability" were terms dictated by WHO member states, and thus there was a need to speak to disabled communities about terms they would like others to use when referring to them. In brief, for the purpose of international public health policies, as an international body, WHO is aware of linguistic consequences in naming disabled persons socially and person-first structures are perceived to be neutral.

DISCUSSION AND CONCLUSION

Both corpus and interview data have highlighted that naming strategies are dependent on the membership and perspectives of the represented voices in the multi-perspective discourse in question. To medical professionals, medical terms are crucial for professional efficiency and accurate diagnoses and interventions. Some disability groups have also reclaimed terms once considered negative, for instance "deaf", "blind" and even "crip" (Linton, 1998). For institutions such as the authorities and WHO, terminology has to be polite, neutral and applicable in multiple contexts, promote a positive vision, and maintain positive images of the institutions. In journalism, choices and forms of words are affected by experiences and considerations of time and space. While certain words are accurate for certain parties, others may not be comfortable with them.

In attempts to speak the right language for pragmatic purposes of face-saving and observing politeness, particularly by non-disabled and institutional voices, person-first phrases and euphemisms have been overused to disguise the power of naming. This emphasises the relative powerlessness of disabled persons instead of fostering respect and dignity. Such practice has become a means of labelling and bracketing disabled persons into marginalised sectors, thus reflecting a paternalistic practice in society.

Naming is central to identity formation. A person is identified through names and names become "words of identity" that affect both the "namer" and the person being named (Stone, 1962). In other words, naming is a co-constructed process. In this case, naming disabled persons is constructed and measured against the so-called "norm" and this gives rise to the identification of the non-disabled self too. Hence, the definitional power of names is socially distributed, in particular how the power of the mainstream is orchestrated by classifications by the institutional power (Valentine, 1998). This also aligns with Bourdieu's (1986) view that the power of names not only grants the "namer" the power of defining but also legitimises the status of the self. In this study, the practices of institutional power through the voices of professionals in journalism and international bodies appear to have largely determined and influenced what are deemed acceptable or unacceptable, discriminatory or non-discriminatory, and inevitably, a sided perspective determined by institutions.

The naming of disabled persons is also viewed as a labelling of a stigmatised bodily difference. Goffman claimed that "stigma" is a language of relationships between attributes and stereotypes. Disability and disabled persons are presented as stereotyped categorisations and their disabilities are negatively construed as the loss of attributes and capacity, which diminishes life chances. A person becomes reduced in our minds from a whole to a discounted one. Such an attribute is a stigma, especially when its discrediting effect causes us to reclassify individuals in terms of their social categories. The deviance or this spoilt identity that stigmatises one type of possessor can confirm the usualness of another (Goffman, 1963).

Generally, this chapter has presented how the multiplicity of voices in discourse influences naming processes. Each voice represents a perspective with a different social agenda vis-à-vis the Bakhtinian view of "heteroglossia", within discursive and ideological formations with reference to Pêcheux and Althusser. Thus, we propose a reconsideration of the "unrecognised discrimination and unfairness" against disabled persons (Reah, 2002, p. 53) that ensues from naming practices. There is a need to recognise the forms of exclusion that they embody instead of disguising them under the veil of altruism, rationality, or morality (Mouffe, 1999).

REFERENCES

Althusser, L. (1971). *Lenin and philosophy and other essays* (B. Brewster, Trans). Monthly Review Press.

Andrews, E. E., Forber-Pratt, A. J., Mona, L. R., Lund, E. M., Pilarski, C. R., & Balter, R. (2019). #SaytheWord: A disability culture commentary on the erasure of "disability". *Rehabilitation Psychology, 64*(2), 111–118. DOI:10.1037/rep0000258

Ang, P. S. (2015). *Naming and visualising people in the discourses of disability* [Doctoral dissertation, Macquarie University].

Ang, P. S., & Yeo, S. L. (2018). Exclusionary visual depiction of disabled persons in Malaysian news photographs. *Discourse & Communication, 12*(5), 457–477. DOI:10.1177/1750481318766922

Audit Bureau of Circulations. (2018). Audit Bureau Report 2018. Retrieved from http://abcm.org.my/report/latest-audit-reports-january-to-june-2018/

Bakhtin, M. M. (1981). *The dialogic imagination: Four essays* (C. Emerson & M. Holquist, Trans.). University of Texas Press. (Original work published 1953)

Bourdieu, P. (1986). The forms of capital. In J. Richardson (Ed.), *Handbook of theory and research for the sociology of education* (pp. 241–258). Greenwood.

Burridge, K. (2017). Euphemisms and dysphemisms. In *Oxford Bibliographies in Linguistics*. Oxford University Press.

Campbell, F. K. (2009). *Contours of ableism: The production of disability and abledness*. Palgrave.

Candlin, C. N., & Crichton, J. (2011). *Discourses of deficit*. Palgrave Macmillan.

Coghlan, D., & Brydon-Miller, M. (Eds.) (2014). *The SAGE encyclopaedia of action research*. Sage.

Collier, R. (2012). Person-first language: Noble intent but to what effect? *CMAJ: Canadian Medical Association Journal, 184*(18), 1977–1978. DOI:10.1503/cmaj.109-4319

Commonwealth Style Manual. (1994). *Style for authors, editors and printers* (5th ed.). Australian Government Publishing.

Corbett, J. (1996). *Bad-mouthing: The language of special needs*. Falmer Press.

CT State Department of Education. (2007). *Guidelines for identifying children with intellectual disability*. Connecticut State Department of Education.

Darrow, A., & White, G. W. (1998). Sticks and stones ... and words can hurt: Eliminating handicapping language. *Music Therapy Perspectives, 16*(2), 81–83.

Fairclough, N. (2003). *Analysing discourse: Textual analysis for social research.* Routledge.

Garland-Thomson, R. (2002). Politics of staring: Visual rhetorics of disability in popular photography. In S. L. Snyder, B. J. Brueggemann, & R. G. Thomson (Eds.), *Disability studies: Enabling the humanities* (pp. 56–75). Modern Language Association of America.

Gernsbacher, M. A. (2017). The use of person-first language in scholarly writing may accentuate stigma. *Journal of Child Psychology and Psychiatry, 58*(7), 859–861.

Gernsbacher, M. A., Raimond, A. R., Balinghasay, M. T., & Boston, J. S. (2016). "Special needs" is an ineffective euphemism. *Cognitive Research: Principles and Implications, 1*(1), 29. DOI:10.1186/s41235-016-0025-4

Goffman, E. (1963). *Stigma: Notes on the management of spoiled identity.* Simon & Schuster.

Goodley, D. (2014). *Dis/ability studies: Theorising disablism and ableism.* Routledge.

Haller, B. (2010). *Representing disability in an ableist world: Essays on mass media.* Advocado Press.

Haller, B., Dorries, B., & Rahn, J. (2006). Media labeling versus the US disability community identity: A study of shifting cultural language. *Disability & Society, 21*(1), 61–75. DOI:10.1080/09687590500375416

Halmari, H. (2011). Political correctness, euphemism, and language change: The case of 'people first'. *Journal of Pragmatics, 43*(3), 828–840. DOI:10.1016/j.pragma.2010.09.016

Jernigan, K. (2005). A definition of blindness. *Low vision and blindness: Special Issue, 24*(3).

Kasper, G. (1990). Linguistic politeness: Current research issues. *Journal of Pragmatics, 14*(2), 193–218. DOI:http://dx.doi.org/10.1016/0378-2166(90)90080-W

Kelman, I. & Stough, L. (2015). *(Dis)ability and (dis)aster.* Palgrave.

Leech, G. (1981). *Semantics: The study of meaning* (2nd ed.). Penguin Books.

Limoncin, E., Galli, D., Ciocca, G., Gravina, G. L., Carosa, E., Mollaioli, D., Lenzi, A., & Jannini, E. A. (2014). The psychosexual profile of sexual assistants: An internet-based explorative study. *PLoS ONE, 9*(6): e98413. DOI:10.1371/journal.pone.0098413

Linton, S. (1998). *Claiming disability: Knowledge and identity*. New York University Press.

Mouffe, C. (1999). Deliberative democracy or agonistic pluralism? *Social Research, 66*(3), 745–758. DOI:10.2307/40971349

National Federation of the Blind US. (1993). Resolution 93-01 [Press release].

NSW Physical Disability Council. (2010). *Word matters: Language guide*. Physical Disability Council of NSW.

Ohio Coalition for the Education of Children With Disabilities. (2015). Ohio special education profile. Retrieved from https://www.ocecd.org/Downloads/Special%20Educ%20Profile%20Report%203%205%202015.pdf

Pêcheux, M. (1982) *Language, semantics and ideology: Stating the obvious* (H. Nagpal, Trans.). Macmillan.

Penn, D. L., & Nowlin-Drummond, A. (2001). Politically correct labels and schizophrenia: A rose by any other name? *Schizophrenia Bulletin, 27*(2), 197–203.

Reah, D. (2002). *The language of newspapers*. Routledge.

Stone, G. P. (1962). Appearance of the self. In M. Arnold Rose (Ed.), *Human behaviour and social processes* (pp. 86–118). Houghton Mifflin.

United Nations. (2010). Monitoring the convention of the rights of persons with disabilities: Guidance for human rights monitors. Retrieved from https://www.ohchr.org/Documents/Publications/Disabilities_training_17EN.pdf

Valentine, J. (1998). Naming the other: Power, politeness and the inflation of euphemisms. *Sociological Research Online, 3*(4), 1–17. DOI:10.5153/sro.184

Whorf, B. (1956). Science and linguistics. In J. B. Carroll (Ed.), *Language, thought and reality*. MIT Press.

Woodward, K. (1997). *Identity and difference*. Sage.

Zola, I. K. (1993). Self, identity and the naming question: Reflections on the language of disability. *Social Science & Medicine, 36*(2), 167–173. DOI:10.1016/0277-9536(93)90208-L

Appendix: Breakdown of frequencies of name phrases according to structures and voices that employed them

Reference Type \ Voice	Family	Disabled persons	Disabled columnists	Journalists	Authorities/ Political figures	Private service providers	Caregivers/ Volunteers	Charity personnel	Educators/ Trainers	NGOs/Advocates	Medical/Allied health workers	Researchers	Public	Total
Non-discriminatory														
People with	39	46	158	232	174	131	5	0	23	297	146	99	16	1366
People who have	1	1	0	3	0	6	0	1	0	5	7	3	0	27
People having/ living with	0	0	2	2	1	0	0	0	0	2	3	1	0	11
Attributive	2	9	1	87	37	9	1	34	7	19	0	4	1	211
The +	1	5	1	18	17	5	0	8	0	16	0	3	1	75
(Condition) + survivor	0	1	0	8	0	1	0	0	0	2	9	0	1	22
Attributive "special"	2	3	1	6	6	1	1	8	2	4	0	0	0	34
Sub-total	*45*	*65*	*163*	*356*	*235*	*153*	*7*	*51*	*32*	*345*	*165*	*110*	*19*	***1746***
Discriminatory														
Attributive	41	58	112	333	94	7	0	31	49	448	28	12	12	1225
The +	16	52	138	181	78	20	2	34	31	247	12	9	11	831
Discriminatory lexicon	3	9	24	56	15	0	15	7	1	16	62	16	2	226
Subtotal	*60*	*119*	*274*	*570*	*187*	*27*	*17*	*72*	*81*	*711*	*102*	*37*	*25*	***2282***
TOTAL	*75*	*259*	*437*	*626*	*422*	*180*	*24*	*123*	*113*	*1056*	*267*	*147*	*44*	***4028***

Chapter 7

Voices of Fear: Nightmare Landscapes in Western Fantasy Literature and Fantastic Painting

Elżbieta Chrzanowska-Kluczewska*

ABSTRACT

The chapter analyses the construction of nightmarish landscapes in 19th- and 20th-century European and North American fantasy literature, showing that lexical choices and stylistic devices applied to this end in poetry and prose draw from a similar set. Figuration helps readers to visualise fantastic landscapes and be emotionally affected by the uncanny, which is related directly to a basic emotion, fear. The author then turns to pictorial means applied in European fantasy paintings. The construction of linguistic and visual landscapes turns out to rely on a set of similar strategies, well captured by such concepts as *the rhetoric of the image* (Barthes, 1964/1977). The interpretation of *verbal and visual voices of fear* is worth conducting according to Bakhtin's (1975/1981) model of *dialogism*, later renamed *intertextuality* by Kristeva (1966a/1980a).

Keywords Rhetoric of the image, dialogism, heteroglossia, polyphony, (semiotic) intertextuality

* Jagiellonian University, Poland

INTRODUCTION

Fantasy literature and fantastic art have been present in European culture for centuries and it would be difficult to trace their origins to some well-defined dates. Although *fantasy* as a literary metagenre[1] is mostly associated with 20th- and 21st-century prose, its predecessors are conspicuous in the tradition of Romanticism, which programmatically[2] focused its attention on the supernatural, the uncanny, the legendary, and the spiritual. Nightmare and horror entered late 18th- and 19th-century literature with that tide and have been present in literary and, consecutively, cinematographic creation ever since (cf. Berthelot, 2008). In turn, modern fantastic painting, whose beginnings are sometimes associated with the *oeuvre* of the Dutch painter Hieronymus Bosch (1450–1516), had its representatives in all Western countries from that time on and has never formed a definite current or artistic school (cf. Schurian, 2005). It is associated specifically with such periods as Mannerism, Romanticism, Symbolism and Surrealism, though 18th-century and contemporary art may also boast fantastic elements. Fantasy literature and painting draw heavily from the pictorial resources of our imaginations, dream experiences and—not infrequently—mental disturbances.

Being an extension of my short study (Chrzanowska-Kluczewska, 2020) on the interplay of the sublime and the nightmarish in the construction of landscapes by Mary Shelley in her famous Gothic novel *Frankenstein* (1818), this article analyses the construction of nightmarish landscapes in European and North American fantasy literature, drawing on Robert Browning's *Childe Roland to The Dark Tower Came* (1855) and excerpts taken from two classics of high fantasy: *The Two Towers* by JRR Tolkien (the second part of *The Lord of the Rings*, 1954) and *The Farthest Shore* by Ursula K Le Guin (the last part of *The Earthsea Trilogy*, 1972). I focus my attention on those lexical choices and stylistic devices that are meant to help the reader not only to visualise a fantastic landscape but also to be emotionally affected and even

1 Jones (2008, p. 160) treats the term *fantasy* as the umbrella term for "disparate works characterized by a degree of explicit anti-realism". She includes the following genres within its scope: horror, high fantasy, dark fantasy, science fiction, cyberpunk, futurism, Gothic fiction, ghost stories, magical realism, myths, folklore and fairy tales.

2 This means according to a programme as used in arts discourse.

attracted by it. The overall purpose of such strategies is to raise excitement in the reader, related to the feeling of terror. All three works analysed have a common leitmotif—a perilous journey in search of some important truth. Since the underlying theme is the eternal struggle between good and evil, the allegorical and symbolic interpretations of the texts have to be taken for granted.

I then switch to the analysis of purely pictorial means applied in the fantastic currents present in European painting, concentrating on the classics of this type, namely *The Nightmare* by Johann Heinrich Füssli (1781, 1790/1791) and *The Isle of the Dead* by Arnold Böcklin (1880), followed by its modern travesty *The Presences* by Fabrizio Clerici (1974), in order to show that painters apply instruments akin to those used in the linguistic medium to create similar emotions. It is thus worth considering to what extent the strategies utilised in the process of fantastic imagery creation converge in literature and the fine arts.

Be it a piece of literature or a visual artwork, the nightmarish effect it can carry is an instance of a very conspicuous *voice of fear* that comes mainly from the writer/painter who wants to impress the reader/viewer in a specific way.

VERBAL AND VISUAL ARTISTIC VOICES OF FEAR

Fear: A universal emotion

Ekman (1992) provided a list of *basic emotions*, such as anger, disgust, disdain, enjoyment, fear, sadness and surprise. "Basic" refers to the universality of those emotions, in the sense of their not being related to a specific cultural upbringing. Not surprisingly, in Schurian's (2005) opinion, fantastic painting arouses two human emotions from the list above—fear and sadness, which play a regulatory and stimulating part in our existence. Undoubtedly, the same can be claimed about fantasy literature with its frequent nightmare and horror themes and motifs.

Although we all know, experientially, what fear is, there has been no consensus on its unique definition. Gałuszka (2019, p. 24) provides the following definition of fear (after the *Merriam-Webster Online Dictionary*): "an unpleasant[,] often strong emotion caused by anticipation or awareness of danger". A very distinct category of fear has been identified, namely the *fear of death* (Greenberg et al., 1997, and their Terror Management Theory, cited in Castano et al., 2011, p. 603). It is this particular type of fear, connected to our inevitable mortality, that lies at the core of several nightmare and horror effects as visualised in literature, painting, and film. It will also be a leitmotif in all the excerpts of fantasy literature to be discussed in Section 3.

MM Bakhtin and J Kristeva: The interrelations of voices across artistic texts

Since the leading subject of this collected monograph is the concept of *voices*, it seems very proper to assume as a theoretical model two interlinked theories of language in general and of artistic texts in particular, to wit the Bakhtin-Kristeva paradigm of texts engaging with other texts in an incessant dialogue. For several years, Bakhtin (1972/1984, 1975/1981), a Russian literary critic, developed a theory of natural language as inseparable from its social and ideological context. His main claim, meandering through several of his works and directed against purely formal poetics, was that language is never truly our individual possession but is shared by a community of speakers: "The life of the word is contained in its transfer from one mouth to another, from one context to another context, from one social collective to another, from one generation to another generation" (Bakhtin, 1984, p. 202).

Although Bakhtin's main interest was the language of literature, his ideas can be easily mapped onto a wider, semiotic scene, which also covers texts produced in non-verbal media. Most certainly, art is also communal, always dependent on a specific aesthetic, historical and cultural context. Starting its life as a creation of an individual artist, sooner or later every artefact becomes immersed in a community of its viewers, listeners, and interpreters. Related to this idea is the Bakhtinian theory of *dialogism*, highlighting a conversational quality of each and every text. Dialogism can assume two distinct forms dubbed *heteroglossia* and *polyphony*. Heteroglossia refers to the presence—sometimes unrealised—of other, alien voices within the author's own voice. Indeed, we never create completely novel utterances or texts—the voices of our predecessors show through our own creations: "World views, trends, viewpoints, and opinions always have verbal expression. All this is others' speech" (Bakhtin, 1979/1986, p. 94). Polyphony, on the other hand, is a concurrent existence of different voices (perspectives, points of view) within a text. Taking the novel as an exemplary literary creation, Bakhtin points to the voice of the author, the narrator(s), and the characters as expressing separate ideological stances.

In *Problems of Dostoyevsky's Poetics* (1984), Bakhtin claims that *dialogue* is the ultimate purpose of all human communication. He does not use the term *intertextuality*, which belongs to Kristeva (1966/1980), but all his theorising introduces this concept in an explicit way, especially when he says that an utterance adjoins not only the previous but also the subsequent links in a discursive chain. This means that every artistic text refers backwards to its various sources of inspiration and also anticipates a reaction from its audience, possibly as well from imitators in the future. Bakhtin's (1986) ultimate idea is that a word (read: a text) is a drama in which three agents participate: the author, all the voices present in the author's language, and the interpreting community.

Kristeva takes this idea further, stating famously in her essay "The bounded text" (1966a/1980a) that "any text is constructed as a mosaic of quotations" (p. 36). In another essay "Word, dialogue and novel" (1966b/1980b), she also elaborates the notion of *menippea*—a carnivalesque, satirical and parodistic genre of literature, with its sources in Graeco-Roman antiquity. This kind of literary creation often contains elements of symbolism and phantasmagoria, mixed with sombre naturalism. Not infrequently, this broadly conceived genre draws its inspiration from madness, hallucinations, and dreams. The menippean current is of prime interest to our considerations of literary and visual nightmare.

Let us turn to a more detailed analysis of verbal and pictorial voices of fear.

NIGHTMARISH LANDSCAPES IN FANTASY LITERATURE

Childe Roland to the Dark Tower Came by Robert Browning

This epic poem of 34 stanzas, written by Browning over the period 1852–1855, with its title an intertextual borrowing from *King Lear*,[3] exemplifies a (post-)Romantic "phantasmagoria" of a desperate quest, with several allusive and allegorical undertones (cf. Bloom, 1975/2003; Browning, 2004, p. 670). What appears of particular interest to our discussion, the way landscapes are described by Browning, is traceable to the treatise *The Art of Painting, in All its Branches* authored by the Dutch painter Gerard de Lairesse (1707/1778), especially the part "Of things deformed and broken" (cf. Browning, 2004, p. 670). In consequence, we are dealing here with an instance of *semiotic intertextuality/intermediality*, namely the application of techniques recommended for the visual arts to the shaping of literary language.

Construction of landscape

Let us consider first a number of salient elements that build the landscape in the poem. I list them in the chronological order in which they appear to the travelling Childe Roland.

Scenery: a dusty thoroughfare, barren grey plains, a horrid stream with unknown animals, bogs, rubble, mud, a circle of mountains ("ugly heights and heaps", l. 166), the ominous tower awaiting the hero at journey's end.

Creatures: a hoary cripple as deformed as the surrounding landscape, a moribund starved blind horse, a black bird with "dragon-penned" wings (l. 161), a bat, toads, wild cats, ghostly apparitions of the protagonist's dead friends.

Deformed plants: thistles with their heads chopped off and ragged stalks, scrubby alders, drenched willows, palsied oaks.

[3] In medieval terminology, a "child(e)" was a wellborn youth aspiring for knighthood. Other sources of poetic influence on Browning were *The Song of Roland* and Lord Byron's *Childe Harold's Pilgrimage* (1814–1818) (cf. Bloom, 2003).

Colouring: lack of greenness (colour of life), grey, rusty red (soil mixed with blood), black, brown (stones of the Tower), a sheet of flame.

Sound effects: silence ("no sound", l. 105), a shriek of an unidentified water-creature, a click as of a closing trap, an unbearable growing noise (knell of a bell), the blowing of a horn.

From the "props" listed above, readers quickly construct in their imaginations the image of a depressing, desolate and fearsome landscape that not only serves as the background against which the travel takes place, but is actually also an inherent emotional element of the quest itself.

Lexical choices that build the atmosphere of horror

In their exposition of the way in which linguistic stylistics can be practically applied to evaluate the style of an artistic text (mostly prose), Leech and Short (1981/2007, Ch. 2 and 3) propose a "checklist" that consists of the following descriptive tools: (a) lexical categories, (b) grammatical categories, (c) figures of speech, and (d) cohesive and contextual devices. My own analysis, much more limited in scope and aimed only at specifying a *semantico-stylistic field* related to nightmarish effects, will be narrowed to two tools: (a) major lexical categories (with the exclusion of adverbs, since in the excerpts analysed they appear to play a minor role), and (b) stylistic (figurative) devices. I also extend this analytical apparatus to epic poetry, in which style markers can be expected to mirror those applied in prose.

The three main parts of speech responsible for creating the overall mood of Browning's poem are *nouns, verbs* and *adjectives*. A rough count and selection of the most important "atmosphere-building" examples yields the following items.[4]

[4] It would be of theoretical interest to carry out the so-called *keyness analysis*, that is, a selection and count of key words/parts of speech for the three texts described below (especially prose). Since my analysis focuses only on highly representative excerpts taken from Tolkien and Le Guin (and the entire poem by Browning), there was no technical need to apply electronic tools. The subject definitely deserves a separate, more expanded stylometric analysis, with a corpus created from several samples of the texts responsible for the evocation of a nightmarish ambience.

Nouns (approx. 35), e.g. *epitaph, inertness, penury, brute, leprosy, blood, grotesqueness, woe, pain, gloom, fiend, despair, dusk, trap, den, sunset.*

Verbs (approx. 34), e.g. *ensnare, waylay, suffer, bruise, prick, strain, spear, tangle, trample, reel, not see, not hear, surprise, trap, stab, end, toll.*

Adjectives (approx. 46), e.g. *skull-like, ominous, dreary, ragged, harsh, bruised, scant, stupefied, gaunt, wicked, fiendish, dismal, spiteful, suicidal, dank, fell, horrid, trampled, stubbed, desperate, distorted, scalped, squat, blind.*

Whereas the number of atmosphere-creating nouns, functioning as subjects and objects of sentences, and of verbs with similar semantics used as predicates are comparable, a relatively large number of adjectives, applied as modifiers in nominal constructions, is notable. Thus, adjectives appear to play an important role in constructing the imagery of the text.

Predominant stylistic devices

According to the functional tropological model developed in my previous work (Chrzanowska-Kluczewska, 2013), the three levels of figuration can be distinguished within a literary text: (1) the level of *microfigures* (*microtropes*) that operate within phrases and sentences, (2) the level of *macrofigures* (*macrotropes*) that shape longer sections of text, e.g. extended similes and metaphors, and (3) the level of *megafigures* (*megatropes*), which is the most abstract holistic level of interpretation, with figures operating in a covert way. The analysis below makes recourse to this taxonomy, mostly at the overt levels of micro- and macrofiguration.

The simplest and quite effective device employed in the poem is a consistent application of *epithets*, noun phrases with typically adjectival modification, such as a "skull-like laugh" (l. 10), "one grim red leer" (ll. 47–8), "grey plain all round" (l. 52), "starved ignoble nature" (l. 56) and "the round squat turret ... without a counterpart [i]n the whole world" (ll. 182–184). The last quote is an instance of an *extended epithet*.

Similes and *comparisons* organise the text both at the *micro-level* (phrases and sentences) and the *macro-level* (e.g. a stanza). The ones with the highest imagistic potential follow: the hero feels resigned and compares himself to a "sick man very near to death" (l. 25); a "skull-like laugh" (l. 10, an interesting case of an epithet that contains a simile at the morphological level); "quiet as despair" (l. 43); "as scant as hair in leprosy" (ll. 73–74); "it sounded like a baby's shriek" (l. 126); "a cleft in him [an oak] [l]ike a distorted mouth" (ll. 154–155); "as when a trap shuts" (l. 174); "those two hills ... crouched like two bulls locked horn in horn in fight" (ll. 176–177); "the Tower ..., blind as the fool's heart" (ll. 181–182); "noise ... tolled increasing like a bell" (ll. 193–194). All these similes create unpleasant associations with sickness, warfare and death, except for "as a man calls for wine before he fights" (l. 86), which brings in a meagre allusion to a short-lived joy.

Extended similes are less frequent. The poet utilises them whenever he feels that a regular micro-comparison will fail to express the mood adequately. One of the most interesting cases is below (the dehumanising metaphor, "the game", is embedded within the simile):

> The hills, like giants at a hunting, lay,
> Chin upon hand, to see the game at bay,—
> 'Now stab and end the creature—to the heft!' (stanza xxii, ll. 190–193)

Metaphors, less numerous than similes, mostly take the form of *animisations* and *personifications*. The hills, for instance, are first likened to bulls and then compared to giants; the trees (stanza xx) and the Tower are animised/ personified as well, yet human beings are treated like animals ("the game"), exemplifying an animalising metaphor.

Hysteron-proteron, viz. a transposition of events in time, appears twice at the beginning of the story as "my epitaph" (l. 11) and "that ominous tract" (l. 14), creating suspense and adding to the expectation of a fatal development of the events narrated. The comparison of Childe Roland to "a sick man very near to death" (l. 25) alludes additionally to the expected resolution of the story.

Finally, auditory and visual *antithesis* appears at some crucial moments. Through it, the poet juxtaposes the silence of the plain traversed by Roland with a terrible noise at his journey's end, and plays on light effects that contrast darkness with a burst of flame.

Skilful choice of emotively marked vocabulary, heightened by stylistic effects achieved via "atmospheric" figuration, endows the poem with a vivid, painting-like quality.

The Two Towers by JRR Tolkien: Nightmarish effects in 20th-century British high fantasy prose

This novel—the middle part of the famed trilogy, possibly the most dense in terrifying effects—takes up a similar motif of an allegorical journey and a dangerous quest that symbolises the unending fight between good and evil to gain power and control over life. In order to compare the linguistic means chosen by the novelist to create the atmosphere of terror (a century after Browning's poetic efforts), I will concentrate on two excerpts that describe two significant events of the plot: (1) the passage through the Dead Marshes by Frodo, Sam and Gollum, followed by the description of a ghastly view of Mordor (Tolkien, 1954/1974, pp. 209–210) and 2) the same group passing the ghostly tower of Minas Morgul (pp. 277–279).

Construction of ghastly landscapes

Similar to section 2.1.1, I concentrate on selected elements presented in the order of their appearance in the text.

Scenery: ominous mountains, barren dry plains, the Dead Marshes, poisonous pits, ghostly architecture (walls, towers, bridge), demented forms, shadows.

Creatures: Ringwraiths (faceless Black Riders), their fearsome horses, black winged shadows, the Eye (synecdochic reference to the Dark Lord).

Deformation: flowers horrible in shape, corrupt and loathsome figures carved on the bridge.

Colour palette: black (rocks), grey (earth), dark (sky and earth), pale white (sickly corpse-light, defiled and without radiance), livid (lightning), blue (flame), red and crimson (flashes).

Sound effects: silence predominates (synaesthetic "heavy stillness", p. 178), torn by harsh voices as of birds of prey; a rending screech with a piercing pitch beyond the range of hearing; sickening cries; wails; neighing; a rumble of thunder.

Smells: bitter reek, foul fumes and smoke, exhalation of decay, odour of rottenness, charnel-smell of flowers, stench of vapours.

Temperature: coldness, chill.

The "stage setting" is very rich, compared with Browning's text. The sensations invoked appeal not only to sight and hearing, but also to smell and temperature. The Alan Lee illustrations (in the edition of *The Lord of the Rings* published by HarperCollins in 1991), especially the coloured ones, help the reader visualise the landscape. Actually, some of these illustrations could accompany Browning's poem just as well, which only points to the fact that in both cases the nightmarish landscapes are built out of well-defined stock details.

Lexical choices

As previously, my selection concerns only the vocabulary that creates the atmosphere of dread, either in a direct or indirect way. This time *nouns* (approx. 33 and 32 in excerpt 1 and 2, respectively) and *adjectives* (approx. 39 and 40) appear to play the most prominent role. Adjectives are slightly more numerous than nouns but the rough count of these key parts of speech displays a good balance.

Nouns, e.g. *terror, horror, shadow, fear, rottenness, ash, mud, filth, slag, desolation, nightmare, darkness, peril, decay, emptiness, chasm.*

Adjectives, e.g. *ominous, grim, dismal, dead, barren, stony, cruel, weary, harsh, bitter, dreadful, loathsome, lurking, forbidding, ghostly, corrupt, fierce, violent, sullen, sickly.*

Several of these lexemes belong to exactly the same semantic fields as those evoked in Browning's poem. What is striking is the explicit use of highly expressive words such as *terror, horror* and *nightmare,* which leave no room for doubt as to what emotional states the story wishes to arouse in its receivers.

Figurative devices

Not surprisingly, pre- and post-modifying *epithets* predominate. To quote just a few: "accursed hills" (p. 208), "shadow of horror" (p. 208), "dismal waste" (p. 209), "slopes, barren and pitiless" (p. 209), "leprous growths" (p. 209), "a land defiled, diseased beyond all healing" (p. 209), "unseen eyes" (p. 280).

Similes come next in number and are often indicative of an oneiric and sickly atmosphere: (1) "they cowered ... like worms" (p. 208); "as if the mountains had vomited the filth of their entrails" (combined with an animising metaphor, p. 209); "high mounds ... stood like an obscene graveyard" (p. 209); "they stood ... like men on the edge of a sleep where nightmare lurks" (p. 210); (2) "rock ... darker than the dark sky behind" (p. 277); "windows ... like countless black holes" (p. 277); "flowers ... like the demented forms in an uneasy dream" (p. 278); "ridges like notched knives" (p. 279).

Animising/personifying metaphors abound, showing landscape and architecture as superficially dead yet obscenely alive at the same time: (1) "the winged terror" (p. 209); "crawling muds" (p. 209); "leprous growth" (p. 209); "gasping pools" (p. 209); (2) "the moon ailing" (p. 277); the upper part of Minas Morgul described as "a huge ghostly head leering into the night" (p. 277); "a black mouth" of the city's gate (p. 278); "the earth groaned" (p. 279); "its cavernous gate, shaped like an open mouth with gleaming teeth, gaping wide" (a combination of simile and metaphor, p. 280).

Synaesthetic effects are very strong throughout the passages analysed, bringing together sight, hearing, smell, and touch, e.g. "a bitter reek that ... parched their mouths" (p. 209); moonlight "like a noisome exhalation of decay" (p. 277).

Synecdoches include the Eye and ghastly wings (p. 208).

Oxymoronic constructions meant to arrest the reader's attention include "a corpse-light ... that illuminated nothing" (p. 277); "flowers ... beautiful and yet horrible of shape" (p. 278); "water ... steamed, but the vapour ... was deadly cold" (p. 278).

The choice of both vocabulary and figuration in the Tolkien excerpts is strikingly similar to the means applied by Browning, which indicates that epic poetry and prose draw from a common stylistic repertoire in creating the imagery and mood of the fantastic.

The Farthest Shore by Ursula K Le Guin: Nightmarish landscapes in a classic of American high fantasy prose

This is the third part of *The Earthsea Trilogy* (1972/1975), younger by two decades than the Tolkien trilogy. A perilous journey to the Land of the Dead is undertaken by the wizard Sparrowhawk (Ged) and his young disciple Arren. Below, I consider briefly one excerpt from the novel, namely the description of the Dry Land, where the dead abide (pp. 171–187), which occupies an entire chapter.

Construction of a nightmarish landscape

As before, I concentrate on selected linguistic and stylistic elements, following the order of their appearance in the text.

Scenery: a valley under the mountains; the dust, cold and silence; the Dry River and its source (a black hole); the eyeless Cob (the immortal magician); boulders and steep gorges of the Mountains of Pain; empty pools; volcanic rocks and lava slag; spurs and chasms; no motion; emptiness: "No tree or thorn or blade of grass" (Le Guin, 1972/1975, p. 174). The leitmotif is the uncanny stars:

> They were no stars that he had ever seen. Unmoving they shone, unwinking. They were those stars that do not rise or set, nor are they hidden by any cloud, nor does any sunrise dim them. Still and small they shine on the dry land. (Le Guin, 1972/1975, p. 172)

Creatures: dragons at the entrance to the Dry Land, souls of the dead, Cob—a terrifying magician.

No deformation: the dead are whole and healed of the pain and burden of their existence, neither frightening nor loathsome, with no marks of illness, but without hope in their eyes. This contrasts with the *deformation* in Cob's facial appearance (empty eye-sockets) as well as the emptiness of the Dry River and its unnatural source.

Colouring: blackness, darkness, dim starlight.

Sound effects: the overwhelming silence of the Dry Land; only rocks clattering and gritting under the travellers' feet; Cob's false and uncanny laughter; Ged's voice ringing like iron; a roll of thunder.

Touch: the earth burning and searing the travellers' hands and feet; dry throats.

Temperature: the piercing cold of the Dry Land creeping into flesh and spirit; dour, chill, dull air (synaesthetic effect).

The way Le Guin builds her landscape is reminiscent of Tolkien. Not only visual but also auditory and tactile effects, along with the sensation of temperature, are equally important in evoking the mood of dread.

Lexical choices

The threatening landscape is described mainly through the use of *nouns* and *adjectives*, not differing in this respect from the way Tolkien constructed his landscapes. *Verbs* are less strikingly important in regard to mood-evoking.

Nouns, e.g. *emptiness, despair, terror, fear, hatred, silence, desolation, shadows, dusk, hollowness, nothingness, (black) blood, pain, torment, thirst.*

Adjectives, e.g. *cold, dry, dusty, barren, silent, steep, empty, still, unmoving, hopeless, abominable, terrible, rough, numb, unmerciful.*

Verbs, e.g. *to weather, grit, burn, sear, choke, strangle, die.*

Both Tolkien and Le Guin utilise what seems a very straightforward lexis, whose aim is to excite and frighten readers through reference to a wide range of mostly unpleasant bodily sensations.

Figuration

As can be expected, the selection of figurative devices in Le Guin's prose does not differ substantially from those applied by Browning and Tolkien.

Similes and *comparisons* occupy an important position, taking precedence over metaphors: "it was only as if something deep within him grieved, like an animal shut up in a room and chained" (double simile, p. 172); "rocks ... and boulders ... , rough to the touch like scoria" (p. 176); "it was as if this narrow valley might be ... the course of a river of fire, long since cold" (p. 176); "as if the current of the Dry River were darkness itself" (p. 177); "as if he were a star fallen on earth" (p. 183); "burning their hands like molten iron" (p. 186).

Metaphors, relatively less frequent, are basically of the animising, personifying or reifying type: "cold ... crept into his spirit, which was, here, also his flesh" (animisation, p. 173); "Here they drink dust" (p. 175); "black unmerciful peaks" (personification, p. 176); "the Dry River, where only night and no water ran" (reification of night, p. 181); "old darkness" (animisation, p. 182); "a steep gorge choked with stones" (animisation, p. 182).

Lexical recurrence and *structural parallelism* are noticeable characteristics of the text, which is highly repetitive (for instance, the motif of the unwinking and unsetting stars is repeated as many as six times).

List of three, one of the most forceful rhetorical devices, is also outstanding: "the potter's wheel was still, the loom empty, the stove cold" (apart from the listing of three elements, this is also an instance of a *metonymical/synecdochical chain,* p. 173); "No tree or thorn or blade of grass grew in the stony earth under the unsetting stars" (p. 174); "darkness and weariness and horror within him" (p. 176); "into the dust and cold and silence" (p. 181).

Having gained a general idea as to the techniques with which poets and novelists are capable of sharing with their readers visions of fantastic landscapes, brought to life in their imaginations and translated into language, which—in turn—recreates visual and other sensual effects, aural and tactile in particular, we can now ask what strategies are available to painters of fantasy *oeuvres* and set them against the poetic, stylistic and rhetorical means utilised by writers.

NIGHTMARISH SCENES IN FANTASTIC PAINTING

In line with our previous ponderings on fantasy literature, I have selected three works as exemplars of the late 18th-, 19th- and 20th-century painting of this genre. Yet, before we move on to more detailed discussion, I want to briefly devote some attention to a theoretical concept that may come in useful in our analysis.

Roland Barthes' *Rhetoric of the Image*

In his well-known essay *Rhetoric of the Image* (1964/1977) Barthes points to the presence of two messages within a picture:

(1) The first level of interpretation is a coded iconic message, *denotational* and *literal* (called *iconographic* by art historians, cf. Chrzanowska-Kluczewska, 2012);

(2) The second level of interpretation is a coded iconic message, *connotational*, open to several readings (called *iconological* by art historians). At this level, so-called *connotators* operate (*symbols, allegories* and other tropes). They produce a multi-level significance of the image, analogous to verbal texts, in which meaning is also hierarchically arranged. The second level of interpretation crucially depends on what Barthes dubbed *anthropological* and *cultural codes*. Hence the recognition and understanding of nightmarish effects both in literature and the arts will be heavily dependent on interpreters' ability to recognise symbols and tropes and their knowledge of pertinent socio-cultural contexts, including Bakhtinian *voices of others*. The discussion of the three paintings presented below will be conducted with respect to Barthesian double-level rhetoric of the visuals.

Nightmare by Johann Heinrich Füssli (1781, 1790/1791)

Webster's Third New International Dictionary of the English Language (Babcock Gove & the Merriam-Webster Editorial Board, 1961, p. 1527) provides the following three definitions of the word *nightmare*: "1) an evil spirit (*mare*) formerly thought to oppress people during sleep as a) [an] *incubus...*; 2) a frightening dream accompanied by a sense of oppression or suffocation that usu. awakens the sleeper; 3) something producing a feeling of burden, agitation, anxiety, or terror". The famous picture by the Swiss artist Füssli explicitly refers to the first two meanings. In its earlier version (1781, Institute of Arts, Detroit, reproduced in Bolaños Atienza, 2007/2008, p. 98), kept in dark hues with a contrasting sharp spot of light colour in the centre, it shows a young blonde woman asleep in a curtained bedroom. Reminiscent of a Greek sculpture due to the marble-white colouring of her body, she lies with her arms outstretched and her head hanging over the bed's edge. Actually, she looks lifeless, yet the title of the composition suggests a tormented sleep. The bed and curtains are dark-purple and brown. On the woman's breasts sits an ugly half-monkey, half-humanoid creature. According to ancient tradition (cf. Bolaños Atienza, 2007/2008), this legendary creature, suffocating the sleeper, could assume the shape of a bird, cat or monster. The Greek name for such a daemon was *efialtes*, called *incubus* in Latin. The English term *nightmare* makes direct reference to a female horse (*mare*), since according to Saxon legend, this night monster arrives on horseback. Indeed, a fiendish horse with bulging yellowish eyes appears in the background, amidst the heavy curtains. The atmosphere of horror is created with the help of ominous dark colours of the bedroom furniture, the brown hair covering the *incubus* and the blackness of the horse. The neighing of the mare, an acoustic effect suggested by her open mouth, adds to the frightening ambience of this visualisation. All these, conjointly, deploy visually the *voices of fear* drawn from different cultural resources.

Bolaños Atienza (2007/2008) claims that the painting juxtaposes *the poetics of beauty*—represented by the girl's perfectly shaped figure—with *the poetics of horror*, whose embodiments are the incubus and its mare. The second version of this picture (1790/1791, Goethe-Museum, Frankfurt, reproduced in Schurian, 2005, p. 18) has preserved the setting and figures. This time, the palette and arrangement of the protagonists have been changed. The colour white is more prominent in the female figure, the bed-linen, and the night-table cover. The horrific horse, peeping through the curtains, is also white and her glowing, bulging eyes remain unseeing as before. The Frankfurt version proves that the light colour-palette can equally well create a nightmarish atmosphere, which in Western culture tends to be associated with sombre hues and darkness (cf. Chrzanowska-Kluczewska, 2020, pp. 75–77).

The Isle of the Dead (*Die Toteninsel*) by Arnold Böcklin (1880)

This iconic fantasy painting (Kunstmuseum, Basel, reproduced in Schurian, 2005, p. 27) was commissioned from the young Böcklin as a "picture for sleep" and later repeated in four successive versions. The subject is a mysterious Mediterranean island (Ischia) approached by a boat in which two figures escort a sarcophagus covered with a white shroud. The landscape depicted is ideal in its classic composition but simultaneously terrifying. The overall atmosphere of this strange, unreal place is oneiric and although the execution of the painting is realistic, the eschatological reading becomes quite clear.

Scenery is composed of a number of elements: high cliffs, cypresses (associated with cemeteries in Mediterranean tradition), white tombs with entrances hewn in rock (suggesting entrance to Hades?), unknown figures shown from the back—one a red-haired woman rowing (impersonation of Charon), the other a standing figure in a cream-coloured robe (Death?), a sarcophagus and still sea-water (suggesting lifelessness).

Colouring includes a palette of *hues* such as navy blue, black, dark brown and dark green, orange, white, cream, yellow and reddish, and plays on an unnatural *sharpness* of the sunset light.

The painting has its peculiar stylistics based on *antitheticality* at the denotational and connotational level of interpretation: light is opposed to darkness, day competes with night, life is juxtaposed with death, reality with unreality; and, above all, quietude and stillness are set against the disturbing sensation of fear, dread and uncertainty. Again, the work presents itself as a perfect fusion of the poetics of beauty and horror, being elegant and somewhat frightening at the same time. The Mediterranean perfection of the island contrasts with the repulsion the living usually feel for the dead (cf. Chrzanowska-Kluczewska, 2020, pp. 87–88). Böcklin—a Romantic symbolist—has, indeed, created a disconcerting masterpiece of fantasy, a *polyphony* of artistic voices of beauty and fear, embedded in an eerie quietude of the landscape and seascape combined.

***The Presences* by Fabrizio Clerici (1974)**

This picture by an Italian painter (Galleria Forni, Bologna, reproduced in Schurian, 2005, p. 79) is a surrealist travesty of Böcklin's work, a case of *semiotic intertextuality* (within the pictorial mode). It has also been classified as an example of *magical realism* in painting (Schurian, 2005, p. 78). Clerici takes one section of the Böcklin picture and plays with it, as if it were part of a stage setting, hanging on the back wall. From the stage itself (foreground) protrude upper parts of cypresses and rocky elements "borrowed" from *Die Toteninsel*. We are faced, actually, by a picture (Böcklin's) within another picture (Clerici's), an instance of visual embedding, a pictorial commentary on another painting.

The point is that the "dissection" of Böcklin's work and the playful changes introduced into its subject matter and technique of execution have subdued the sense of terror present in Böcklin's vision, though the mood of Clerici's painting remains surreal. This has been achieved in the following manner:

The original *Toteninsel* has been dissected and the so-called *Japanese framing* utilised (only parts of the scenery are shown, the rest cut off).

The *scenery* plays very clearly with fragments of *stage design* and various arrangements of *props/sculptures*. This *intersemiotic dialogue* with the theatre, architecture and sculpture reflects Clerici's education and activity as an architect, painter, stage designer, art collector, and literary expert.

The feeling of terror has been *removed*, although disquieting details are still present (sheer rocks, tombs, cypresses, a gate, snakes). The picture is now *dehumanised*—the boat and the two strange persons in it have disappeared; direct reference to death has been eliminated from the title, if not from the painting itself.

New details have been added in the form of likenesses of snakes incorporated into the rock fragments. They are not only decorative but possibly symbolic (snakes as chthonic gods of the underground, water, rain and life).

Colouring has greatly changed and now includes hues such as: grey, off-white, light/yellowish green, yellow, orange, light and darker purple.

A major *shift of temporal perspective and light* has occurred: evening/sunset has become daylight, the gloomy dusk of the original has been replaced with the sun penetrating through mist.

What is important is that the techniques applied by the artist have greatly influenced the mood of the Böcklin original—nightmarish effects have been largely suppressed, but the painting remains a piece of surreal fantasy.

LANGUAGE VS THE VISUAL ARTS IN FANTASY CREATION: VERBAL VS PICTORIAL VOICES

The time has come for a summary of our findings and an attempt to answer a query about whether verbal language can compete with visual media, such as painting, in creating fictional imagery that accompanies the subgenre of fantasy associated with nightmarish and macabre experiences.

The rhetoric of visual texts

The lexical and stylistic devices listed in Section 3, skilfully selected and applied, are extremely effective in building nightmarish scenes in literary works. Figuration plays an important role here and a predilection for using similes at the micro- and macro-level of interpretation is conspicuous. Among metaphors, synaesthesia seems to play a prominent part. The fact that all three texts discussed rely mostly on relatively simple stylistic devices such as epithets and similes makes them rather straightforward. It seems that in building an atmosphere of fear and sustained terror, the above-mentioned authors of fantastic fiction, instead of applying indirect allusions and metaphors, prefer to use explicit comparisons and very direct vocabulary. This superficially "simplistic" strategy, the outcome of difficulties experienced by the authors in transmitting their imagery to the readers, has had excellent results, judging by the positions Tolkien's and Le Guin's (and to a lesser extent Browning's) fantasy works have been enjoying.

The difficulties we encounter in transposing the visual into a linguistic description have long underlain the arguments for and against the *semiotic untranslatability* of pictorial effects into language, to mention only Foucault's (1966/2009) or Gombrich's (1996) opinions about the disparity of the two media of expression. And yet, though it seems hopeless to equate the aesthetic value of a picture with its literary description, excellent as it may be, the two media—natural language and painting—draw from a similar repertoire of techniques in creating atmospheres of dread, as hopefully our analysis has shown. A selection of the instruments proper to the rhetoric of texts/images—scenery, figures, colours, perspective, playing with forms (deformation), figurative techniques (like antithetical juxtaposition), and unexpected details—are utilised both in literary and visual media. Still, natural language has an undeniable superiority over painting in its ability to invoke bodily sensations other than sight—aural, tactile, olfactory, etc.

Fantasy literature and fantastic painting, while referring to a similar set of elements of the physical world, have their own strategies and techniques that partly overlap. Each of the two media can boast its own peculiar assets and neither should be treated as radically superior or inferior in creating the intriguing world of nightmare, as fascinating as it is repulsive. The rhetoric of the image finds its counterpart in the multi-level interpretation of verbal texts and both verbal and pictorial texts crucially rely on contextualisation, Barthesian *cultural codes* or Bakhtinian *voices*, in order to be fully appreciated.

These cultural codes have to be taken not as random individual artistic voices of poets, novelists or painters, but rather as a powerful *collective voice* formed over a longer span of time and related to tradition and cultural heritage of particular nations or communities. In order to fully appreciate a work of art, whether in a verbal or visual medium, and to recognise its "rhetoric" at various levels of interpretation, we need to be able to contextualise a given artistic text in various aspects: aesthetic and cultural (including at least religious, social and national references and undertones). Sooner or later, we will discover Bakhtinian heteroglossia in every artwork: the combination of the author's individual voice with all the voices that make up a culture in which a given work has been embedded.

Our examples of nightmarish creations have all been instances of Western sensibility—mostly European, related to such countries as Great Britain (Browning and Tolkien), Switzerland (Füssli and Böcklin), Italy (Clerici), and the United States (Le Guin), connected through language (English and German) or religious references (Greek and Roman paganism, Anglo-Saxon myths, Christian eschatological beliefs). This rich polyphony of artistic voices of fear overlaps with the phenomenon of dialogism. All of them have been addressed to readers/viewers, without whose *voices of interpretation* the recognition of the effects of terror, of the dread shown in the face of the uncanny and of death would fall flat. To be shocked, emotionally aroused or scared, the reader/viewer has to recognise the nightmare and sometimes be ready to tame it.

Aesthetic and cognitive value of fantasy in intertextual practice

The instances of fantastic art briefly described in this study well exemplify various forms of intertextuality as envisaged by Bakhtin and Kristeva. In the literary part, Browning looks back to chivalric ideas of Roland's song and Lord Byron's story of Childe Harold, Tolkien converses with Anglo-Saxon legends and myths and Le Guin, in a sense, talks to Tolkien (or, rather, Tolkien's voice perspires through her fantasy). In the visual company, Füssli talks *intratextually* to Füssli in producing a remake of the same subject in a different colour palette,[5] while Böcklin converses with Böcklin over five versions of the same image, realised in slightly different hues and with certain alternations of motifs. As far as intertextuality *per se* goes, Clerici enters into dialogue with Böcklin and some Graeco-Roman myths. All these *aesthetic voices* audible across a range of texts of fantasy involve the authors and the

5 In Chrzanowska-Kluczewska (2020), I point to a striking similarity between a description provided by Mary Shelley in *Frankenstein* of the dead body of Elizabeth, murdered by the Monster, and Füssli's representation of a girl tormented by an incubus. Shelley must have been acquainted with the painter's works, if only through her family connections.

audiences in an ongoing conversation over how to express and respond to fear, the emotion resting ambiguously between displeasure and excitement.

Caillois (1966, cited also in Schurian, 2005, p. 15) states that the world of fantasy has a peculiar characteristic: it discloses "scandals, fissures and strange cracks, which would be unbearable in the real world" (translation mine). The value of such discontinuities and rifts in our life and thought was discussed *in extenso* by Foucault (2009). Fantasy, apart from its ability to uncover hidden layers of cognition, also appeals to its receivers emotionally. This well explains the popularity of and demand for nightmare and horror in works of literature, the visual arts, cinematography, and video games. The fantastic, through the suspension of rationality, does not cease to offer excitement and ultimately even satisfaction to its addressees. No wonder, then, that its works, whether transmitted through language or vision and other senses, unceasingly fascinate us, judging by the huge readership and viewership of this *transtextual genre*. This article has focused on Western fantasy only, but future research could hopefully turn to some comparative analyses of fear-inducing verbal and visual imagery and motifs in the artistic creations of Eastern cultures.

REFERENCES

Babcock Gove, P., & the Merriam-Webster Editorial Board. (1961). Nightmare. In *Webster's third new international dictionary of the English language, unabridged* (p. 1527). G. & C. Merriam.

Bakhtin, M. M. (1981). *The dialogic imagination: Four essays*. M. Holquist (Ed.) (C. Emerson & M. Holquist, Trans.). University of Texas Press. (Original work published 1975)

Bakhtin, M. M. (1984). *Problems of Dostoyevsky's poetics*. University of Minnesota Press. (Original work published 1972)

Bakhtin, M. M. (1986). *Speech genres and other late essays* (V. W. McGee, Trans.). University of Texas Press. (Original work published 1979)

Barthes, R. (1977). *Image music text*. Essays selected and translated by S. Heath. FontanaPress. (Original work published 1964)

Berthelot, F. (2008). Fantastic, the. In D. Herman, M. Jahn & M-L. Ryan (Eds.), *Routledge encyclopedia of narrative theory* (pp. 159–160).

Bloom, H. (2003). Testing the map: Browning's *Childe Roland*. In H. Bloom, *A map of misreading* (pp. 106–122). Oxford University Press. (Original work published 1975)

Bolaños Atienza, M. (2007). *Interpretar el arte*. Libsa (Polish edition: 2008. *Jak czytać sztukę* [How to read art?]. Buchmann).

Browning, R. (2004). Childe Roland to the Dark Tower came. In *The best poems of the English language*, selected and with commentary by H. Bloom (pp. 670–677). HarperCollins. (Original work published 1855)

Caillois, R. (1966). *Images, images...: Essais sur le role et les pouvoirs de l'imagination* [Images, images...: Essays on the role and powers of imagination]. José Corti.

Castano, E., Leidner, B., Bonacossa, A., Nikkah, J., Perrulli, R., Spencer, B., & Humphrey, N. (2011). Ideology, fear of death, and death anxiety. *Political Psychology, 32*(4), 601–621.

Chrzanowska-Kluczewska, E. (2012). Can tropes be seen? *Journal of Kyiv National Linguistic University, Series Philology, 15*(2), 71–80.

Chrzanowska-Kluczewska, E. (2013). *Much more than metaphor: Master tropes of artistic language and imagination*. Peter Lang Edition.

Chrzanowska-Kluczewska, E. (2020). The aesthetics of *Frankenstein*: Nightmarish landscapes in European Romantic and Symbolic fantasy literature and fantastic painting. In D. Petzold & K. Seibel (Eds.), *Frankenstein 1818-2018.–Parabel der Moderne/Parable of the modern age. Symposium 2018 in Ingolstadt* (pp. 73–90). Peter Lang.

Ekman, P. (1992). An argument for basic emotions. *Cognition & Emotion, 6*(3–4), 169–200.

Foucault, M. (2009). *The order of things: An archaeology of human sciences*. Routledge. (Original work published 1966)

Gałuszka, K. (2019). *The discourse of fear in the mass media: A comparison of articles from liberal and conservative British and American online newspapers (2017–2018)* [Unpublished MA thesis]. Institute of English Studies, Jagiellonian University.

Gombrich, E. H. (1996). *The essential Gombrich*. Selected and edited by R. Woodfield. Phaidon Press.

Herman, D., Jahn, M., & Ryan, M-L. (Eds.). (2008). *Routledge encyclopedia of narrative theory*. Routledge.

Jones, S. G. (2008). Fantasy. In D. Herman, M. Jahn & M-L. Ryan (Eds.), *Routledge encyclopedia of narrative theory* (pp. 160–161).

Kristeva, J. (1980a). The bounded text. In L. S. Roudiez (Ed.), *Desire in language* (pp. 36–63) (T. Gora, A. Jardine & L. S. Roudiez, Trans.). Columbia University Press. (Original work published 1966a)

Kristeva, J. (1980b). Word, dialogue and novel. In L. S. Roudiez (Ed.), *Desire in language* (pp. 64–91). (Original work published 1966b)

de Lairesse, G. (1778). *The art of painting, in all its branches* (J. F. Fritsch, Trans.). S. Vandenbergh. (Original work published 1707)

Leech, G., & Short, M. (2007). *Style in fiction: A linguistic introduction to English fictional prose*. Pearson Longman. (Original work published 1981)

Le Guin, U. K. (1975). *The farthest shore*. Bantam Books/Atheneum. (Original work published 1972)

Schurian, W. (2005). *Fantastic art*. Taschen/TMC Art.

Tolkien, J. R. R. (1974). *The two towers*. George Allen & Unwin. (Original work published 1954)

Tolkien, J. R. R. (1991). *The lord of the rings*, illustrated by Alan Lee. HarperCollins Publishers.

Chapter 8

Translating English Political Discourse into Arabic: Roles of Translator, Context, and Voice

Kais Amir Kadhim*

ABSTRACT

This chapter critically examines Arabic translations of English political discourses, taken from BBC News, drawing on two notions, namely context (*field, mode,* and *tenor*) and voices of translators. It aims to answer two research questions: (1) to what extent are "messages" in Arabic translations sustained in terms of *field, tenor* and *mode*?, and (2) to what extent are translators' voices reflected in translations, particularly in their communicative and societal functions? A translator is usually a dominant writer and therefore determines the way in which his or her imaginary audience responds to his or her message. In other words, he or she utilises a wide variety of voices to enable an audience to relate to him or her. The chapter adopts Halliday and Hassan's (1985) functionality and Hatim's (1997) sociocultural method of interpreting translation texts.

Keywords Context, culture, society, translation, message, voice

* Sohar University, Oman

INTRODUCTION

The notions of context and contextual factors and their effect on meaning have grabbed the attention of many linguists whose works not only led to the development and clarification of these notions but also had a tremendous effect on the field of pragmatics as a whole. Lewis (1970) states that his "proposals regarding the nature of meanings will not conform to the expectations of those linguists who conceive of semantic interpretation as the assignment to sentences and their constituents or components of 'semantic markers' or the like" (p. 18). According to Lewis's approach (1970), context is a specification of the identity of the speaker, the audience, time and place of the utterance, the identification of any indicated or salient objects, the previous discourse and "anything else that is needed" (pp. 24–25).

In addition to context, translators are the main decision-makers. Hence "voice" refers to the characteristic, individual physical sounds of speech, singing, and so forth that convey values, viewpoints, ideas, and other types of content. The notion can also be used metaphorically, as has been done in translation studies (Alvstad, 2013). It has been used to describe several partly overlapping phenomena, related to the different perspectives or influence of the many agents involved in the shaping and reception of translated texts (Buzelin, 2011; Jansen & Wegener, 2013). "Voice" has sometimes been used for the stylistic preferences of specific translators (Munday, 2008) and for the voices of literary characters and narrators, as well as for the discursive presence of translators in translated texts (Bosseaux, 2007; Mossop, 2007). Therefore, observing voices of translation on both textual and contextual levels not only reveals a more complex and complete picture but is also indispensable for a reliable analysis.

Of all the paratextual and contextual factors, the impact of the source and target cultures and the effect of any divergence between them have caught the attention and concern of linguists and translators. The impact of differences between the source and target cultures can be seen, most importantly, in the existence of a great deal of culture-specific terms that are specific to one culture rather than another (Kadhim, 2009). The impact of cultural differences can also be detected in other aspects, such as the differences in the connotative meaning or referential value of some lexical items between languages due to cultural considerations, as well as the differences in the degree of sensitivity of people of different cultures to certain topics. For example, people in the Arab and Western worlds differ in their sensitivity to certain topics, such as religion, sex, and political issues (Kadhim, 2011).

Towards that end, this study focuses on the role or effect of context and voice in the translating of political discourse, which is channelled through electronic media discourse. It looks at one of the three variables of situational features identified by Halliday (1978, p. 32) that determine registers—*tenor* (the two others being *field* and *mode*). The data for this study were drawn from BBC News on the Internet. All of the original English messages (source texts) were rendered in Arabic. The major focus in the analysis is the role structure into which the participants in the discourse fit and how this determined how they made and interpreted meaning in the political discourse. This study looks at the Arabic translation of English news from the view of the functions of the news texts, especially in terms of *field*, *tenor* and *mode* as conceptualised in Halliday and Hasan (1985). This study also considers the texts in terms of their communicative functions, as viewed in Hatim's (1997) sociolinguistic view that language is, to a large extent, a reflection of the society which uses it.

TRANSLATOR'S VOICE

"Voice" is usually related to the author's voice or presence as perceived through the act of narration (Booth, 1961). Chatman (1978) uses "voice" to refer to "the speech or other overt means through which events and existents are communicated to the audience" (p. 153). Peden Sayers (1987, p. 9) defines voice as "the way something is communicated: The way the tale is told; the way the poem is sung". Voice is also regarded as an element to show an author's subjectivity. For instance, Greenall (2015, p. 98) defines voice as the "dialogically constituted, but also unique, subjectivity". Taivalkoski-Shilov (2015) considers voice as a set of textual cues characterising a subjective or collective identity in a text. The author's voice can take various forms. It can be overt if the author makes direct obtrusions, like commentary or summary in the narrative texts. It can also be obvious when he or she shifts his or her point of view by moving into or out of a character's mind (Booth,

1961). Even if the author's voice is hidden at times, it is always in the text. The concept of translator's voice is firstly discussed by Venuti (1995) in presenting the translator's invisibility in a translated text: "The voice that the reader hears in any translation made on the basis of simpatico is always recognised as the author's, never as a translator's, nor even as some hybrid of the two" (Venuti, 1995, p. 238). Thus, he calls for the use of non-fluent, non-standard, and heterogeneous language by producing "foreignised" rather than "domesticated" texts so that translators can make themselves visible and their voices detectable. Hermans (2014) for the first time puts forward the notion of translator's voice. He points out that "the translated narrative discourse always contains more than one voice ... as an index of the Translator's discursive presence" (Hermans, 1996, p. 27). He refers to the "second voice" (Hermans, 1996, p. 27) as the translator's voice, which may remain entirely hidden, unable to be detected, and may be directly or forcefully present in paratexts, like prefaces, footnotes, and translator's notes. Hermans (1996, p. 27) furthers his concept of translator's voice by focusing less on formal translatorial intrusions and more on the translator's role in mediating the values inscribed in the translation to its prospective readers. By viewing translation as "a reported discourse" and "echoic speech", he holds that as the study of translation turns increasingly to the translator's social and ethical roles, it becomes more urgent to trace the translator's position, by way of identifying things like voice, views, values, and attitudes (Hermans, 1996, p. 27). In this way, Hermans' understanding of a translator's "voice" goes beyond the range of a translated text itself and puts more focus on its sociological implications. A translator's voice is always present in a translated text along with the author's. In the whole translating process, the translator is both a receiver of the source text and at the same time the producer of the translation whose target readers are in every sense temporally, geographically, and linguistically different from the source text readers. In talking about the relationship between the author's voice and the translator's voice, Schiavi (1996) points out that the translator's voice is "in part standing in for the author's and in part autonomous" (p. 2). Barnstone (1993) considers that there are two possibilities: the voice of the source language author is retained in the target text, and the translator's is thus "suppressed (in deference to the author)", or else the translator's voice comes to dominate (pp. 28–29). Munday (2008) contends that the translator's voice generally mixes more subtly with that of the author's and generally passes unnoticed unless the target is compared to its source. He also argues that translators filter, alter, or distort the voices of the source text author and narrator, "creating something new with a subtly distinct voice" (Munday, 2008, p. 14). The translator reworks the already sculpted material of the author's words into new words in the target language which may bear the fingerprint of the translator's idiolect or preferred translation strategies (Munday, 2008). Scholars also put much emphasis on the subjectivity of translations. Baker (2006) maintains that the translator may deliberately re-mould the target text to fit a pre-existing personal and public ideological framework or narrative. Greenall (2015) argues that it is up to the translator to decide whether or not to make his or her voice manifest.

METHODOLOGY

For the purpose of this article, we employ a composite methodology derived from Halliday and Hasan's functional model (1985) and ideas of Hatim (1997), which are summarised below.

Halliday and Hassan's (1985) functional model

Halliday and Hasan's theory of functions (1985) relates to the stylistic, sociolinguistic, and rhetorical aspects of language. The two authors are more general and at the same time more restrictive in their theory of functions. They are more general in the sense that they suggest three functional categories of language: the ideational (i.e. experiential), the interpersonal, and the textual. They are more restrictive in the sense that their explanation of the systematic realisation of the context of a sentence is confined to three things, namely *field*, *tenor* and *mode*, through the three respective functional components of the semantic system mentioned above.

In the ideational function, Halliday and Hasan's theory relies on and departs from the text to detect the real meaning. It must refer to our experience of the real world. For them, the interpersonal meaning of the language functions as a way of acting, a progression from the semantic meaning to the pragmatic one and to text as a communicative intercourse vehicle. As for the textual meaning of a text, they refer to grammatical features, texture, structure, and generic features of language. In this study, the main focus of the analysis of the translated Arabic news messages will be only on *field, tenor* and *mode.* The term *field* refers to "what is happening, to the nature of the social action that is taking place", while *tenor* has to do with who are taking part in the transaction as well as the nature of the participants, their status and roles, and *mode* is concerned with "what it is that the participants of a transaction are expecting language to do for them in that situation" (Halliday and Hasan, 1985, p. 12).

Hatim's (1997) ideas on communication across cultures

Hatim (1997, p. xiii) notes that a careful consideration to a given text means "someone attempts to mediate in communicating its 'import' across both linguistic and cultural boundaries", and such an attempt is "one way of making sure that we do not settle for a partial view of what goes on inside that text". Hence, he suggests that cultural elements play an important role in communication among nations and in the process of translation. Hatim has studied texts based on two main elements: (1) Western and Islamic-Arab cultures, and (2) the sociolinguistic element in situations when they are in contact, by using texts that people from different cultures can reach and use to understand the culture of one another properly (Hatim, 1997). Hatim's (1997) ideas are to view a text within and across a number of cultural boundaries so as to enable a language user from either of the two cultures in question to operate felicitously within the rhetorical conventions not only of the target culture but also those of his or her own.

With regard to English and Arabic texts, Hatim (1997) identifies two kinds of audiences that the procedures of the two texts assume: *counter-arguments* which are typically addressed to the sceptical, and *through-arguments* which assume a supportive audience. On the matter of the nature of the occurrence of audiences with respect to text, Hatim (1997) notes that some texts are more oral than others. While this can certainly affect text type, it does not necessarily make morality an exclusive property of Arabic, English, or any other language. Furthermore, some languages tend to display a particular preference for one or another strategy, but this does not make tendency questionable. These are merely preferences, tendencies, and trends. For example, Arabic prefers through-argument whereas English orients its rhetorical strategy the other way, towards counter-argument.

DATA

The data presented in this article were collected from BBC News online from January 2005 to April 2006. One hundred cases were collected as part of our study. However, this study will analyse four types of data and their Arabic translations in terms of *field, tenor* and *mode*, since those articles were taken from BBC News texts on the Internet.

Data Analysis

"The fugitive al-Qaeda leader"

In this section, we will examine the phrase *the fugitive al-Qaeda leader* in terms of *field, tenor* and *mode.*

Consider the following Table 1:

Table 1 The field of "the fugitive al-Qaeda leader"

Source text (ST): BBC	Bin Laden call falls on deaf ears US intelligence believes the audio tape aired by an Arab TV channel is genuine, making it the fugitive al-Qaeda leader's first message since January.
Target text (TT): BBC	قال اسامة بن لادن زعيم تنظيم القاعدة في تسجيل صوتي منسوب اليه Qala osama bin laden za'eem tanzeem al qa'da fi tasjeel sauti mansub elayh
Glosses	said Osama Bin Laden leader organising al qa'eda in sound recorder attributed to him

In Table 1, we are concerned with the phrase *the fugitive al-Qaeda leader* in the source text (ST) and its corresponding Arabic translation (underlined), and the impact it has upon the perception of Arabic news readers. It is notable that the *field* of the ST regards Bin Laden as a fugitive, which is evidenced from the noun phrase *the fugitive al-Qaeda leader.* The translator used his own voice and shifted the meaning of the lexical words "the fugitive" into Arabic as زعيم تنظيم القاعدة (*za'eem tanzeem al-qa'eda*), "leader organising al-Qa'eda", which is also a noun phrase describing Bin Laden's merits. That is, the translator has replaced "the fugitive" of the ST with the word تنظيم (*tanzeem*), "organising", to reflect the general perception of Arab readers of Bin Laden's character as one who is highly esteemed, respectable, and acceptable in Arab society. In a sense, the meritorious leadership quality of Bin Laden in the ST is sustained in the corresponding Arabic target text (TT), in that the focus of the message remains the same while the emphasis has shifted from regarding him as a fugitive to one who is capable in leading his organisation. In these respects, the translation is not fully literal but rather semi-literal.

The English ST describes a *field* pertaining to a political matter. The phrase *the fugitive al-Qaeda leader* is used to describe Bin Laden as a leader of an organisation with the enemy in hot pursuit. The repetitive and continuous use of the nouns to describe him is evidently a way of emphasising the seriousness of the West in perceiving his character in the world of the media. In this respect, the translator has attempted to emulate that kind of portrayal by having a similar repetitive technique in the Arabic version: زعيم تنظيم القاعدة (*za'eem tanzeem al-qa'eda*), "leader organising al-Qa'eda". However, although the focus is the same, namely Bin Laden being a leader, the emphasis in the ST and the TT is somewhat different. In the ST, he is portrayed as a fugitive leader, while in the TT, he is seen as a well-organised leader. The fugitive (i.e. negative connotation) part has been suppressed. Such an approach whereby the translator has empathised with the readers' perception of Bin Laden can be seen as befitting the Arab societal-cultural milieu only when we fall back on Hatim's (1997) view of translating across different cultures or nations; we have to be seen as communicating in that new cultural setting. Also, in the new context of this TT and bearing in mind the field of the discourse, another explanation why the translator acts the way he does must be considered; that is, from the metaphorical use of the word *al-Qaeda*. The original message does not change the name *al-Qaeda*. In the Arab world, *al-Qaeda* is not just any organisation; for example, metaphorically *al-Qaeda* in the TT represents Bin Laden's foundation or ideology, to which no negative quality should be attached.

Next, we reconsider the data in Table 1 but we do so now in terms of the *tenor* of the text as represented in Table 2:

Table 2 The tenor of "the fugitive al-Qaeda leader"

ST: BBC	Bin Laden call falls on deaf ears US intelligence believes the audio tape aired by an Arab TV channel is genuine, making it the fugitive al-Qaeda leader's first message since January.
TT: BBC	قال اسامة بن لادن زعيم تنظيم القاعدة في تسجيل صوتي منسوب اليه Qala osama bin laden za'eem tanzeem al qa'da fi tasjeel sauti mansub elayh
Glosses	said Osama Bin Laden leader organising al qa'eda in sound recorder attributed to him

In the above table, we still focus on the underlined constituents. It is notable that the *tenor* of the ST is one in which Bin Laden is conveyed as *the fugitive al-Qaeda leader*. This functional role of Bin Laden has been translated into زعيم تنظيم القاعدة (*za'eem tanzeem al-qa'eda*), "leader organising al-Qa'eda", which also reflects Bin Laden's merits and ideology. Here, the translator has changed the character of Bin Laden from being portrayed as a *fugitive* in the ST to an individual who is, in the Arab world, very capable in leading and *organising* something.

That is, while the participant remains Bin Laden, his role is certainly viewed positively. Also, while the ST sees the negative quality of Bin Laden as a *fugitive*, the translator stresses his positive quality and role of an organiser to Arabic news readers. Hence from the viewpoint of his role, the original message is only partially retained. Therefore, it is a semi-literal translation.

Finally, we look at the same text in terms of its *mode*: that is, the nature and purposes of the linguistic expressions. We present it in Table 3:

Table 3 The mode of "the fugitive al-Qaeda leader"

ST: BBC	Bin Laden call falls on deaf ears US intelligence believes the audio tape aired by an Arab TV channel is genuine, making it the fugitive al-Qaeda leader's first message since January.
TT: BBC	قال اسامة بن لادن زعيم تنظيم القاعدة في تسجيل صوتي منسوب اليه Qala osama bin laden za'eem tanzeem al qa'da fi tasjeel sauti mansub elayh
Glosses	said Osama Bin Laden leader organising al qa'eda in sound recorder attributed to him

The phrase *the fugitive al-Qaeda leader* is expressed in a declarative sentence. This implies that the speech function of the original message is thematic with a purpose, such as announcing the negative character of Bin Laden. That is, Bin Laden is a fugitive and leader of the al-Qaeda organisation. To that end, the writer of the ST describes Bin Laden in a declarative statement in a series of cohesive nouns as *fugitive, al-Qaeda,* and *leader.* Such a structural schematisation conveys a proposition of intensity in the original message to ST readers. As evidenced from the opening phrase قال اسامة بن لادن (*Qala osama bin laden*), "Said Osama Bin Laden", the same technique of a declarative sentence as well as word repetition has been employed by the Arabic translator's view; but instead of choosing an Arabic equivalent of *fugitive,* he has chosen the word تنظيم (*tandem*), "organising". By so doing while he has been able to maintain the intensity of the original message, he simultaneously creates a new purpose, namely to shift the emphasis to a positive quality of Bin Laden, the ability to organise. In this sense, the result is a semi-literal translation. In terms of the sociolinguistic views here, the translator's choice of linguistic terms merely portrays Bin Laden as he is naturally seen by Arabs in the Arab world.

To summarise this section, from the perspective of *field, tenor* and *mode,* it is observed that the Arabic translation of the English phrase *the fugitive al-Qaeda leader* does not fit squarely into the term *literal translation,* as within the similarities there is still some degree of difference of information between the ST and the TT. Hence, it is a semi-literal translation that the translator uses while translating the English phrase *the fugitive al-Qaeda leader* into Arabic.

"Parliamentary speaker"

In this section, we examine the phrase *parliamentary speaker* in terms of *field, tenor* and *mode*. We will consider Table 4:

Table 4 The field of "parliamentary speaker"

ST: BBC	Maliki endorsed as new Iraq PM Maliki also gave the post of parliamentary speaker to Mahmood Al Mashhadani, a Sunni Arab.
TT: BBC	اختير محمود المشهداني و هو سني رئيسا للجمعية الوطنية Ekhteera mahmood al mashadani wa hua suni raesan lil jam'eeyah al wataneeya
Glosses	Chosen Mahmood Mashadani and he Sunni president for the association the nationalism

Regarding the data in Table 4, we are concerned with the underlined constituents only. It is notable that the *field* of the ST is the appointment of a *parliamentary speaker*. In the perception of the Arabic translator befitting the socio-cultural milieu of Arab readers, this event has been extended as the appointment of رئيسا (*raesan*), "president", للجمعية (*lil al jam'eeyah*), "the association", and الوطنية (*al wataneeya*), "the nationalism", which is also a noun phrase describing Mashhadani's political post. As a consequence, the translator has expressed his view and widened the *field* of the ST, the nominal *parliamentary speaker,* to nouns. In addition, surrounding the appointment of a *parliamentary speaker*, the original message has been elaborated to include detailed information about the nominated candidate. To the name of *Mahmood Al Mashhadani*, the writer has also provided his religious sector, *Sunni*, and his race, *Arab,* suggesting the completeness of the announcement of Mashhadani's appointment in the political media. Although the same range of information is found in the TT, the appointment is noticeably given greater emphasis by virtue of the fact that political terms such as للجمعية الوطنية (*lil jam'eeyah al wataneeya*), "the association the nationalism", encompass a greater scope of an association and nation.

Next, we will reconsider the data in Table 4 but will do so now in terms of the *tenor* of the text as represented in Table 5:

Table 5 The tenor of "parliamentary speaker"

ST: BBC	Maliki endorsed as new Iraq PM Maliki also gave the post of parliamentary speaker to Mahmood Al Mashhadani, a Sunni Arab.
TT: BBC	اختير محمود المشهداني و هو سني رئيسا للجمعية الوطنية Ekhteera mahmood al mashadani wa huwa suni raesan lil jam'eeyah al wataneeya
Glosses	Chosen Mahmood Mashadani and he Sunni president for the association the nationalism

In the ST, the participant is mentioned as *Mahmood Al Mashhadani* who is a Sunni Arab. The same range of information has been well translated in the Arabic TT as محمود المشهداني وهو سني (*mahmood al mashadani wa huwa suni*), "Mahmood Mashhadani and he (is a) Sunni". As we move to his role, however, there is a difference in the way it is perceived in the ST to that in the TT. In the TT, *Mahmood Al Mashhadani* has been voiced by the translator not merely as a person whose function is within the confines of parliament, but more than that; his role is very much respected within the country. It is a perception that is very natural within the Arab social-cultural context. As a consequence, the translator has provided a broader concept to the new political role of *Mahmood Al Mashhadani* in the TT compared to the information in the ST.

We move on to reconsider the data in Table 5 in terms of *mode* as presented in Table 6:

Table 6 The mode of "parliamentary speaker"

ST: BBC	Maliki endorsed as new Iraq PM Maliki also gave the post of parliamentary speaker to Mahmood Al Mashhadani, a Sunni Arab.
TT: BBC	...اختير محمود المشهداني و هو سني رئيسا للجمعية الوطنية Ekhteera mahmood al mashadani wa huwa suni raesan lil jam'eeyah al wataneeya
Glosses	Chosen Mahmood Mashadani and he Sunni president for the association the nationalism

Here, the declarative sentence is to inform the readers of an important appointment to a political office, that of *parliamentary speaker*. The personality is *Mahmood Mashadani*. There is additional information, namely that he is an Arab who is a Sunni. The Arabic version also comprises a declarative sentence whose purpose is also to inform. Insofar as the personality and the appointment to a political office are concerned, the Arab TT contains the same information. There is a difference, however, in the nature of noun that is declared. While the ST declares it as a simple post of *parliamentary speaker*, the target text declares much more than that. It declares a position that assumes a three-in-one post رئيسا للجمعية الوطنية (*raesan lil jam'eeyah al wataneeya*), "president for the association the nationalism", which is a reflection of the sociolinguistic and cultural perception of Arabic speakers in Iraq.

"Traders"

In this section, we examine the translation of the English word *traders* to Arabic in terms of *field, tenor* and *mode*. First, we consider Table 7:

Table 7 The field of "traders"

ST: BBC	Iran fears drive oil to new high But traders say that in the short term the price could rise as high as 75 dollars per barrel.
TT: BBC	و يرى محللون ان استمرار التوتر سيدفع ا لا سعار في ا لاتجاه المزيد بشكل يتجاوز تقريبا سعر 75 دولار للبرميل Wa yara muhalilun ana estimrar al tawater sa yadf' al asa'r fi etijah al mazeed bi shakel yataj waz taqreeban se'r dular llibermeel
Glosses	And analysts see that continuing the tension will push the prices in the high direction which access 75 dollars per barrel

With regard to the English word *traders* in the above text, it concerns the activities of buying and selling oil, in which prices are buoyant and there is a continual fear of rising price. The word has been translated as محللون (*muhalilun*), "analysts". In the first reading of the target text, this information is also obtained. However, in the absence of the word النفط (*al naft*), "the oil", in the context of the sentence when the word محللون (*muhalilun*), "analysts", is considered in a broader scope, the word محللون (*muhalilun*) may have a second interpretation, namely that of analysts in general. Due to these two possibilities, the translator's choice of the word محللون (*muhalilun*), although not incorrect, is somewhat inappropriate and makes the target text potentially ambiguous. Hence, it is an ambiguous translation.

From the perspective of the *tenor* of the text of the word *traders*, we will examine the data in Table 8:

Table 8 The tenor of "traders"

ST: BBC	Iran fears drive oil to new high But traders say that in the short term the price could rise as high as 75 dollars per barrel.
TT: BBC	و يرى ان استمرار التوتر سيدفع ا لا سعار في ا لاتجاه المزيد بشكل يتجاوز تقريبا سعر 75 دولار للبر ميل Wa yara muhaliluun ana estimrar al tawater sa yadf' al asa'r fi etijah al mazeed bi shakel yataj waz taqreeban se'r dular llibermeel
Glosses	And analysts see that continuing the tension will push the prices in the high direction which access 75 dollars per barrel

In the above data, it is notable that the *tenor* of the ST contains the lexical plural noun *traders* which in a business society can refer to business people who usually deal in oil, such as oil producers, agents, buyers, and sellers. The favourite reading of the Arabic TT محللون (*muhalilun*), "analysts", also conveys this range of participants. However, due to another possibility of a wider range of usage of the Arabic word, or various repertoires and networks of sociolinguistic communication in Arab society according to Hatim (1997), it may have an additional, though less popular, reading of a "general analyst". Hence, from the perspective of the *tenor* of the Arabic text, there is a possibility of the Arabic translation being ambiguous.

We move on to reconsider the data from the perspective of the *mode* of the text as presented in Table 9:

Table 9 The mode of "traders"

ST: BBC	Iran fears drive oil to new high But traders say that in the short term the price could rise as high as 75 dollars per barrel.
TT: BBC	و يرى محللون ان استمرار التوتر سيدفع ا لا سعار في ا لاتجاه المزيد بشكل يتجاوز تقريبا سعر 75 دولار للبرميل Wa yara muhaliluun ana estimrar al tawater sa yadf' al asa'r fi etijah al mazeed bi shakel yataj waz taqreeban se'r dular llibermeel
Glosses	And analysts see that continuing the tension will push the prices in the high direction which access 75 dollars per barrel

By virtue of the sentential conjunction *but*, the *mode* of the language of the ST is expressed in a contrastive sense, giving rise to a declarative-contrastive meaning. In other words, due to the fear of Iran, the oil traders hold the negative view that the price of oil will keep increasing. In terms of *mode*, the use of the word *traders* in the context of "drive oil to new high" can only refer to people who deal in oil and handle oil. In the case of the Arab translator's style, the use of the conjunction و (*wa*), "and", suggests that the first reading holds true; however, its use together with the word محللون (*muhalilun*), "analysts", where the phrase النفط (*al naft*), "the oil", is not also used, may give rise to another interpretation, namely "the analysts on matters other than oil"; that is, an idea that does not convey the sense and meaning of the original message. In this sense, the translation is an ambiguous one.

"Have reduced the number of weapons"

In this section, we will examine the verb phrase *have reduced the number of weapons* in terms of *field, tenor* and *mode.* We consider the data in Table 10 which presents the verb phrase in terms of *field*:

Table 10 The field of the verb phrase "have reduced the number of weapons"

ST: BBC	Iraq tribe 'taking on al-Qaeda' They set up the salvation council for Anbar and claim to have reduced the number of weapons and foreign fighters coming into this area.
TT: BBC	و اسست هذه العشائر "مجلس انقاذ الا نبار" و زعمت انها ساهمت في خفض عدد الاسلحة و المقاتلين الا جانب في هذه المنطقة Wa asasat hathi al 'shaer magles inqath al anbar wa za'mat enha sahamat fi khefd 'dad al asliha wa al muqateleen al ajaneb fi hathih al mantaqa
Glosses	And these tribes established 'AL anbar rescue committee' and claimed that she (AL anbar rescue committee') participated in reduced number of the weapons and the foreign fighters in this area

In the above data, the *field* of the English ST is about the political events in Iraq at a certain time. These events are set out in the present perfect tense. They are the setting-up of the salvation council for the city of Anbar and the reduction of weapons and foreign fighters. The same political situation in Anbar, however, is set by the translator in the past tense in the Arabic ST, namely by the use of the verb خفض (*khefd*), "reduced". As a consequence, the translator has perceived the message somewhat differently from that found in the TT. That is, he sees these events as completed ones. Thus, in terms of *field*, there is a dislocation of time frame from present perfect to past tense and, therefore, grammatically the result is an incorrect translation.

The same data above will be analysed in terms of its *tenor* as laid out in Table 11. Here, we are interested in the identity and nature of the participants:

Table 11 The tenor of the verb phrase "have reduced the number of weapons"

ST: BBC	Iraq tribe 'taking on al-Qaeda' They set up the salvation council for Anbar and claim to have reduced the number of weapons and foreign fighters coming into this area.
TT: BBC	و اسست هذه العشائر "مجلس انقاذ الا نبار" و زعمت انها ساهمت في خفض عدد الاسلحة و المقاتلين الا جانب في هذه المنطقة Wa asasat hathi al 'shaer ' magles inqath al anbar' wa z'emat enha sahamat fi khefd 'dad al asliha wa al muqateleen al ajaneb fi hathih al mantaqa
Glosses	And these tribes established 'AL anbar rescue committee' and claimed that she (AL anbar rescue committee') participated in reduced number of the weapons and the foreign fighters in this area

In the above data, the scope and nature of the participants are the same in the source text and the target text. These are the tribes, the people of Anbar, the committee, the weapons, and the fighters. What is different between the two texts is the timing and the manner of the reduction of some of the participants.

In the source text, the reduction is an ongoing process and nearing completion; but the use of the past tense in خفض (*khefd*), "reduced", suggests that the translator is not interested in what has gone before, but rather is more focused on the fact that the reduction of weapons and fighters was completed. As a consequence, in terms of its *tenor* the translator has given an incorrect translation.

Now we move on to reconsider the text from the perspective of *mode* as shown in Table 12:

Table 12 The mode of the verb phrase "have reduced the number of weapons"

ST: BBC	Iraq tribe 'taking on al-Qaeda' They set up the salvation council for Anbar and claim to have reduced the number of weapons and foreign fighters coming into this area.
TT: BBC	و اسست هذه العشائر "مجلس انقاذ الا نبار" و زعمت انها ساهمت في خفض عدد الاسلحة و المقاتلين الا جانب في هذه المنطقة Wa asasat hathi al 'shaer magles inqath al anbar' wa z'emat enha sahamat fi khefd 'dad al asliha wa al muqateleen al ajaneb fi hathih al mantaqa.
Glosses	And these tribes established 'AL anbar rescue committee' and claimed that she (AL anbar rescue committee') participated in reduced number of the weapons and the foreign fighters in this area

The source text in the above table is set in a conjoined declarative sentence putting together a number of participants and events. Its declarative purpose is to express a thematic sense that action has been taken to reduce the number of weapons and that the process is almost completed. In the Arabic version, however, while the same declarative and conjoined structures are used to put together all the participants, and thematically to report an action of weapon reduction, the translator sees the action as only having been fully completed. There is a shift in focus. Maybe this is the way the action is naturally seen from the perspective of the Arabic language. If so, this is congruent with Hatim's (1997) view that linguistic expressions are reflections of the perceptions of their speakers about their surroundings. Therefore, although the *mode* of the situation of the original source text message, *have reduced,* has been changed to past tense in the Arabic target text, Arabic readers can still accept it as having some standard and readable form. Nonetheless, the fact remains that literally the result shows an incorrect translation.

CONCLUSION

Theoretically, *field, tenor and mode* are useful in the examination of data from the perspective of events, participants, context, and language; but they do not work as well in the examination of a message in terms of the hidden cultural elements and ideology that may exist in a text. From the four texts that have been examined, it is also found that the translators seem to have been keen to use language which can be understood by different social classes. In other words, there have been attempts to pitch the language of the target text to one standard that is readable by the masses. To that end, one case has been ambiguously translated while another receives an "incorrect" representation (translation). In this regard, Hatim's (1997) views on communication across different cultures and nations in translation studies serve as useful tools in understanding more clearly the nature of STs and TTs as well as translation problems. In particular, Hatim's ideas help us understand the data (of both the STs and the TTs) better, especially in order for us to be more careful in our examination of the data, as different words, phrases, and clauses can have different connotations in different nations and cultures. Against such difficult backgrounds, in general, we find the translators have done fairly well; this is so because, apart from the few cases of overtranslation, overall their translation outputs are noticeably acceptable to a wide circle of readers who come from different social classes and educational and cultural backgrounds.

REFERENCES

Alvstad, C. (2013). Voices in translation. In Y. Gambier & L. van Doorslaer (Eds.), *Handbook of translation studies* (4th ed., pp. 207–210). John Benjamins.

Baker, M. (2006). *Translation and conflict: A narrative account*. Routledge.

Barnstone, W. (1993). *The poetics of translation*. Yale University Press.

Booth, C. (1961). *The rhetoric of fiction*. Chicago University Press.

Bosseaux, C. (2007). *How does it feel? point of view in translation: The case of Virginia Woolf into French*. Rodopi.

Buzelin, H. (2011). Agents of translation. In Y. Gambier & L. van Doorslaer, *Handbook of translation studies* (Vol. 2, pp. 6–12). John Benjamins.

Chatman, S. (1978). *Story and discourse: Narrative structure in fiction and film*. Cornell University Press.

Greenall, K. (2015). Translators' voices in Norwegian retranslations of Bob Dylan's songs. *Target, 27*(1), 40–57.

Halliday, M. A. K. (1978). *Language as social semiotic: The social interpretation of language and meaning*. Edward Arnold.

Halliday, M. A. K., & Hasan, R. (1985). *Language, context and text: Aspects of language in a social-semiotic perspective*. Deakin University Press.

Hatim, B. (1997). *Communication across cultures: Translation theory and contrastive text linguistics*. University of Exeter Press.

Hermans, T. (1996). The translator's voice in translated narrative. *Target: International Journal of Translation Studies, 8*(1), 23–48.

Hermans, T. (2014). Positioning translators: Voices, views and values in translation. *Language and Literature, 23*(3), 285–301.

Jansen, H., & Wegener, A. (2013). Multiple translatorship. In H. Jansen & A. Wegener (Eds.), *Authorial and editorial voices in translation: Collaborative relationships between authors, translators, and performers* (Vol. 1, pp. 1–39). Éditions québécoises de l'œuvre.

Kadhim, K. A. (2009). The sociolinguistics and cultural considerations of English-Arabic translation of political news. *Journal of Language, 9*(3), 71–81.

Kadhim, K. A. (2011). The translation of English BBC political news into Arabic: Thematic analysis. *International Journal of Humanity and Social Sciences, 1*(1), 6–14.

Lewis, D. (1970). General semantics. *Synthese, 22*(1), 18–67.

Mossop, B. (2007). The translator's intervention through voice selection. In J. Munday (Ed.), *Translation as intervention* (pp. 18–37). Continuum.

Munday, J. (2008). *Style and ideology in translation: Latin American Writing in English*. Routledge.

Peden Sayers, M. (1987). Telling others' tales. *Translation Review, 24–25*(1), 9–12.

Schiavi, G. (1996). There is always a teller in a tale. *Target, 8*(1), 1–21.

Taivalkoski-Shilov, K. (2015). Friday in Finnish: A character's and (re)translators' voices in six Finnish retranslations of Daniel Defoe's Robinson Crusoe. *Target, 27*(1), 58–74.

Venuti, L. (1995). *The translator's invisibility: A history of translation*. Routledge.

Chapter 9

Investigating the Shift in Voice and Rhetoric of United States Administrations Regarding the Middle East 2001–2016

Mourhaf Kazzaz*

ABSTRACT

This chapter attempts to apply the character-interlocutor-narrator voice model to the discourse of United States (US) administrations between 2003 and 2016. It also investigates the representation of the self and the other as well as the threat representation of the other. The data for the study are composed of key speeches given by presidents George W Bush and Barack Obama while in office. The findings of the study show that a shift can be detected in the administrations' approaches to representing identity and the relationship with the other that transforms from a conservative neo-realist worldview to a more interdependent liberal one. Additionally, a unique mediator voice emerges in the speeches of Barack Obama, characterised by the use of indexical demonstrative expressions.

Keywords Ideological square, international relations, political discourse analysis, proximisation, representation, political theory, voice

* OP Jindal Global University, India

INTRODUCTION

The speeches of US presidents regarding the Middle East are of particular importance and dire consequences for several reasons. For instance, US foreign policy is influenced directly and/or dictated by the political position expressed in presidential speeches. The authority of a US presidential speech is a binding force both in cultural and political terms. President Donald Trump's campaign and inauguration speech, for example, included anti-immigration rhetoric that was translated to strict policy within the first hundred days of his administration. Yet, perhaps the most important reason why US presidential speeches are important is that they are bound to trigger cultural and political reactions from receivers in the Middle East and elsewhere. These communities, which are often on the receiving end of such speeches and accompanying policies, are forced to manoeuvre their way around representational strategies in these speeches into a working relationship with every new US administration. This chapter attempts to investigate the presence and shifts of identity constructions and threat representation strategies in select US presidential speeches by both the Bush and Obama administrations.

The study of discursive representation in foreign policy and International Relations (IR) is constant but on the margin of IR research (cf. Mearsheimer, 2011; Neumann, 1992, 1996; Shapiro & Schall, 1990). This stems from the fact that mainstream IR theories such as neo-realism, realism and liberalism provide limited space for political linguistic research of all sorts including Discourse Analysis. On the other hand, "Most scholars doing political discourse analysis are linguists and discourse analysts" (van Dijk, 1997, p. 12). This chapter argues that this gap between discourse analysts and political scientists can be bridged by linking critical discourse analysis with political theory. It also argues that political analysis cannot dispense with discourse analysis in a great many cases because a political event boils down to language use and policy.

POLITICAL TERMINOLOGY

Realism is mainly a state-centric theory that lends no space for a discussion of individualism or categories. It concerns itself with the assumption that objective laws govern the world and bases its analysis on an inherently competitive and insatiable human nature. It also views the state as the only political actor. Thus, it lacks the ability to explain the roles of non-state actors, cooperation between states, and the transformational impact of self-contained ideas on state policy. Neo-realism is a less state-centric version of Realism. It attempts to explain the state of instability between states as a lack of balance rather than the driving force of a merely competitive human nature. However, it relies heavily on the rational choice theory, which assumes the state, as an actor, knows everything it needs to know and does not offer explanations of how identity formation or ideational concepts could affect state policy (cf. Hay, 2002). The administration of George W Bush is an example of this conservative worldview because, in the words of Mearsheimer in his comments about the Iraq War, the Bush administration "basically steamrollered [*sic*] their way on this, and the price is we won't have the debate we should" (Payne, 2007, p. 504). The ideological framework here is that the state knows everything it needs to know to make a decision and to legitimise military action.

Liberalism is fundamentally different from Neorealist/Realist thought in its attention to non-state actors and cooperation between states. It argues that interdependence and economic relations can be grounds for international cooperation and stability. Military choice is seen as only one in a set of tools rather than the only tool. Defenders of the Obama legacy view him as liberal when compared to Bush. This comes from Obama's insistence on the importance of global institutions such as the United Nations to govern the relationship between states, and that this relationship does not have to be a zero-sum game. Critics of his administration, however, cite Obama's reluctance to use force or deploy troops in conflicts around the world as Realist tactics or at best pragmatist liberalism that he employed to protect his legacy.

Either way, in this chapter, it is argued that at the level of language, one can clearly detect the ideological and political paradigms within which both George W Bush and Barack Obama operated by employing critical discourse analysis and linking it to IR.

METHODOLOGY

Traditional political analysis concerns itself with actors, events, statistics, and concepts. Political scientists already use a range of methods such as rational choice theory, systems theory, economic analysis, and statistical models. Within this context, political discourse analysis is a fringe element that can only be used in political analysis when it has valuable input to offer. For discourse analysis to be used in political analysis, it has to present an analysis of actors, recipients, practices, and events (van Dijk, 1997). It is also expected to give an account of abstractions of political concerns such as hegemony, power, and domination within these events and encounters (van Dijk, 1997). For these reasons, conducting a discourse analysis of political discourse is not the same as doing political analysis in the political theory sense.

This chapter attempts to advance a model of political analysis that comprises certain critical discourse analysis concepts. This model, argumentatively, attempts to cover a range of areas that are of political interest and can only be accessed for political analysis through methods of critical discourse analysis. Data for the study comprise the following speeches:

Table 1 Data for the study

George W Bush	Barack Obama
State of the Union address, January 29, 2002	Turkish Parliament address, April 7, 2009
State of the Union address, January 28, 2003	Cairo University speech: "A New Beginning", June 4, 2009
News conference, August 21, 2006	

Dialogic voice and engaging the public

Critical Discourse Analysis (CDA) and Dialogism (dialogic understanding of language) share numerous assumptions about language (Pietikäinen & Dufva, 2006). Both currents view language as a tool to construct meaning as opposed to being solely a rhetorical device. They also agree on the importance of the social makings of meaning. Most importantly, CDA and Dialogism agree on the importance of context (Pietikäinen & Dufva, 2006). The latter is an important framework for any research that explores invocations and references to shared, cultural, historical, ethnic, or national events and memories.

These assumptions play a significant role in political discourse analysis whereby politicians can be thought of as assuming the role of a narrator, interlocutor, or character (Koven, 2007; Reyes, 2011). Each of these roles has its own distinctive dialogic voice that is both constitutive and reflective of the discourse these politicians attempt to establish. Each of these voices can also be seen as a political tactic that seeks to establish legitimisation. While the narrator voice is used to "present objectivity and therefore validate the story or the facts presented" (Reyes, 2011, p. 3), an interlocutor's voice is a display of interactivity and closeness on the part of the politician that manifests in the form of casual interjections, questions, and the use of first and second person pronouns with the audience. These interactions are intended to create a sense of "false" solidarity (Reyes, 2011, p. 95). The character voice, on the other hand, is used by politicians to reiterate and re-contextualise statements, quotations, or stories told by influential historical figures to borrow the legitimacy thereof and extend it to their own statements.

"Us", "inclusive Us", and "Them"

Identity construction is indispensable to the language of politics. A political speech or an election campaign would be unimaginable without the invocation of a heroic past, references to shared values, or arousal of nationalistic fervour of a given community. These seem most visible at times of (international) political tension (e.g. US-Iran) as well as when nation-states are marred with unrest (e.g. Syria and Iraq).

These invocations and references presuppose the existence of a dichotomy of political camps, usually followed by emphasis on the moral weight of one camp over the other. Hence, dividing the public into different categories based on temporal, spatial, religious and ethnic considerations and parameters becomes a vital strategy that a politician cannot do without.

Perhaps the most fundamental tool to study the shift in categorisation techniques between the two administrations is the Ideological Square (van Dijk, 1992, 1995, 2013). In its simplest definition, it is the study of ideological representational structures, one that typically "emphasizes positive properties of Us, the ingroup, and negative properties of Them, the outgroup" (van Dijk, 2013, p. 222).

As will be exemplified later in the chapter from speech excerpts, the war rhetoric of the Bush administration constructed a dichotomy of entities of the good "Us" versus the bad "Them". It maintained this construction even when it adopted an axiological strategy 10 months into the war upon failure to present evidence of Iraq's weapons of mass destruction (WMD) (Cap, 2013b). In comparison, Obama's administration constructed three entities, or a trichotomy. It employed physical, temporal, and spatial strategies to herald a new era of dealing with the Middle East. Obama's inclusive approach marks a clear shift from Bush's binary categorisation. Perhaps more importantly, Obama's approach simultaneously engaged in both exclusivist as well as inclusivist processes, such that it required a modification of the analytical method, i.e. the Ideological Square, to account for all three different entities that Obama classified.

Proximisation and threat portrayal

Proximisation as a concept (Chilton, 2004) and theory (Cap, 2008, 2010, 2013a, 2013b) studies strategic regularities underlying "forced" constructions in political discourse (Cap, 2013b, p. 294). As a research project, it emerged to explore legitimisation in the interventionist discourse of the Bush administration concerning the war on Iraq in 2003. By definition, proximisation is a discursive strategy of presenting physically and temporally distant events and states of affairs as increasingly and negatively consequential to the speaker and their addressee (Cap, 2013b). Proximisation explores legitimisation of (interventionist) action against these negative imminent events. Proximisation can be Spatial (whereby the discourse peripheral entities or "aliens" encroach physically upon the discourse central entities "addressee" and "speaker"), Temporal (whereby a conflict is portrayed as imminent and dangerous, requiring preventive measures), or Axiological or Ideological (whereby "home values" are under constant potential threat by "foreign values" regardless of the state of the current conflict, opening a window for further legitimisation and change of strategy based on eclecticism).

ANALYSIS OF FINDINGS

Dialogic voice

Based on the narrator-interlocutor-character model (Koven, 2007; Reyes, 2011), we can argue that both Bush (example [1]a) and Obama (example [1]b) use the narrator's voice to present a certain interpretation of reality as "real, truthful, and reliable" (Reyes, 2011, p. 44). They present it as a fact.

(1) a. Iraq continues to flaunt its hostility toward America and to support terror. The Iraqi regime has plotted to develop anthrax. (Bush, 2002)

b. For decades, there has been a stalemate: two peoples with legitimate aspirations, each with a painful history that makes compromise elusive. ... The only resolution is for the aspirations of both sides to be met through two states, where Israelis and Palestinians each live in peace and security. (Obama, 2009b)

This employment of the narrator's voice in both excerpts and other locations in the speeches creates a distance between what is being said and the sayer. It shields the sayer from criticisms of ideological manipulation. The statements made with this voice inspire an assimilation effect on the part of the receiver because they fall within "latitude of acceptance" (O'Donnell & Jowett, 2012, p. 180), whereby the receiver expects and identifies with the message (cf. Cap, 2008). Bush lists what he perceives as facts about Iraq in a third-person narrator voice and excludes certain other facts related to the interests of his administration in Iraq, such as oil and regional security concerns. Obama's narrator voice is employed to present a certain version of history as authentic. He presupposes the existence of two powers at play that are equal in military might; however, Palestinians' present situation is far from that of Israel as a state with an actual army.

This interlocutor voice is not present in Obama's speeches due to the formality constraints of the genre of political speeches. Despite this formality, however, Bush employs instances of interlocutor's voice (example [2]) in which he frequently poses questions to invite the audience into his line of thinking. More importantly, he creates a sense of "false" solidarity (Reyes, 2011, p. 95) and connection with the audience because he uses his position and power as a speaker to answer his own questions without genuine interest in the supposed replies.

(2) Saddam Hussein has gone to elaborate lengths ... to build and keep weapons of mass destruction. But why? The only possible explanation, the only possible use he could have for those weapons, is to dominate, intimidate or attack. (Bush, 2003)

Both Bush and Obama use a character voice in their speeches. Bush tells stories in the voice of an everyday person to evoke a moral standard or invoke a moral response (example [3]a). He follows his stories with refrains of recommitment to these moral standards.

(3) Story:

Last month, at the grave of her husband, Michael, a CIA officer and Marine who died in Mazur-e-Sharif, Shannon Spann said these words of farewell: 'Semper Fi, my love.'

Refrain:

Shannon, I assure you and all who have lost a loved one that ... our country will never forget the debt we owe Michael and all who gave their lives for freedom. (Bush, 2002)

Obama's employment of the character voice, as in (4), is more historically bound. He chooses quotations of historical figures and re-contextualises the morals of the quotations in the here and now to evoke a moral standard.

(4) The Holy Koran tells us, 'O mankind! ... we have made you into nations and tribes so that you may know one another.' The Talmud tells us: 'The whole of the Torah is for the purpose of promoting peace.' ... [T]hat must be our work here on Earth. (Obama, 2009b)

The argument of liberal versus realist view can be further supported by studying a unique feature in Obama's speeches (example [5]) that is lacking in Bush's. Obama's liberal mission of finding a compromise and establishing interdependence between actors manifests itself in his inclination to provide explanations and justifications throughout his speeches.

(5) a. All nations have a stake in overcoming [challenges]. That is why we must listen to one another ... That is why we must build on our mutual interests. (Obama, 2009a)

b. Freedom in America is indivisible from the freedom to practice one's religion. That is why there is a mosque in every state in our union. (Obama, 2009b)

Demonstrative discourse deixis such as *this* or *that* (Cornish, 2007) denotes a metaphorical understanding of discourse as time and time as space. It also functions as a deictic reference to a portion of a discourse relative to the speaker's current point in the discourse. This entails a physical vision of discourse as space whereby *this* is a "location" in the text as opposed to *that*. The speaker can identify himself or herself with either *this* or *that* and the modal distance from the other deixis can be studied for ideological framing (Cornish, 2007).

This understanding can also be extended to show causality in the employment of demonstrative discourse deixis. More specifically, indexical demonstrative expressions such as "this/that is why" and "that/this is what" are interesting to the purpose of this chapter because they occur frequently in Obama's speeches and are absent in Bush's. These expressions function as proximal markers that bridge the gap between a referent as it is and the way Obama identifies with it. In other words, Obama uses these structures to explain, augment, and promote what he sees as potential reality characterised by cooperation as opposed to the current situation of the referent reality. This reconciliatory and persuasive approach sets Obama apart from Bush and marks his policies.

The Ideological Square

From the data available in the speeches of Bush (Table 2) we can argue that the "Us" entity is lexicalised as overwhelmingly positive. For example, "Us" is spoken of as a "government" as opposed to the regime of "Them". "Us" is expected to advance a "freedom agenda". On the other hand, the negative "Us" is de-emphasised. For instance, "Us" did not wage war on Iraq; rather, it "went into" Iraq. "Us" did not make a mistake in the national strategic estimate of the war objectives; rather, "Us" "thought" Saddam/Iraq had WMDs.

Table 2 Sample of Bush's ideological construction

Us		Them		
Positive	**Negative**	**Positive**	**Negative**	
prevent	thought	he didn't	terrorists	uranium
civilized	went into		nuclear weapons	chemical
government			axis of evil	hostility
advance			regimes	hide
freedom agenda			flaunt	biological
			plot	

Negative "Them" is emphasised in numerous examples, but there is only one mention of a positive "Them" and it is de-emphasised: "Iraq/Saddam did not have WMDs" becomes "he didn't".

As a fundamentally different approach, Obama dedicates a whole section of his speeches to dwell on the middle area between "Us" and "Them". In this research, this area will be termed "inclusive Us" because it seems to represent a third entity in the speech. This entity is so essential to the political argument presented that it cannot be overlooked.

The classical positive "Us" in the speeches of Obama (Table 3) is emphasised as a "sweeping change" that is characterised by "modernity and globalization". It is also "[n]ot at war with Islam", which is an important step to establishing common ground. Apart from the ideational construction, "Us" is also emphasised by processes such as when Obama "prohibited the use of torture" and "closed Guantanamo Bay".

The negative "Us" is de-emphasised in several locations of the speech. For example, in the opening section, Obama argues that the current state of "tension" was fed by "colonialism that denied rights to many Muslims".

Table 3 Sample of Obama's ideological construction

Us		**Inclusive Us**	**Them**	
Positive	Negative	Positive	Positive	Negative
sweeping change	led Muslims to believe it is hostile	not exclusive		exploited
modernity	tension	not in competition	small minority	but potent minority
globalization	colonialism denied rights	share common principles		hostile not only to America
not at war with Islam		justice, progress, tolerance, dignity, respect		operate
prohibited the use of torture		Civilization debt, Islamic culture		killed
Ordered Guantanamo Bay closed		innovation		

He also argues that a "sweeping change of modernity and globalization" is what led Muslims to view the US as hostile. A closer look at this argument reveals that the lexeme "tension" is a downgrade from "conflict", which would be a better alternative to describe the state of affairs in the Middle East, particularly in Iraq where there are insurgents and US-backed government forces. Additionally, it is argued that it was colonialism that "denied rights" and not the US. In other words, an infamous historical third party denied the rights and the US cannot be held accountable if parties need to reach common ground. Finally, viewing the US as hostile by Muslims seems to be represented as a mere misunderstanding of modernity and globalisation. Agency here is given to Muslims in this misunderstanding rather than US policies in the Middle East.

Obama then turns to the description and construction of "Them". This concept is essential as it serves as a point of reference against which "inclusive Us" is judged. Negative "Them" is emphasised by the use of verbs such as "exploit", "operate", and "kill". Negative "Them" also seems to be emphasised by certain modifiers and emphatic grammatical structures such as "small but potent minority" and "hostile". A clear contrast with Bush's discourse, however, is in the use of the term "violent extremists" which has less of an impact than Bush's "terrorists".

Obama's speeches are markedly different from Bush's. Bush tends to compartmentalise people into two groups. Obama, in an effort to focus on cooperation and establishment of common ground, constructs and maintains three entities, all of which are important to his political argument. Obama defines a special group that will be termed "inclusive Us" in this paper. He sets this group apart from "Them", i.e. "violent extremists", and presents it as slightly different from the "Us" entity introduced earlier. The characteristics of this new entity merit a separate categorisation because of the foreign element it still retains, i.e. "Islamic identity", and the fact that Obama's elaborate argument depends on this entity to express comparison and contrast with both "Us" and "Them".

In the construction of this entity, Obama recognises "civilization's debt to Islam" and that "Islamic culture" is a "part of America's story". These two references are the founding tenets for the "inclusive Us" that holds the key to an era of liberal cooperation and interdependence. "Inclusive Us" is the combination of "America and Islam, [which] are not exclusive" and are "not in competition". A positive "inclusive Us" is emphasised with attributes such as "common principles—principles of justice and progress; tolerance and ... dignity".

Proximisation

The research from which proximisation emanated as a theory was the rhetoric revolving around the "War on Terror". Proximisation focused particularly on investigating the legitimisation of interventionist preventive measures against external threats in political discourse (Cap, 2013b). It attempts to account for the symbolic construal of relations between entities in the discourse space (DS) whereby the threat comes from DS peripheral entities, in this case Iraq, and is conceptualised to be crossing to invade the inside-deictic-centre elements. The threat is both spatiotemporal and ideological.

Building on Cap's (2010, 2013a) examination of legitimisation through proximisation in the speeches by George W Bush leading to the war on Iraq, the texts selected for this chapter show an argument for Iraq acquiring WMDs and that because of the historical antagonism between Saddam Hussein and the US and the ideology of Iraq as an adversary that is completely opposite to American "home values", a pre-emptive military intervention was legitimate.

Lexico-grammatical choices in Bush's speeches such as "Iraq continues to flaunt its hostility towards America" and "axis of evil" refer to an antagonistic history between the US, i.e. the deictic centre, and the outside peripheral Iraq. This reference to things that are assumed to have happened before is part of legitimisation through a spatiotemporal proximisation whereby the American addressee, as Patricia Dunmire (as cited in Cap, 2013b) argues, is predisposed to recognise and identify with the stated purpose of the interventionist discourse based on experience in the First Gulf War and World War II. "Axis of evil" elevates the threat represented by Iraq as a rogue state into the gravity of World War II, thereby legitimising and requiring a moral response.

The assertions that Bush makes such as "We must prevent", "Iraq continues to flaunt", and "the need to advance a freedom agenda" are given in the form of "facts". The statement of these "facts" is well within Bush's expected capacity as a US President and they are available for him to build on.

The direct physical threat that the peripheral poses is represented as urgent and encroaching on the centre. It is both imminent and ready to materialise. Lexical items to this effect include "This is a regime that has something to hide from the civilized world", "Saddam Hussein recently sought significant quantities of uranium from Africa", and "Iraq continues to support terror".

This direct threat portrayal, however, did not hold its water when weapons of mass destruction were nowhere to be found in Iraq. In a 2006 conference, Bush deflects from the physical to the ideological. With value-ridden argument and lexical items, Bush plays down the failure to find weapons of mass destruction using lexical items such as "We thought he had WMD. It turned out he didn't" and "He had the capacity to make" them. He highlights the home values "advancing [the] freedom agenda" of the centre as opposed to the destructive values and "human suffering" imposed by the peripheral. Unlike the physical threat, the ideational threat against home values is always ready to materialise and hence requires a reaction. In this way, Bush adds an axiological dimension to his argument that makes it stand regardless of the failure of the socio-temporal proximisation discussed earlier.

Obama's threat portrayal registers a marked difference from Bush's. We have discussed in the Ideological Square section that Obama creates three entities, "Us", "inclusive Us" and "Them". The first entity corresponds to the inside-deictic-circle (IDC) element of proximisation theory. It holds "home values" and tradition. "Inclusive Us" is a peripheral outside-deictic-circle (ODC) element but it poses no threat to IDC. Rather, a relationship of cooperation and interdependence can be seen in it, both in physical proximity and in the values it shares with IDC. It remains, however, an outsider to the deictic centre on account of its own values, which it brings to enrich the IDC values. It is also important to note that in the construction of Obama's discourse, this entity is important for him to draw parallels with "Them" and differentiate between the good ODC and the bad ODC, as it were. This is why it cannot be said to be the same as the IDC. In juxtaposition, "Them" corresponds to the peripheral ODC element that represents the direct physical threat as well as the ideological threat, not only to the IDC but also to the other ODCs that are considered vital in the struggle against it.

Obama's spatiotemporal proximisation strategies revolve around delivering the message that the US is not at war with Islam while also stressing the need to eradicate "violent extremists". This premise helps Obama distance himself and his administration from previous choices made in the name of the war on terror and herald a new era that he terms "A New Beginning". It also helps him exclude "violent extremists" from the type of Islam that he recognises and with which he is ready to work. This exclusion by categorisation results in two peripheral entities in relation to one central entity. This exclusion also helps Obama in his call upon one ODC group to help in the fight against the other. A shared history, mutual agreements, and previous coalitions are among the concepts that Obama mentions to make his case for the moderate "Islam" represented by Ankara and Cairo. The threat from "violent extremists" to both "Islam" and "America" is presented as both real and constant. It continues to be alarming and has to be dealt with, and this is a common goal between America and its allies, in this case Ankara's and Cairo's Islam. In Obama's discourse, the physical threat is manageable by cooperation; in Bush's, by war.

The exclusion by categorisation is also based on moral and axiological grounds. "Islam" has more to share with the US than "violent extremists" do. Obama's premise can be seen as reconciliatory in comparison with Bush's. We notice that Obama is more concerned with the ideational and axiological argument than with the actual portrayal of a direct threat. He lists values that are important to the speaker, the American addressee, and the "good" ODC addressee. He links the temporal in the historical sense with the axiological rather than with the spatial. This ideational argument legitimises co-operational responses over direct interventionist actions. Obama's lexical choice of the term "violent extremists" over Bush's "terrorists" is in itself an axiological strategy. "Terrorists" as a category requires a direct physical response. "Violent extremists", on the other hand, is not as direct or urgent a threat. Extremism is not as serious or threatening as "terrorism" because it is not always accompanied by violent life-claiming acts. One can think of extremist rhetoric by some scholars that remains rhetorical which, in Obama's world, can be fought with re-education and rehabilitation by Arabic-speaking US allies. Thus, for "extremism" to be elevated to the same threat threshold inherent in "terrorism", it has to satisfy another condition, namely "violent", before a moral military response is needed. This change in lexico-pragmatic choices and employing an ideational argument to depict threats mark Obama's liberalist speeches and set them apart from the interventionist realist discourse of Bush.

Perhaps the choice of venues for speeches is one of the simplest and most direct applications to study this shift. This choice was essential to the overall political messages both presidents tried to deliver. Their choices were in tandem with their ideological categorisation of political entities as well as their proximisation strategies regarding these entities. These choices reflected the threat perception the presidents tried to impart in their speeches and were contingent on the political context and ideological framing.

President Bush began his war on terror with the proclamation:

> Every nation, in every region, now has a decision to make. Either you are with us, or you are with the terrorists. (Bush, 2001)

This binary categorisation assumes that only the physical space on US soil or provided by its allies in this war is a safe space. A speech by the president, then, can only happen in a location within this safe space. Furthermore, to project an image of power, Bush's choices were limited to locations that were fortified. For example, his declaration of the war on terror was televised from the White House. His speech ending major combat operations in Iraq took place aboard USS Abraham Lincoln on May 1st, 2003 with a "Mission Accomplished" banner in the background. Perhaps the only time this careful power projection was contested on a symbolic level was in a conference in the prime minister's palace in Baghdad, Iraq in December 2008. On this occasion, an Iraqi journalist, Muntadhar al-Zaidi, threw a pair of shoes at President Bush as a "farewell kiss" (Myers & Rubin, 2008). Incidentally, this palace is at the centre of the Green Zone, a US fortified neighbourhood that includes the US embassy building.

By comparison, Obama's speech to the Muslim world took place at the Turkish Parliament in Ankara, Turkey—a country that is a long-time ally of the US. This speech took place on friendly peripheral soil, or ODC in proximisation terms, at a venue that the US (IDC) recognises as politically legitimate.

On the other hand, Obama's speech to the Arab world took place at Cairo University, Egypt, which constitutes an ODC. Al Azhar University co-hosted the event and was referenced in the speech. The speech did not take place at an Egyptian political or legislative venue, nor did it take place at the American University in Cairo, an IDC.

It can be argued, therefore, that Obama recognised the impact of Egypt on Middle East "Muslim" affairs. He considered it an important ally in the region. But he chose to distance the US from political issues arising from political affiliation with its regime and pre-emptively undermined any attempts of Egypt's regime to politically capitalise on his visit. His choice not to speak at the American University can be seen as Obama distancing himself from his predecessor's choices of fortified US-affiliated venues for his speeches. Obama in a reconciliatory endeavour projected himself as a liberal president looking forward to cooperation with the Middle East by maintaining a sensitive and delicate balance of religious openness and political recognition. More on the religious and political context of venues will follow in the political contextualisation.

Political contextualisation

The US national interests and national security were targeted by a terrorist act on September 11, 2001, leaving the US united and its citizens awaiting retaliation. It is understandable, according to Mearsheimer (2011, p. 127), that "to ensure that the country adopts the correct foreign policy, it is necessary to inflate the threat by deploying lies about the adversary". Politicians like George W Bush may lie in an effort to unite the public to support wars. The reason for this is that given the semi-isolated geographical place the US occupies, only an act on a 9/11 magnitude would actually represent imminent and looming danger. Rogue states seeking WMD are constant reminders that the war on terror that began with Afghanistan is yet to be completed.

It is, therefore, not surprising that Bush had this to say:

> The British government has learned that Saddam Hussein recently sought significant quantities of uranium from Africa. (Bush, 2003)

This much-discussed 16-word sentence was used despite intelligence agencies advising him against it, and despite the 2015 declassified National Intelligence Estimate (NIE) dated October 2002 on WMDs (cf. Eisner & Royce,

2007). The reason for this sentence usage can be explained by Mearsheimer's argument (2011, p. 69): "Fearmongering has played an important role in U.S. foreign policy over the past seventy years ... in hopes of dragging a reluctant American public into war".

Based on the discourse analysis in this paper, we can argue that the understanding of the war on terror between the two administrations morphed from regarding it as an aggressive war in a binary world marked by immediate physical threats into a more reconciliatory understanding of this world.

The nature and legitimacy of the war on terror are based on the ideological and political framework within which each administration operates. They also depend on the different understanding and employment of the subtle differences between nuanced concepts such as fundamentalism, radicalism, extremism, and terrorism.

In the case of terrorism, for example, despite the large amount of literature on terrorism research, a globally acceptable definition of the term "terrorism" is yet to be established. Adopting a definition is both a lexical and political problem.

In terms of lexicalisation, the terms *radical* and *extremist* agree in their potentiality of non-violence; that is, they do not necessarily espouse lethal actions. Extremist views include interpretations of religious texts that can be discredited or accepted through discourse and dialogue between the parties concerned. Thus, to have an extreme view is a fundamental human right. These extreme views are found in most zealous religious discourses. Extremism can also be a non-religious understanding of an event or movement. For example, populist understanding of immigration and the extreme policies emanating from this understanding are forms of political extremism. Thus, while terrorism is, in fact, taking radicalisation to the next level as an intellectual, social, emotional, and religious decision, to be radical is actually "merely to reject the status quo, and not necessarily in a problematic or violent way" (Bartlet & Miller, 2012, p. 2).

In terms of politics, terrorism requires a set of endless permissive factors. Among these factors are socio-economic conditions, religious tensions, and foreign military intervention. These factors, *inter alia*, create the "sense that the West is on a crusade to oppress the Muslim world" (Bartlet & Miller, 2012, p. 1). This is why many people in the Middle East and in Muslim communities took offence at what was described as "a slip of the tongue" on the part of George W Bush when he said "This crusade [pause], this war on terror is going to take a while" (Bhatia, 2004, p. 2). Many in the Middle East considered the invasion of Iraq as state terrorism on the part of the US. Radicals capitalised on this and similar references to build an alternative narrative to US interventionist discourse in an effort to radicalise more and more youths in the fight against the US, arguing that "the West, for [its] geopolitical interests, oppress[es] Muslims" (Bartlet & Miller, 2012, p. 6).

The lack of a global definition of terrorism and the complex nature of terrorism as a lexical and political phenomenon made President George W Bush's legacy an irksome inheritance for President Obama. Obama, coming from a liberal strand of IR theory, chose a less confrontational term to describe Bush's *terrorists* in his Cairo speech, namely "violent extremists". The more subtle nuance of the term lent him space to negotiate interdependence with the states he visited, where the US is not necessarily welcome. At the same time, the modifier *violent* kept the status of "extremists" at the same level as *terrorists*. *Violent* in itself does not necessarily mean terror as it lacks the lethal aspect thereof. But the combination of the modifier and the lexeme constructs the same meaning of *terrorism*. It can be argued, then, that Obama made it harder to speak of *terrorism* because radical elements now needed to satisfy two conditions to fit the category. Yet both *terrorism* and *violent extremists* described an urgent problem that had to be tackled.

Another reason why Obama used a different term from *terrorism* is that the usage of such a term could be used against the US by the more radical elements of the host countries, i.e. Egypt and Turkey. Many of these elements and their radical scholars viewed the antagonistic actions of the US in Iraq and Afghanistan as constitutive of state terrorism.

In fact, one can validate the whole argument of this chapter by Obama's campaign slogan, i.e. *Change*. On one level, *change* is seen as a way to answer the Bush administration's famous question in its assessment of the terrorist attacks of 9/11, "Why do they hate us?" (cf. Dunn, 2005, p. 13). On another level, *change* is seen as a change in policy towards the Middle East evidenced by Obama's inauguration speech's invitation to the people of the Third World: "We will extend a hand if you are willing to unclench your fist" (Prashad, 2012, p. 22).

Additionally, *change* comes to represent not only this "change in policy" but rather a "policy of change" of regimes and states in the Middle East. Hence, Obama's *Change* is not an objective process. It is a deliberate decision to project an image of tolerance and understanding while at the same time issue a statement of the US's interest in the necessity of effecting a regime change in the Middle East using means other than military intervention. This argument explains why Obama chose Egypt and Turkey and not Saudi Arabia, for example. Most of the perpetrators of the 9/11 terrorist attacks were Saudis. One of these, Osama Bin Laden, Saudi head of Al-Qaeda, was still at large at the time of the speeches. These reasons made Obama choose carefully the countries he wanted to project as allies in the Middle East and his administration's level of recognition of them, whether as political and religious allies such as Turkey or solely religious actors such as Egypt.

Incidentally, the countries in which Obama chose to project his shift in policy are those that try to incorporate modernist exegesis of Islam into their IR models, whereby the presumption of friendliness and peace relations between states replaces the juristic division of the world in the foundational period of Islamic history into Islamic territory and non-Islamic/war territory (Fadel, 2018). This difference in the interpretation of Islamic Sharia means that Turkey, Egypt and similar countries can, in fact, have peaceful and interdependent relations with the US and that these relations can be sanctioned and approved by their religious institutions. These countries can help Obama's administration in de-radicalising detainees and former jihadists by initiating re-education and rehabilitative programmes. Closing Guantanamo Bay and Abu Ghraib prisons, then, became possible, removing one infamous barrier between the Middle East and the US. The burden of re-educating former inmates can be outsourced to these allies. On the other hand, entities that still embrace the earlier Islamic/non-Islamic territory understanding such as the Wahabi brand of Salafism have limited or no chance of cooperation with the

US. We note, then, that the model of international relations that Obama tried to advance is fundamentally different from that of Bush, and the difference owes a great deal to the political framework of each and the political language employed.

CONCLUSION

This chapter presents an argument for a political analysis model that contextualises discourse analysis within political theory. It investigates *otherness* and identity formation in selected presidential speeches of George W Bush and Barack Obama in relation to the Middle East. The methods for this study were an extended Ideological Square based on van Dijk's model and the application of a multimodal approach to proximisation theory.

The findings of this chapter include registering a shift in identity construction and political representation, whereby Bush's view of the political world differed from Obama's due to their realist/liberal differences. The study also registers a shift in threat portrayal employed by each president and the impact of this portrayal on the venues of their speeches as an example. These shifts required slight modifications and extensions in the analytical methods, and the findings were then discussed in detail within a social constructivist political framework that provides a space for ideational analysis of the findings.

REFERENCES

Bartlet, J., & Miller, C. (2012). The edge of violence: Towards telling the difference between violent and non-violent radicalization. *Terrorism and Political Violence, 24*(1), 1–21. DOI:10.1080/09546553.2011.594923

Bhatia, U. (2004). *The war on terrorism: A crusade?* S Rajaratnam School of International Studies. https://www.rsis.edu.sg/rsis-publication/rsis/618-the-war-on-terrorism-a-crusad/#.XWkNW-gzZPY"

Bush, G. W. (2001, September 21). *President Bush's address to a joint session of Congress*. CNN. http://edition.cnn.com/2001/US/09/20/gen.bush.transcript

Bush, G. W. (2002, January 29). Text of President Bush's 2002 state of the union address. *The Washington Post.* https://www.washingtonpost.com/wp-srv/onpolitics/transcripts/sou012902.htm

Bush, G. W. (2003, January 28). Text of President Bush's 2003 state of the union address. *The Washington Post.* https://www.washingtonpost.com/wp-srv/onpolitics/transcripts/bushtext_012803.html

Bush, G. W. (2006, August 21). News conference August 21, 2006. *Democracy Now.* https://www.democracynow.org/2006/8/22/president_bush_admits_iraq_had_no

Cap, P. (2008). Towards the proximization model of the analysis of legitimization in political discourse. *Journal of Pragmatics, 40*(1), 17–41. DOI:10.1016/j.pragma.2007.10.002

Cap, P. (2010). *Legitimisation in political discourse: A cross-disciplinary perspective on the modern US war rhetoric* (2nd ed.). Cambridge Scholars Publishing.

Cap, P. (2013a). *Proximization: The pragmatics of symbolic distance crossing.* John Benjamins.

Cap, P. (2013b). Proximization theory and critical discourse studies: A promising connection? *International Review of Pragmatics, 5*(2), 292–316. DOI:10.1163/18773109-13050208

Chilton, P. (2004). *Analysing political discourse: Theory and practice.* Routledge.

Cornish, F. (2007). English demonstratives: Discourse deixis and anaphora. A Discourse-Pragmatic Account. In R. A. Nilson, N. A. A. Amfo, & K. Borthen (Eds.), Interpreting utterances: *Pragmatics and its interfaces: Essays in honour ofThorstein Fretheim.* Novus Press.

Dunn, D. H. (2005). Bush, 11 September and the conflicting strategies of the "War onTerrorism." *Irish Studies in International Affairs, 16,* 11–33.

Eisner, P., & Royce, K. (2007). *The Italian letter: How the Bush administration used a fake letter to build the case for war in Iraq.* Rodale.

Fadel, M. (2018). Modern Islamic international law between accommodation and resistance: The case of Israel and BDS. *Yearbook of Islamic and Middle Eastern Law, 19,* 247–278.

Hay, C. (2002). *Political analysis: A critical introduction.* Palgrave.

Koven, M. (2007). *Selves in two Languages: Bilinguals' verbal enactments of identity in French and Portuguese.* John Benjamins. Retrieved from 978902724 1450,9027241457,9789027291899

Mearsheimer, J. J. (2011). *Why leaders lie: The truth about lying in international politics.* Oxford University Press.

Myers, S. L., & Rubin, A. J. (2008). *Iraqi journalist hurls shoes at Bush and denounces him on TV as a 'Dog'.* The New York Times. https://www.nytimes.com/2008/12/15/world/middleeast/15prexy.html

Neumann, I. B. (1992). Identity and security. *Journal of Peace Research, 29*(2), 221–226. DOI:10.1177/0022343392029002009

Neumann, I. B. (1996). Self and other in international relations. *European Journal of International Relations, 2*(2), 139–174. DOI: 10.1177/1354066196002002001

Obama, B. (2009a, April 6). *Remarks by President Obama to the Turkish Parliament.* The White House: President Barack Obama. https://obamawhitehouse.archives.gov/the-press-office/remarks-president-obama-turkish-parliament

Obama, B. (2009b, June 4). *President Obama's speech in Cairo: A New Beginning.* The White House: President Barack Obama. https://obamawhitehouse.archives.gov/new-beginning

O'Donnell, V., & Jowett, G. (2012). *Propaganda and persuasion* (5th ed.). SAGE Publications.

Payne, R. A., (2007). Neorealists as critical theorists: The purpose of foreign policy debate. *Perspectives on Politics, 5*(3), 503–514.

Pietikäinen, S., & Dufva, H. (2006). Voices in discourses: Dialogism, critical discourse analysis and ethnic identity. *Journal of Sociolinguistics, 10*(2), 205–224. DOI: 10.1111/j.1360-6441.2006.00325.x

Prashad, V. (2012). *Arab spring, Libyan winter.* AK Press.

Reyes, A. (2011). *Voices in political discourse: Castro, Chávez, Bush and their strategic use of language.* Continuum.

Shapiro, G. L., & Schall, M. S. (1990). Rhetorical rules and organization–cultures: Identification, maintenance, and change. *Human Resource Development Quarterly, 1*(4), 321–337. DOI: 10.1002/hrdq.3920010403

van Dijk, T. A. (1992). Discourse and the denial of racism. *Discourse & Society, 3*(1), 87–118. DOI:10.1177/0957926592003001005

van Dijk, T. A. (1995). Discourse semantics and ideology. *Discourse & Society, 6*(2), 243–289.

van Dijk, T. A. (1997). What is political discourse analysis? *Belgian Journal of Linguistics, 11*, 11–52. DOI:10.1075/bjl.11.03dij

van Dijk, T. A. (2013). Ideology and discourse. In M. Freeden, L. T. Sargent, & M. Stears (Eds.), *The Oxford handbook of political ideologies.* Oxford University Press.

Chapter 10

Critically Negotiating British and American Englishes: Voices from Indonesia[1]

Ribut Wahyudi*

ABSTRACT

This article investigates the critical negotiation of British and American Englishes (BAE) through the problematisation of these two varieties in the newspaper *The Jakarta Post*. In this paper, the word "problematisation" is used to question the dominant construction of BAE as the only legitimate varieties. Firstly, I map the areas of problematisation addressed by two Indonesian scholars and place these areas in the field of critical applied linguistics. Secondly, the historical context of English Language Teaching (ELT) in Indonesia is explained to understand why the hegemonic structure of BAE remains uninterrupted. The problematisation of BAE focuses on "standard" versus "non-standard" English(es), ownership, intelligibility and English as a Foreign Language (EFL) users' identities, including the capitalisation of sociocultural contexts and the shifts of subject positions as the strategies. The problematisation is also used to unpack the socio-economic, political and historical constructions of BAE by problematising the netizens' subjectivities favouring BAE. Bakhtin's concept of dialogism is also used to provide additional analysis.

[1] My presentation at the Universiti Malaya's Discourse and Society International Conference, 2019, was funded by Daftar Isian Penggunaan Anggaran (DIPA) Fakultas Humaniora, UIN Maulana Malik Ibrahim Malang, Indonesia. I would also like to thank the editors of this volume and the reviewer(s) for their feedback to improve the quality of the chapter.

* Universitas Islam Negeri Maulana Malik Ibrahim Malang, Indonesia

Keywords Critical negotiation, problematisation, British and American Englishes, subjectivities, voices

INTRODUCTION

Pioneered by Kachru (1986), a plethora of academic works has extensively discussed World Englishes (WE) and associated issues, such as teaching WE and English as the *lingua franca* (Jenkins, 2006), WE and the implications for international communication and ELT (Kirkpatrick, 2007), cultures, contexts and WE (Kachru & Smith, 2008), global Englishes (Pennycook, 2007), and more current works such as the critical analysis of WE (Saraceni, 2011) and language contact and WE (Onysko, 2016). In the Indonesian context, there have been studies on WE such as an investigation of Englishes to teach after study in Australia (Dewi, 2017) and WE and the possible implications for ELT (Wahyudi, 2018b).

The rising issues of WE have also motivated the establishment of journals devoted explicitly to WE such as *World Englishes* and *Asian Englishes,* associations such as the International Association of World Englishes, WE conferences and courses on WE. However, despite the burgeoning studies on WE, this issue is under-researched in Indonesia. This article aims to discuss the problematisation of Inner Circle Englishes (ICE), primarily American and British English, according to articles written by two Indonesian scholars in *The Jakarta Post*. In the article, I map the area of problematisation addressed by the scholars and extend the possible critical positioning by drawing on the Foucauldian notion of problematisation.

SETTING UP CONTEXTS

First, I would like to explain the reason for article selection and the reason for using existing critical studies in applied linguistics, post-structural and post-colonial works, the scope of *The Jakarta Post,* and its political support for Joko Widodo (popularly referred to in Indonesia as Jokowi) in the 2014 Indonesian presidential election. Uncovering the support for the 2014 presidential election is vital as Usman's (2014) article is about Widodo's English.

Usman's (2014) and Martin's (2016) articles were selected because of the similarity of themes. Both articles discuss two figures' use of English that was criticised by the majority of netizens (at least), as argued by the two authors. That was because their English was considered illegitimate as seen from the ICE perspective.

As stated in her article, Rezia Usman is an English language instructor who had teaching experience (Indonesian language) at Arizona State University, the United States (US), and was under the Fulbright programme, whereas Nelly Martin was finishing her study at the University of Wisconsin, the US, when she wrote her article. Of these two writers, Martin explicitly stated that she had encountered Kachru's work *World Englishes in the Asian Context*. The exposure to this work might have inspired her to gain legitimacy in her current positioning toward ICE as Kachru's works consistently promote Outer and Expanding Circle varieties of English as legitimate (see for example Kachru, 1986; 1998; 2005). 'Outer Circle' refers to the use of Englishes in the former colonies of the United Kingdom (UK) (e.g. Malaysia and India), while 'Expanding Circle' refers to the use of Englishes in countries that have never been colonised by Britain (Kachru, 1998; 2005).

These shared topics have been documented in Critical Applied Linguistic studies such as the works of Pennycook, Canagarajah, and Kumaravadivelu. In that regard, inspired from the post-structural paradigm, I started the analysis from the discursive practices (Walshaw, 2007) in the real world, quoted as data, and situated the data in the existing critical studies. Thus, I could make sense of Usman's (2014) and Martin's (2016) articles from the unlimited and non-reductive approach. What I mean by this approach is that I started my analysis from the data rather than examining the data from the existing theories.

The Jakarta Post is a national English newspaper published online and in print. In 2014, this newspaper supported Widodo for the presidential election (see "Editorial: Endorsing Jokowi", 2014). It is quite understandable that published articles written by Usman (2014) and Martin (2016) were in line with the mission of the media due to media *surveillance*, using Foucault's term (Danaher et al., 2000). Even though Martin's (2016) article was not about

Widodo's English, the position taken by her conforms to Usman's (2014) article in that they both problematise the majority of Indonesians (as they reported) who are in favour of ICE.

In analysing data, following Walshaw's (2007) adoption of Foucauldian discourse, I identified the keywords or discourse in relation to English(es) and subject positions of people, e.g. Widodo in the mainstream and the problematised contexts. I referred to discourse as defined by Foucault (2010), that is, "practices that systematically form the objects of which they speak ... [D]iscourses are not about objects; they do not identify objects, they constitute them" (p. 49). I traced the discursive relations (Foucault, 2010) between what was narrated by Usman (2014) and Martin (2016) in *The Jakarta Post* articles with the relevant studies in what Pennycook (2001) termed *critical applied linguistics*, along with post-structural and postcolonial studies.

MAPPING THE AREAS OF PROBLEMATISATION

Having examined two articles by Usman (2014) and Martin (2016), I found that the shared areas of problematisation were standard, ownership, intelligibility, and identity.

Usman (2014) discussed three crucial topics: standard, ownership and identity. Her opinion arose in the context of many netizens' critiques of President Widodo on his presentation at the CEO Summit of the Asia-Pacific Economic Cooperation. In the presentation, Widodo used simple, Javanese-accented English. Yet his presentation was clear, and he was able to convey the message. It was likely that the delegates in the forum understood his speech, as the author said. Usman (2014) critically questioned commentators on social media because they compared President Widodo with former President Susilo Bambang Yudhoyono and his competitor Prabowo Subianto in the 2009 presidential election. The following is Usman's critical commentary on "standard" English.

(1) On social media platforms, commentators repeatedly compared other political figures' use of English with that of Jokowi. (Usman, 2014, para. 7)

(2) His former rival Prabowo Subianto and predecessor Susilo Bambang Yudhoyono were among those considered to possess the standard of English that many believe a head of state should possess. (Usman, 2014, para. 7)

(3) Such a comparison is inaccurate and not like-with-like. (Usman, 2014, para. 7)

As Usman said, many people in Indonesia indeed appreciate Yudoyono's and Subianto's English as having the features of a native speaker's way of speaking. This "standard" English is believed by social media commentators to be a necessary skill for the President. The term "standard" was first applied to language and literature in the 18th century (McArthur, 1998, cited in Kachru & Nelson, 2006). The term applies more to grammar than pronunciation (Kachru & Nelson, 2006). McArthur argues that this term was the result of intensive codification (Kachru & Nelson, 2006). The above quotes confirm Wahyudi's (2018a) argument that BAE have formed knowledge and shaped ELT lecturers' desire/pleasure.[2] Therefore, going against these two varieties is considered illegitimate. In the quotes, Usman considers the dialogue on English use by Widodo as self and Yudhoyono's & Subiyanto's as others. Furthermore, she attempts to counter social media comments on Widodo's English. Usman's effort resonates with Bakhtin's dialogism which conceptualises life as "dialogic and a shared event" (Coghlan, 2014, p. 2), in which meaning is generated through constant dialogue from all parties.

In the following section, Usman critically highlighted that both Yudhoyono's and Subianto's schooling, training, access and exposure contributed to their native-like English.

(4) Many overlooked the fact that both Yudhoyono and Prabowo studied at Fort Benning, [USA]. (Usman, 2014, para. 8)

(5) Also, Prabowo was born into a privileged family and was briefly educated in London. (Usman, 2014, para. 8)

[2] This desire/pleasure is usually found in post-structural works, especially those inspired by Foucault. In this regard, BAE have become ELT lecturers' comfort zone.

(6) Both had enough access and exposure to study and interact in English that allowed them to speak fluently in a bright [*sic*] accent in favour of the "golden language", a term known for accents or languages that have the upper hand in social and political circumstances. (Usman, 2014, para. 8)

Again, Usman rightly pointed out that both Yudhoyono and Subianto (both having elite military backgrounds) had a chance to study in the United States (US) as a part of military training. Also, Subianto was partly educated in London. This access and exposure to English-speaking countries enabled both Yudhoyono and Subianto to speak English fluently. In contrast, Widodo took his undergraduate degree in Yogyakarta, Indonesia, and did not have the same access and exposure to English. He was also from a non-privileged family. Thus, it was unfair to make such a comparison as Usman noted in the following statement on access to standard English.

(7) This shows that many Indonesians believe that proper English can only be acquired by a handful of people with high [*sic*] access to language education. (Usman, 2014, para. 10)

In the above quote, Usman appeared to be in a dilemma as, on one hand, she problematised standard English, accessible to a limited number of people, which for her was unfair. However, on the other hand, she still used the common term "proper English" (para. 20). Implicitly she could not avoid mentioning a hierarchy of language, as shown below.

(8) Many of us Indonesians still fantasize that good English speakers should have either an American or British accent, history of intensive language training or overseas education. (Usman, 2014, para. 11)

In quote (8), the phrase "should have" suggests that it is compulsory to have an American or British accent. This fact confirms Wahyudi's (2018a) finding that American and British accents have become the reference of "truth" or even disciplinary practice. Thus, those who do not use ICE are excluded discursively. Wahyudi and Chusna (2019) also revealed that having these accents suggests that teachers of English can gain legitimacy. However, in another context, making American and British accents the reference of truth suggests the exclusion of other varieties (Wahyudi, 2018a). American and British accents are also considered to have a higher position than others (Phillipson & Skutnabb-Kangas, 2013). This is a form of linguicism of "ideologies, structures, and practices which are used to legitimate, effectuate, and reproduce an unequal division of power and resources (both material and immaterial) between groups which are defined on the basis of language" (Phillipson, 1992, p. 47; Canagarajah & Said, 2011, p. 390). In quote (8), the metric of "standard" refers to accent. This is not in line with the term "standard", which is argued to be more relevant to grammar (Kachru & Nelson, 2006). In the above quotes, Usman's problematisation appears to be in line with the generation of meanings from "the web of interconnections" between one's English and a personal life history, including one's social, economic and military background, a strategy of Bakhtin's dialogism (Coghlan, 2014, p. 2).

Also as shown in the above quotes, Usman was aware that there were only a limited number of people who have good access to language education. She argued that blaming people who do not have good access to education was unfair. Furthermore, she underlined the fact that many Indonesians still idolise American and British accents, overseas training and education, and native speakerism. Albeit contested (Canagarajah, 1999), the idea of native speakerism is difficult to resist. Problematising those favouring native-like speaking styles further, Usman questioned and commented on the following:

(9) What happens to those who do not have access to these [i.e. overseas training, education, exposure, etc.]? Can they ever be ... good English speaker[s] as well? Do all Indonesian children need to be that privileged so they can conduct presentations on the international stage? (Usman, 2014, para. 12)

(10) Obviously, the judgment of how one is perceived to be speaking English properly is biased and unfair to the disadvantaged. (Usman, 2014, para. 13)

It is interesting that Usman (2014), an English language instructor and a teacher of Indonesian language at Arizona University under the Fulbright programme, was critical about the preference of speaking fluently using BAE accents. She might have been exposed to US and UK English as the dominant varieties in her schooling (see Lauder, 2008; Dardjowidjojo, 2000) and also her time in the US under the Fulbright programme exposed her more to American English. Usman's background as a Surabayan with a heavy Javanese accent reflects her position toward Widodo's English as shown in the following:

(11) As a Surabayan with a thick Javanese accent working in Jakarta, I can relate to that experience. Oftentimes, I have received similar derogatory remarks when speaking in English. (Usman, 2014, para. 13)

Usman may or may not have read post-colonial literature on ELT (Pennycook, 1998) or post-structural work in ELT which appreciates her post-colonial accent (Sayer, 2012) and post-structuralism and identity (Morgan, 2007), but she spoke on behalf of her feelings, of herself and thus her subjectivities (Foucault, 1994). Danaher et al. (2000) explained subjectivity as "[a presentation of] individual identity as the product of discourses, ideologies and institutional practices" (p. xv). However, Usman seemed to be aware that there are localised Englishes, as she briefly mentioned that "Indonesians, inevitably, will have their very own version of English just like the Indians and Singaporeans" (Usman, 2014, para. 25). As Kachru & Nelson (2006) and Kachru (1986) suggested, local versions of English are part of a speaker's contextual realities and nativisation. Furthermore, Usman's subjectivities and experiences of Englishes are noted in the following statements:

(12) Clearly, [Widodo's] limited exposure to English-language training did not hinder him [from] picking up the English language. (Usman, 2014, para. 19)

(13) His vocabulary is probably modest, but it served the purpose for the audience. (Usman, 2014, para. 19)

(14) For that [reason], Jokowi is an ideal representation [to] most Indonesians, who have not had exposure to sophisticated language training. (Usman, 2014, para. 19)

Usman underlined that intelligibility is an important aspect. Kachru and Nelson (2006) defined intelligibility as "the degree of success in communication" (p. 67). Thus, Widodo's choice of modest vocabulary was not a problem to Usman. The use of modest vocabulary employed by Widodo may serve as a strategy of communication to be understood (Baker, 2016) in a *lingua franca* context. Furthermore, when stating that "Jokowi is an ideal representation [to] most Indonesians" (14), Usman shifted Jokowi's subject position (Walshaw, 2007) from being undesirable, i.e. an illegitimate user of English, to desirable. Overall, Usman's quotes above resonate with Bakhtin's understanding of language as a battle in which meanings are formed and reformed, "the constant ebb and flow" (Coghlan, 2014, p. 4) between centrifugal and centripetal forces. Usman's arguments functioned as centrifugal forces which were to pull things apart, while the social media commentators' criticism of Widodo's English served as central forces as they gravitated to the centre, standard English.

In the following statements, Usman tried to deconstruct the obsession with sounding like a native:

(15) Most importantly, it is time to debunk the obsession with trying to sound [like American and British people] or relate ourselves to the 'foreignism' of English language-learning and communication, and start embracing our own accents and language styles. (Usman, 2014, para. 22)

(16) It is time to end the desperate attempt and pressure to sound native when speaking English. Such insecurity will only impede and discourage learning. (Usman, 2014, para. 9)

The keyword *debunk* means "to show that something is less important, less good or less true than it has been made to appear" (Cambridge Advanced Learners Dictionary, 2008). Usman deconstructed the obsession to sound like a native as "insecurity". She shifted the subject position (Walshaw, 2007) of sounding like a native speaker as idealised to "language insecurity" (Usman, 2014, para. 6) on the part of Indonesians. Cook (1999) argued that emulating a native speaker is an unachievable target as native speakers and non-native speakers experience different cognitive thinking processes when using English. Similarly, Wahyudi (2018a) found that one lecturer in his study explicitly encouraged students to not project native speakers as the target, as to her it was impossible. The most important point that Usman made was to encourage EFL learners to stand on their own identities and pride. In that regard, she encouraged EFL learners to exert their agency and selves, and thus their identities. Usman encouraged EFL learners in Indonesia to be more realistic by using locally accented English. This idea resonates with Pennycook's (2000, pp. 107–119) "post-colonial performativity", i.e. speaking from local realities. Usman reminded us to change our belief, which is similar to a call to change attitude (Kumaravadivelu, 2006). Closing her opinion, Usman (2014) wrote a neat statement which problematised the ownership of English:

(17) It is crucial to push the belief that communicating in English confidently is very much doable and possible, albeit in an accented and non-native way, and that English belongs not only to the Americans or British (or any other people from English-speaking countries), but everyone in the world who wishes to speak it. (Usman, 2014, para. 27)

In the above statement, Usman highlighted that the ownership of English is not only with those that use ICE (Kachru, 1986 & 1998). Usman's thought was in line with "translingual practice" (Canagarajah, 2013, p. 69) and Pennycook's (2000) post-colonial performativity which encouraged EFL learners to use English but maintain their own unique pronunciation and accents. In line with this localised use of English, Kachru (1998) defines English in Asian contexts as a means of communication and interaction as well as a means to articulate "local identities within and across Asia" (p. 103). Similarly, Norton (1997) argues that the ownership of English is better understood in terms of its usage. Again, in quote (17) Usman deconstructed the dominant understanding of the ownership of English. Quotes (15), (16) and (17) are in tune with Bakhtinian understanding that utterances contain political and social assumptions which reflect cultural values. The utterances are "multi-voiced and imbued with power" (Coghlan, 2014, p. 3).

In the second article, Martin (2016) questioned the dominance of BAE in Indonesia. She began by discussing an advertisement featuring a popular Korean figure, as shown in the following:

(18) An Indonesian friend of mine recently posted a popular meme featuring Lee Min-ho, a rising South Korean star who advertises an Indonesian coffee brand juxtaposing Korean, English and Indonesian. The post has received a few comments highlighting Lee's English pronunciation. (Martin, 2016, para. 1)

(19) What struck me the most is the nitpicking over one word regarded as mispronounced. Apparently, Lee's inability to pronounce the word 'white' perfectly is enough to suggest he take an English course to improve his pronunciation. (Martin, 2016, para. 2)

The quoted data strongly indicate that dominance of ICE in Indonesia remains pervasive. The quotes are in line with the findings of the author's previous study which showed that BAE have become a regime of truth in two Indonesian universities (Wahyudi, 2018a). That study showed that whoever spoke English in a way that was not in tune with the "standard" would be excluded. In this regard, the "right" pronunciation was used in disciplining someone's (i.e. Lee's) English due to mispronunciation. The act of disciplining others (Walshaw, 2007) was done by suggesting he take an English course for pronunciation improvement.

In quote (19), Martin (2016) scrutinised the social media commentators' comments on the "mispronounced" word uttered by Lee Min-ho. Furthermore, she reminded the readers of the similar negative comments addressed to President Widodo's English. In quotes (18) and (19), Martin tried to generate meanings through a web of interconnection including her friend's criticism through a meme post, a South Korean artist's mispronunciation, and suggestions for the artist to take an English course. In that regard, she constructed the controversy about English use within Bakhtinian dialogism (Coghlan, 2014).

In the following quotes, Martin discussed her language learning trajectory as a way to build her entire argument:

(20) As an Indonesian studying and using English as a second language, I am only too familiar with this criticism. (Martin, 2016, para. 5)

(21) My Indonesian-English pronunciation is often a topic of conversation, and I constantly strive to speak like a Hollywood star. (Martin, 2016, para. 5)

(22) But the more I try, the more I realize that I never will. (Martin, 2016, para. 5)

Martin's argument about the impossibility of her speaking like a Hollywood artist seemed to also reflect the former discourse. Cook (1999) argues that Second Language (L2) speakers need to be treated as speakers in their own right rather than the approximation of monolingual 'native' speakers due to differences in their knowledge of First Language (L1) and L2 and some of their cognitive thinking processes. Martin used her personal language learning history to convince readers that attempting to emulate native speakers was an unrealistic goal. She set the focus of conversation on herself to understand others, e.g. native speakers. In that context, she participated in the debate of ICE versus the use of other Englishes in the Outer and Expanding Circles by providing a response from Indonesia, an Expanding Circle. According to a Bakhtinian concept, she has participated in the dialogue of self and other (Coghlan, 2014).

(23) I was left without any explanation until I encountered Kachru's 'World Englishes' concept from a 1991 book of the same name. (Martin, 2016, para. 6)

(24) I eventually came to understand why variable pronunciation was the target of such stigma, even from fellow second-language users. (Martin, 2016, para. 6)

Similar to Usman's (2014) statement, "the more I try, the more I realize that I never will" was the turning point after Martin read *World Englishes* by Kachru.

This suggests that Kachru's book on World Englishes helped her situate her own experience to be more engaged and sensitive about the importance of social and cultural background in shaping the use of English (Kachru, 1998).

Inspired by Foucault's (1980) thoughts on truth and power, I argued that the dominance of ICE in Indonesia has become entrenched in social bodies such as school and university. It has turned into common knowledge and something that EFL learners cannot escape (Wahyudi, 2018a).

(25) Most Indonesians, like all others who learn English as a second language, are trained to speak like native speakers, be it American or British English. (Martin, 2016, para. 7)

(26) Our English teachers seem to undervalue our social and cultural backgrounds as second-language speakers. (Martin, 2016, para. 8)

The dominance of ICE in Indonesia is not surprising seeing the fact that BAE are favoured in the country (Dewi, 2017; Lauder, 2008). This favour can be traced to the Indonesian government's adoption of a Western ELT curriculum for secondary schools in Indonesia (Gandana, 2014; Wahyudi, 2018a). This history of the adoption of a Western ELT curriculum partly shaped the dominance of ICE. In quotes (23)–(26), Martin (2016) discussed standard and identity concurrently. In quote (23) Martin drew on an intertextual approach, the construction of dynamic meaning resulting from the interconnection between one text and previous texts (Halliday & Hassan, 1985; Barker, 2003), to understand why variation of pronunciation is undesirable as documented in quote (24). In the next quote, she appeared to investigate the historical constitution (Walshaw, 2007) of why "native speakerism" became entrenched. The quote suggests that native speakerism was constituted through formal school pedagogy whereby English language learners were trained to speak like native speakers. Martin then explained in quote (26) that such teaching disadvantaged the social and cultural backgrounds of English learners in Indonesia. From a Bakhtinian perspective, the "native speaker" concept instituted through official discourse in school was in conflict with language learners' social and cultural repertoires (Coghlan, 2014).

The following quote suggests that what was claimed as "standard" pronunciation has created a binary opposition between the superior and inferior. The term "standard" was enacted to exercise power (Foucault, 1982).

(27) The emphasis to speak like those born in New York or in London sets regularity of pronunciation as a standard, relegating second-language speakers to an inferior or peripheral class. (Martin, 2016, para. 9)

In this quote, Martin assumed that teachers of English in Indonesia underestimated learners' social and cultural identity, and referring to the varieties spoken in New York and London as the standard implies that second language speakers are non-standard. In that regard, Martin might have wanted to signpost the issue of identity in second language/foreign language learning as an essential part of the second or foreign language learning process. Relevant to this discussion, Motha et al. (2012) reveal that their social and cultural identities are integrated into their English use and teaching. Concerning "standard", Canagarajah (1999) points out that the domination of the native speaker over the non-native one is rooted in Chomskyan linguistic tradition. The proponents of this camp believe that "the native speaker is the authority on the language and that he/she is the ideal informant provides an understandable advantage to the native speaker in grammaticality judgment" (p. 78). Continued use of native speaker accents, as Canagarajah explained, would only reinforce this Chomskyan notion.

Similar to Usman (2014), Martin (2016) was aware of the fact that English is globally used, and hence English does not belong only to the ICE. This is indicated in the following statements:

(28) Additionally, many underestimate the fact that English is now widely spoken by people outside the UK, the USA, Canada, Australia and New Zealand, plus the other central English-speaking countries. (Martin, 2016, para. 10)

(29) With more and more people across the world learning and speaking English, the language no longer belongs solely to the inhabitants of those countries. (Martin, 2016, para. 11)

(30) English is now spoken in multifarious ways, depending on the geographical area[s] of ... individuals, with social and cultural aspects playing essential roles in shaping and influencing the form English takes. (Martin, 2016, para. 12)

(31) People from all over the world are speaking their own distinctive English: Singaporean English, Indian English, Nigerian English and many others. (Martin, 2016, para. 13)

Quotes (28)–(31) suggest the fact that English has transformed and become mixed with local language. This localised English needs to be taken into account when examining English users' experience in the Outer and Expanding Circles (Kachru & Nelson, 2006). Kachru (1986) calls this phenomenon "linguistic innovations" and "localised functions" (pp. 21–22). In quote (30), Martin was aware of speakers' contextual realities (Kachru & Nelson, 2006), which help the nativisation of English to speakers' use. Furthermore, she seemed aware that geography and socio-cultural aspects had an impact on language use. The proponents of WE in the Outer and Expanding Circles believe that the existence of Englishes depends on their usage, rather than on codification (Kachru & Nelson, 2006, p. 15). From a Bakhtinian lens, Martin highlighted the battle between centripetal forces (quote [27]), whereby New York and London serve as the "standard", and the centrifugal forces reflected in the variety of Englishes used in the Outer and Expanding Circles (quotes [28]–[31]). From a Bakhtinian perspective, there is no winner in the battle, but it results in "a constant ebb and flow" of meanings (Coghlan, 2014, p. 4).

The following are Martin's further problematisation and comments:

(32) They have appropriated English into their own tongues. (Martin, 2016, para. 13)

(33) Who dares to say their English is not 'correct'? (Martin, 2016, para. 13)

In quote (32), Martin used the word "appropriated", which in post-colonial societies means taking over the aspects of "imperial culture" such as "language, forms of writing ... even modes of thought and argument" to help them articulate their own "social and cultural identities" (Ashcroft et al., 2007, p. 15). Martin used "appropriated" as a strategy to nativise and localise ICE function to ensure a legitimate use due to speakers' different contexts and realities (Kachru & Nelson, 2006). She closed the paragraph by posing a rhetorical question in quote (33), "Who dares to say their English is not 'correct'?". Supporters of ICE may still argue that Outer and Expanding Circle Englishes are "not correct". However, from a post-structural perspective, I would argue that how English is used is more important than how it is claimed. Nonetheless, the rhetorical question by Martin may be intended to critically challenge the existing discourses around "standard", "native speaker", "mother tongue", and other similar colonial claims.

(34) Those who still maintain their native-speaker bias must become more socially and culturally observant and aware. (Martin, 2016, para. 14)

As quote (34) suggests, Martin problematised those who maintained native speaker bias to be "socially and culturally observant and aware". The situation suggests that even though the notion of "native speaker" has been problematised (Canagarajah, 1999), this idea remains favoured by many people. In Foucauldian terms, the idea of native speakerism has become "a regime of truth" (Foucault, 1980, p. 131) which is difficult to resist (see Wahyudi, 2018a). Martin used the word "bias", which is adjacent to the word "native-speaker". The *Cambridge Advanced Learners Dictionary* (2008) defines the word "bias" as "often supporting or opposing a particular person or thing in an unfair way by allowing personal opinions to influence your judgment".

Martin's use of the word "bias" appears to have a discursive correlation (Foucault, 2010) with the notion of standard (in which "native speaker" is implicated). The term "standard" has "more to do with ideological than linguistic factors" (Kachru & Nelson, 2006, p. 14). This ideological aspect includes "political, cultural and economic factors" (Marckwardt, 1942, cited in Kachru & Nelson, 2006, p. 14). This bias is in line with Mahboob (2013) who revealed that "nativeness" as the most frequent criterion listed in 77 ELT job advertisements in East Asia and the Middle East makes "non-native" teachers politically and economically disadvantaged. In quote (34) Martin appeared to understand, in the Bakhtinian view, that language is never neutral. It is filled with assumptions, e.g. political and cultural values. Language is also filled with others' intentions (Coghlan, 2014).

Readdressing Lee's and Widodo's pronunciation, Martin made the following comment:

> (35) I have listened to both Jokowi's speech and Lee's ad multiple times, and their variable pronunciation of certain words does not interfere with the message[s]. (Martin, 2016, para. 21)

Quote (35), especially the phrase "does not interfere with the message[s]", has a discursive relation (Foucault, 2010) with a preceding discussion explaining the primary importance of "intelligibility" rather than "standard English" in communication. Intelligibility itself is usually understood as *understanding* while "standard English" is usually desired as it has been intensively researched and codified (Kachru & Nelson, 2006).

> (36) Language is not only a means of communication but also a tool to construct and project our social, historical and cultural values. In their particular cases, both Jokowi and Lee managed to do just that. (Martin, 2016, para. 22)

Quote (36) above reiterates Martin's previous discussion arguing that the use of English is bound to social, historical and cultural values, the centrifugal forces (Coghlan, 2014) by which localised use of English is justifiable. Martin's position resonates with my argument elsewhere that personal and professional histories and cultural geography partly shaped the way lecturers saw the world in the English classroom in two Indonesian universities (Wahyudi, 2018a). Personal and professional histories were integral to these lecturers' lives and identities.

HISTORICAL CONTEXT OF ELT CURRICULUM IN INDONESIA

The trajectory of the ELT curriculum, especially for the secondary sector (such as junior and senior high schools from 1945 to 2013), has been documented in previous studies (Dardjowidjojo, 2000; Mistar, 2005; Lie, 2007) and parts of dissertation sections (Gandana, 2014; Wahyudi, 2018a). From the trajectory, grammar translation was applied from 1945 to 1967, an oral approach was enacted from 1968 to 1974, an audiolingual approach was implemented in between 1975 and 1983 and a communicative approach from 1984 to 2012 with different emphasis and different curriculum names, e.g. "meaning-based" (1994), "competency-based" (2004–2005), "school-based curriculum" (2006–2012) and the 2013 curriculum which foregrounded religiosity, productivity, and innovation (Gandana, 2014; Wahyudi, 2018a).

The provision of the ELT/TESOL scholarship by the Ford Foundation to study Masters and Doctorate degrees in the US, and ELT training conducted by this country and the UK, significantly shaped the adopted English curricula such as grammar translation and oral, audiolingual and communicative approaches (Gandana, 2014; Wahyudi, 2018a). The adoption of this Western ELT curriculum in Indonesian secondary schools partly contributed to Indonesians' way of thinking on what they consider "legitimate" English. This was reflected in the significant positioning of Indonesians toward ICE as problematised by Usman (2014) and Martin (2016) in their articles.

CRITICAL REFLECTIONS OF THE FINDINGS AND DISCUSSION

I would contend that speaking English using Javanese or other local accents is justifiable and legitimate. It is theoretically grounded and should not be blamed. Blaming the use of English with local accents is a form of self-marginalisation in the dominant discourse.

Usman's and Martin's articles echo the discursive traces of debates on standard, ownership, intelligibility and identity as have been documented in Kachru & Nelson (2006) and can also be understood from Pennycook's (2000, p. 107–119) global positioning of English ranging from "colonial celebration" to "colonial performativity". The findings and discussion also confirm Wahyudi's (2018a, 2018b) findings that BAE remain the reference of truth. The hegemony of BAE also reflects the perpetuation of hierarchy and linguicism (Phillipson & Skutnabb-Kangas, 2013; Phillipson, 1992; Canagarajah & Said, 2011) by most Indonesians as narrated by Usman and Martin. The dominance of ICE can also be seen in the act of disciplining others (viz. Lee Min-Ho's critics).

The dominance of ICE in Indonesia needs to be challenged. This endeavour has been made by, among others, Usman and Martin. The discursive construction of the problematisation of ICE by these two was written in the context of a political situation, as this discourse supported President Widodo's English (Usman, 2014). It was absent from the existing discussion of WE in Indonesia.

The problematisation of the dominant ICE needs to be exercised using particular strategies. One strategy was used by the two *The Jakarta Post* contributors by shifting Widodo's and Lee's subject positions from undesirable to desirable ones, and another strategy created a dialogue between self (i.e. voices from the Expanding Circle) and others (i.e. voices from the Inner Circle).

FURTHER PROBLEMATISATION AND CRITICAL POSITIONING TOWARDS ICE

The problematisation of the dominance of BAE is fundamental in Indonesia and other Outer and Expanding Circles. This endeavour is to disrupt the uncritical use of these two varieties of English. Foucault (1994) explained that problematisation is what makes us able to step back from action and reaction. It makes a person "an object of thought" (p. 117) as well as questions meaning, conditions and goals. We need to question the way BAE became dominant and consider it a problem. We need to make the familiar lose its familiarity. This should be done to detach the subject from its social, economic and political processes.

In our discussion, what should be problematised is ICE (e.g. BAE) which disadvantage other speakers' social and cultural values and identities. In

Indonesia, the problematisation of BAE as the standard needs to involve at least six major problematising questions, listed below:

First, who will get the economic benefit if BAE are regarded as the standard? For example, if we want to study overseas, in many cases our English competence is measured by the Test of English as a Foreign Language (an American product) or the International English Language Testing System (a British/Australian product). In such situations, who will get the economic benefit from our tests (Phillipson, 1992)? Why is there no other English test that is inclusive such as proposed by Canagarajah (2006), which embraces other varieties of Englishes? Why are these tests not equally administered by Outer and Expanding Circles?

Second, what are the political motives behind the dominance of standard American and British English in terms of knowledge production? What kinds of control do the US and the UK have by enforcing standard English through major publishers as gate-keepers? What about adding more standards from other countries? What about using plurilingual rather than monolithic approaches in teaching English (Jenkins, 2006)?

Third, if BAE are still maintained as the point of reference, whose socio-cultural aspects will be discussed? Why are others excluded? Is this fair for people in the rest of the world? Are the two varieties able to represent diversity and other peoples' identities?

Fourth, what conditions make BAE prevail? What efforts do the two countries make to maintain their hegemony, especially in ELT?
Fifth, do the US and the UK continue to control the use of English in Outer and Expanding Circles? What institutions, agents, curricula and materials do they use for this purpose?

Sixth, what do the US and the UK do to convince the rest of the world that their Englishes are the standard? What rationales (Foucault, 1982/1983) do they have?

Other critical questions or problematisation can still be raised. The existing critical works have indeed been insightful to interrogate and negotiate the regime of BAE from different perspectives. These include *Linguistic Imperialism* (Phillipson, 1992), *Resisting Linguistic Imperialism* (Canagarajah, 1999), *The Linguistic Imperialism of the Neoliberal Empire* (Phillipson, 2008), *English and the Discourses of Colonialism* (Pennycook, 1998), *Translingual Practice* (Canagarajah, 2013), *Principled Polycentrism and Resourceful Speakers* (Pennycook, 2014), and *Inequalities of Englishes, English speakers, and Languages: A Critical Perspective on Pluralist Approaches to English* (Kubota, 2015). However, asking critical questions above as inspired by Foucault's problematisation is pivotal to help scholars from Outer and Expanding Circles to problematise their subjectivities toward the dominance of ICE as a step to be more critical users of Englishes, e.g. with the use of critical academic voice.

The critical positioning toward BAE needs to be widely advocated in Indonesia and other Outer and Expanding Circle contexts. This positioning needs to be done by avoiding self-marginalisation of English use toward the dominance of BAE, among other things. Furthermore, this critical positioning is the way to inspire confidence in our voices, legitimate accents and identities.

REFERENCES

Ashcroft, B., Griffith, G., & Tiffin, H. (2007). *Post-colonial studies: The key concepts* (2nd ed.). Routledge.

Baker, W. (2016). Culture and language in intercultural communication, English as a lingua franca and English language teaching: Points of convergence and conflict. In P. Holmes & F. Dervin (Eds.), *The cultural and intercultural dimensions of English as a lingua franca* (pp. 70–92). Multilingual Matters.

Barker, C. (2003). *Cultural studies: Theory and practice. Sage.*

Cambridge Advanced Learners Dictionary. (2008). Third Edition [Computer software].

Canagarajah, S. (1999). Interrogating the "Native Speaker Fallacy": Non-linguistics roots, non-pedagogical results. In G. Braine (Ed.), *Non-native educators in English language teaching* (pp. 77–92). Lawrence Erlbaum Associates.

Canagarajah, S. (2006). Changing communicative needs, revised assessment objectives: Testing English as an International Language. *Language Assessment Quarterly, 3*(3), 229–242.

Canagarajah, S., & Said, S. B. (2011). Linguistic imperialism. In J. Simpson (Ed.). *The Routledge handbook of applied linguistics* (pp. 388–400). Routledge.

Canagarajah, S. (2013). *Translingual practice: Global Englishes and cosmopolitan relations.* Routledge.

Coghlan, D. (2014). Bakhtinian dialogism. In D. Coghlan & M. Brydon-Miller (Eds.), *The SAGE encyclopedia of action research.* https://methods.sagepub.com/reference/encyclopedia-of actionresearch/n28.xml#:~:text=Bakhtinian%20dialogism%20refers%20to%20a,level%20that%20dialogue%20takes%20place

Cook, V. (1999). Going beyond the native speaker in language teaching. *TESOL Quarterly, 33*(2), 125–209.

Crystal, D. (2003). *English as a global language.* Cambridge University Press.

Danaher, G., Schirato, T., & Webb, J. (2000). *Understanding Foucault.* Allen & Unwin.

Dardjowidjojo, S. (2000). English teaching in Indonesia. *EA Journal, 18*(1), 22–30.

Dewi, A. (2017). The English(es) to teach after study and life in Australia: A study of Indonesian English language educators. *Asian Englishes, 19*(2), 1–20.

Editorial: Endorsing Jokowi. (2014, July 4). *The Jakarta Post.* https://www.thejakartapost.com/news/2014/07/04/editorial-endorsing-jokowi.html

Foucault, M. (1980). Truth and power. In C. Gordon (Ed.), *Power/knowledge: Selected interviews and other writings 1972–1977 by Michel Foucault* (pp. 109–133). Pantheon Books.

Foucault, M. (1982). The subject and power. *Critical Inquiry, 8*(4), 777–795.

Foucault, M. (1983). *Michel Foucault: Beyond structuralism and hermeneutics.* The University of Chicago Press. (Original work published 1982)

Foucault, M. (1994). *Essential works of Foucault 1954–1984.* Penguin Books.

Foucault, M. (2010). *Archaeology of knowledge.* Vintage Books.

Gandana, I. S. S. (2014). *ELT, interculturality and teacher identity: An inquiry into Indonesian university teachers' beliefs and practices* [Unpublished doctoral dissertation]. Monash University.

Halliday, M. A. K., & Hassan, R. (1985). *Language, context, and text: Aspects of language in a social-semiotic perspective.* Deakin University Press.

Jenkins, J. (2006). Current perspectives on teaching World Englishes and English as a lingua franca. *TESOL Quarterly, 40*(1), 157–181.

Kachru, B. B. (1986). *The alchemy of English.* Pergamon Press.

Kachru, B. B. (1998). English as an Asian language. *Links & Letters, 5,* 89–108.

Kachru, B. B. (2005). *Asian Englishes beyond the canon.* Hongkong University Press.

Kachru, Y., & Nelson, C. L. (2006). *World Englishes in the Asian context.* Hongkong University Press.

Kachru, Y., & Smith, L. E. (2008). *Cultures, context and world Englishes.* Routledge.

Kirkpatrick, A. (2007). Teaching English across cultures: What do English language teachers need to know to teach English. *EA Journal, 23*(2), 20–36.

Kubota, R. (2015). Inequalities of Englishes, English speakers, and Languages: A critical perspective on pluralist approaches to English. In R. Tupas (Ed.), *Unequal Englishes: The politics of Englishes today* (pp. 21–41). Palgrave Macmillan.

Kumaravadivelu, B. (2003). Problematizing cultural stereotypes in TESOL. *TESOL Quarterly, 37*(4), 709–719.

Kumaravadivelu, B. (2006). Dangerous liaison: Globalization, empire and TESOL. In. J. Edge (Ed.), *(Re-)locating TESOL in an age of empire* (pp. 1–32). Palgrave Macmillan.

Lauder, A. (2008). The status and function of English in Indonesia: A review of key factors. *Makara, Sosial Humaniora, 12*(1), 9–20.

Lie, A. (2007). Education policy and EFL curriculum in Indonesia: Between the commitment to competence and the quest for a higher test score. *TEFLIN Journal, 18*(1), 1–14.

Mahboob, A. (2013). Looking for native speakers of English: Discrimination in English Language Teaching job advertisement. *Voices in Asia Journal, 1*(1), 72–81.

Martin, N. (2016, February 6). English in Indonesia: Is it still a matter of British and American? *The Jakarta Post.* http://www.thejakartapost.com/news/2016/02/06/english-indonesia-is-it-still-a-matter-british-or-american.html

Mistar, J. (2005). Teaching English as a foreign language (TEFL) in Indonesia. In G. Braine (Ed.), *Teaching English to the world: History, curriculum and practice* (pp. 75–85). Taylor and Francis.

Morgan, B. (2007). Post-structuralism and applied linguistics: Complementary approaches to culture and identity in ELT. In J. Cummins & C. Davison (Eds.), *International handbook of English language teaching* (pp.1033–1052). Springer.

Motha, S., Jain, R., & Tecle, T. (2012). Translinguistic identity-as-pedagogy: Implications for language teacher education. *International Journal of Innovation in English Language Teaching and Research, 1*(1), 1–28.

Norton, B. (1997). Language, identity and the ownership of English. *TESOL Quarterly, 31*(3), 409–429.

Onysko, A. (2016). Language contact and World Englishes. *World Englishes, 35*(2), 191–195.

Pennycook, A. (1998). *English and the discourses of colonialism.* Routledge.

Pennycook, A. (2000). English, politics and ideology: From colonial celebration to post-colonial performativity. In T. Ricento (Ed.), *Ideologies, politics and language policies: Focus on English* (pp. 107–119). John Benjamins Publishing Company.

Pennycook, A. (2001). *Critical applied linguistics: A critical introduction.* Lawrence Erlbaum Associates.

Pennycook, A. (2007). *Global Englishes and transcultural flows.* Routledge.

Pennycook, A. (2014). Principled polycentrism and resourceful speakers. *The Journal of Asia TEFL, 11*(4), 1–19.

Phillipson, R. (1992). *Linguistic imperialism.* Oxford University Press.

Phillipson, R. (2008). The linguistic imperialism of the neoliberal empire. *Critical Inquiry in Language Studies, 5*(1), 1–43.

Phillipson, R., & Skutnabb-Kangas, T. (2013). Linguistic imperialism and endangered languages. In T. K. Bhatia & W. C. Ritchie (Eds.), *The handbook of multilingualism and bilingualism* (pp. 495–516). Wiley-Blackwell.

Saraceni, M. (2011). Reflections on the rhetorics on the (re-)location of English. *Changing English, 18*(3), 277–285.

Sayer, P. (2012). *Ambiguities and tensions in English Language Teaching: Portraits of EFL teachers as legitimate speakers.* Routledge.

Usman, R. (2014, November 29). Jokowi and English: Beyond language speaking. *The Jakarta Post*. http://www.thejakartapost.com/news/2014/11/29/jokowi-and-english-beyond-language-speaking.html

Wahyudi, R. (2018a). *Situating English language teaching in Indonesia within a critical, global dialogue of theories: A case study of teaching argumentative writing and cross-cultural understanding courses* [Unpublished doctoral dissertation]. Victoria University of Wellington.

Wahyudi, R. (2018b). World Englishes dan beberapa (kemungkinan) implikasinya terhadap pengajaran Bahasa Inggris [World Englishes and some (possible) implications to English Language Teaching]. In M. Huda (Ed.), *Antologi pemikiran linguistik interdisipliner* (Anthology of thoughts on Interdisciplinary Linguistics) (pp. 25–40). UIN MALIKI Press.

Wahyudi, R. & Chusna, S. (2019). Learning from a teacher's classroom discourses to re-modify the EFL framework in the ASEAN context: A possible way forward? In S. Zein (Ed.), *Teacher education for English as a lingua franca: Perspectives from Indonesia* (pp. 156–172). Routledge.

Walshaw, M. (2007). *Working with Foucault in education*. Sense Publishers.

INDEX

D

E

F

G

H

I

Printed and bound by CPI Group (UK) Ltd, Croydon, CR0 4YY

05/05/2026

14871572-0003